Smile

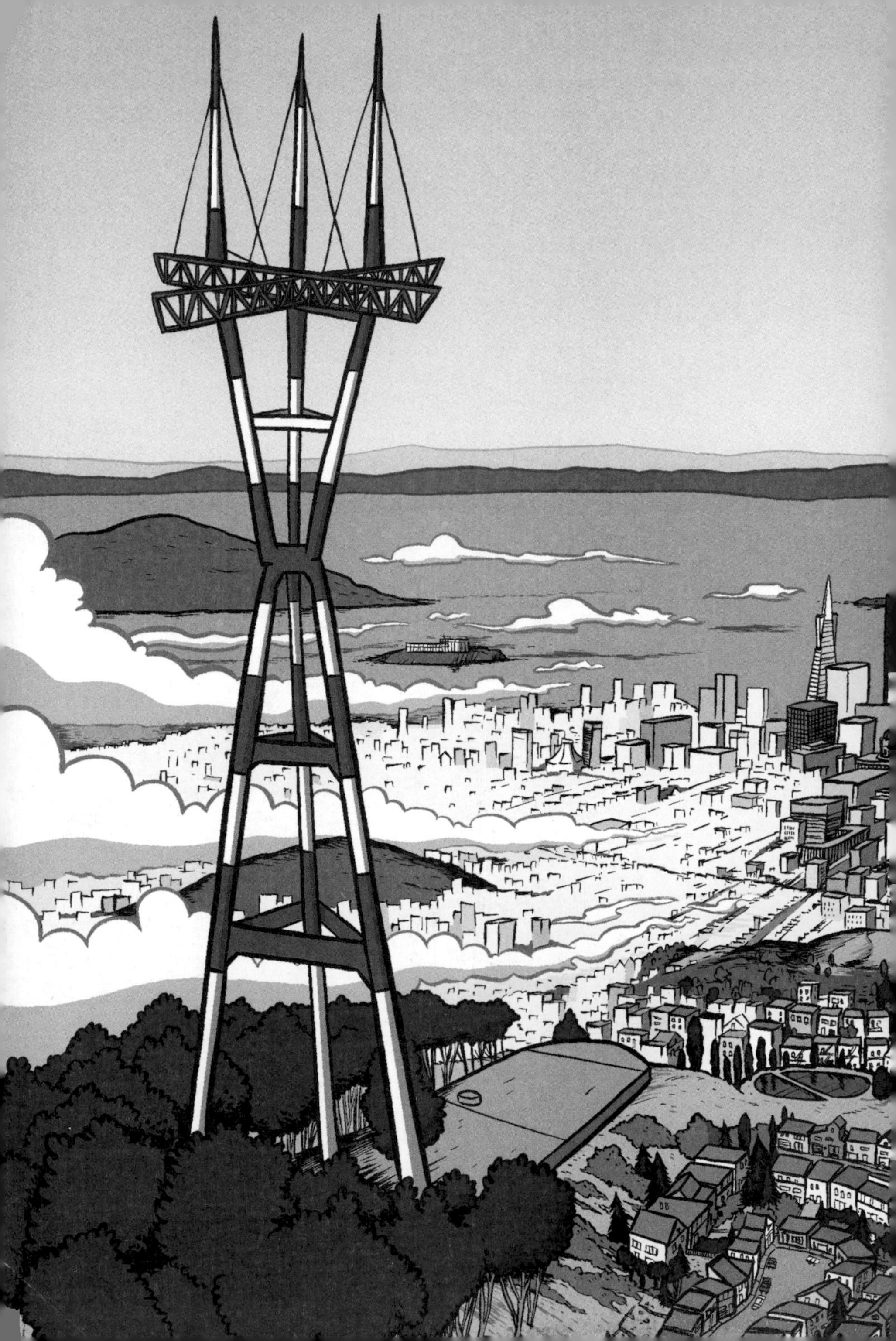

Smile

Raina Telgemeier
with color by Stephanie Yue

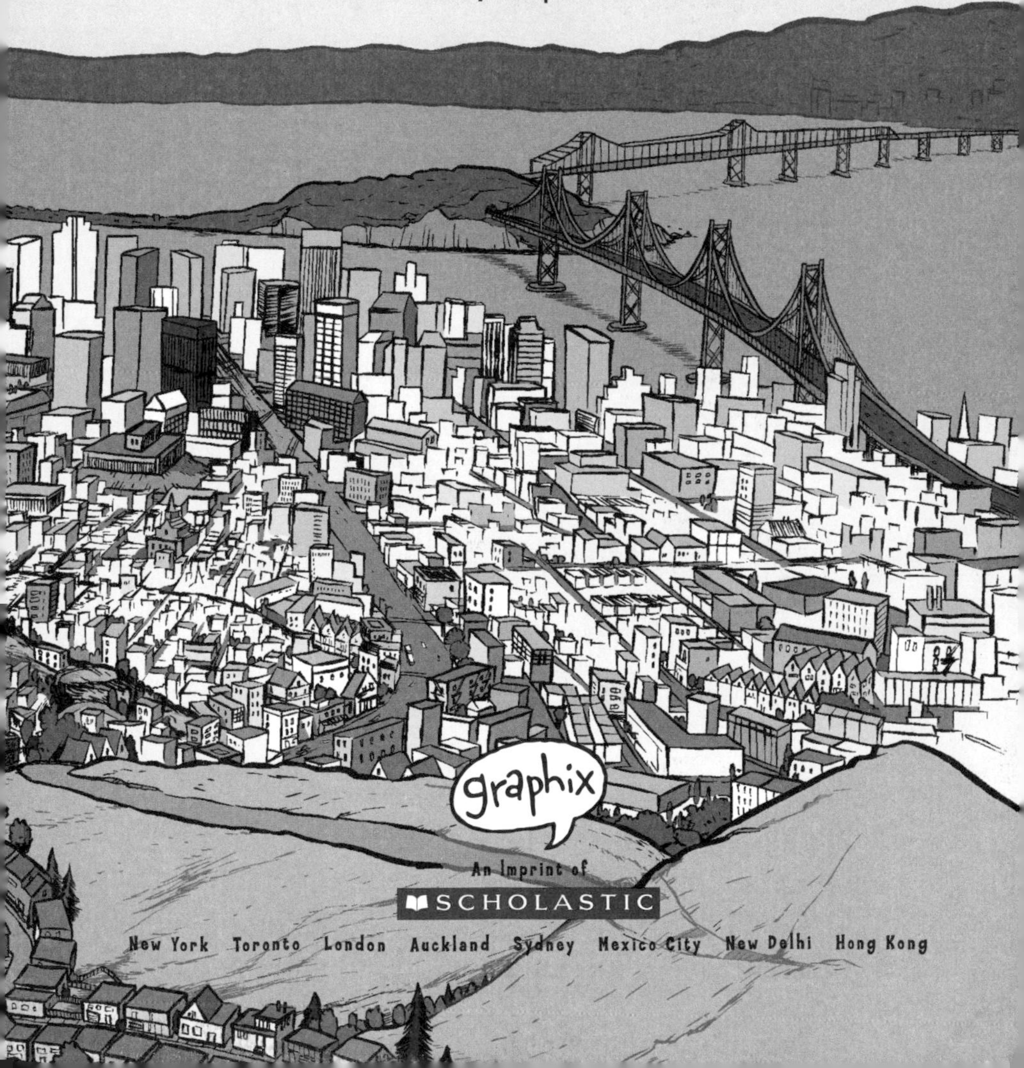

graphix
An Imprint of
SCHOLASTIC
New York Toronto London Auckland Sydney Mexico City New Delhi Hong Kong

All rights reserved. Published by Graphix, an imprint of Scholastic Inc., Publishers since 1920. SCHOLASTIC,
GRAPHIX, and associated logos are trademarks and/or registered trademarks of Scholastic Inc. All other
trademarks are the property of their respective owners and are used without permission.

No part of this publication may be reproduced, stored in a retrieval system, or transmitted in any form or by
any means, electronic, mechanical, photocopying, recording, or otherwise, without written permission of the
publisher. For information regarding permission, write to Scholastic Inc., Attention: Permissions Department,
557 Broadway, New York, NY 10012.

This graphic novel is based on personal experiences, though some names have been changed,
and certain characters, places, and incidents have been modified in service of the story.

Library of Congress Cataloging-in-Publication Data
Telgemeier, Raina.
Smile / Raina Telgemeier. – 1st ed.
p. cm.
ISBN: 978-0-545-13205-3 (hardcover)
ISBN: 978-1-338-74026-4 (paperback)
1. Youth-Dental care. 2. Girls-Dental care. 3. Self-esteem in adolescence.
4. Beauty, Personal. 5. Graphic novels. I. Title.
RK55.Y68.T45 2010
617.6'45-dc22
2008051782

10 9 8 7 6 5 4 3 2 1   20 21 22 23 24

First edition, February 2010
Edited by Cassandra Pelham
Book design by Phil Falco and John Green
Creative Director: David Saylor
Printed in the U.S.A. 40

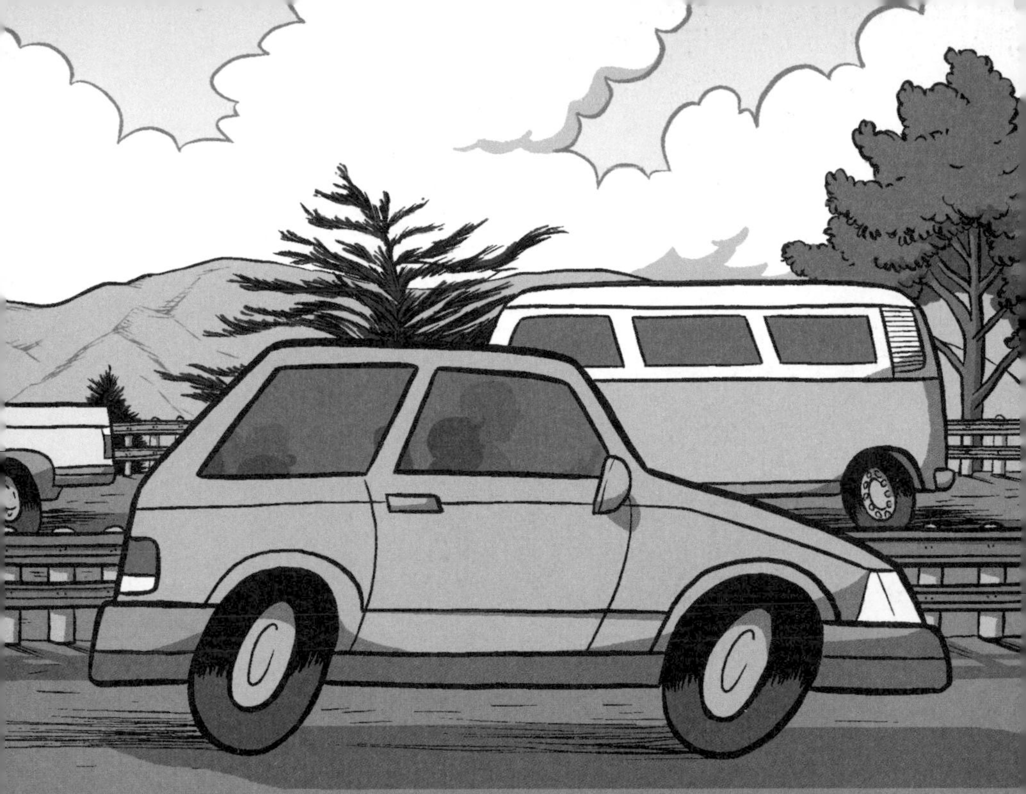

For Dave

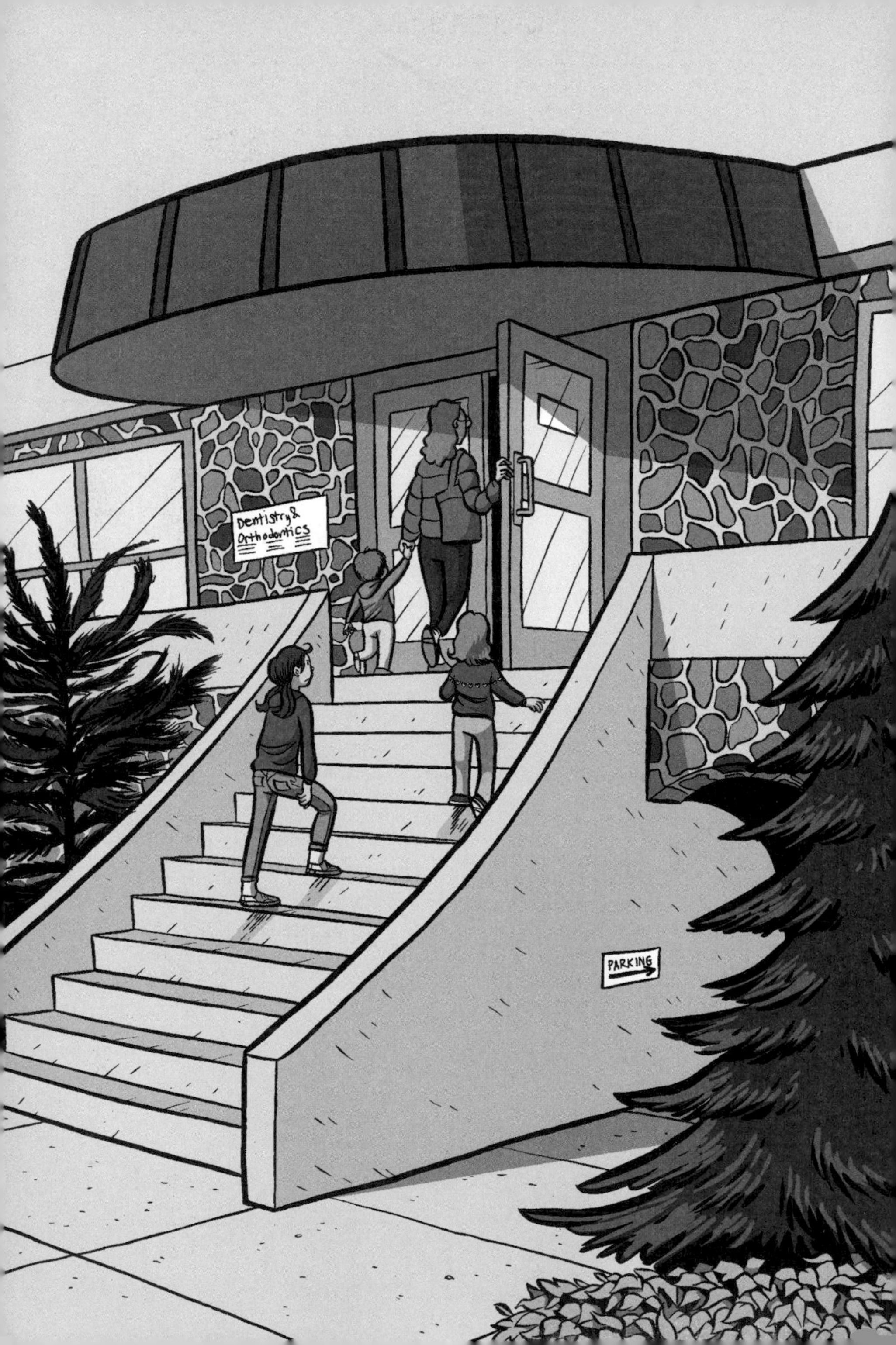
Dentistry &
Orthodontics
PARKING

CHAPTER ONE

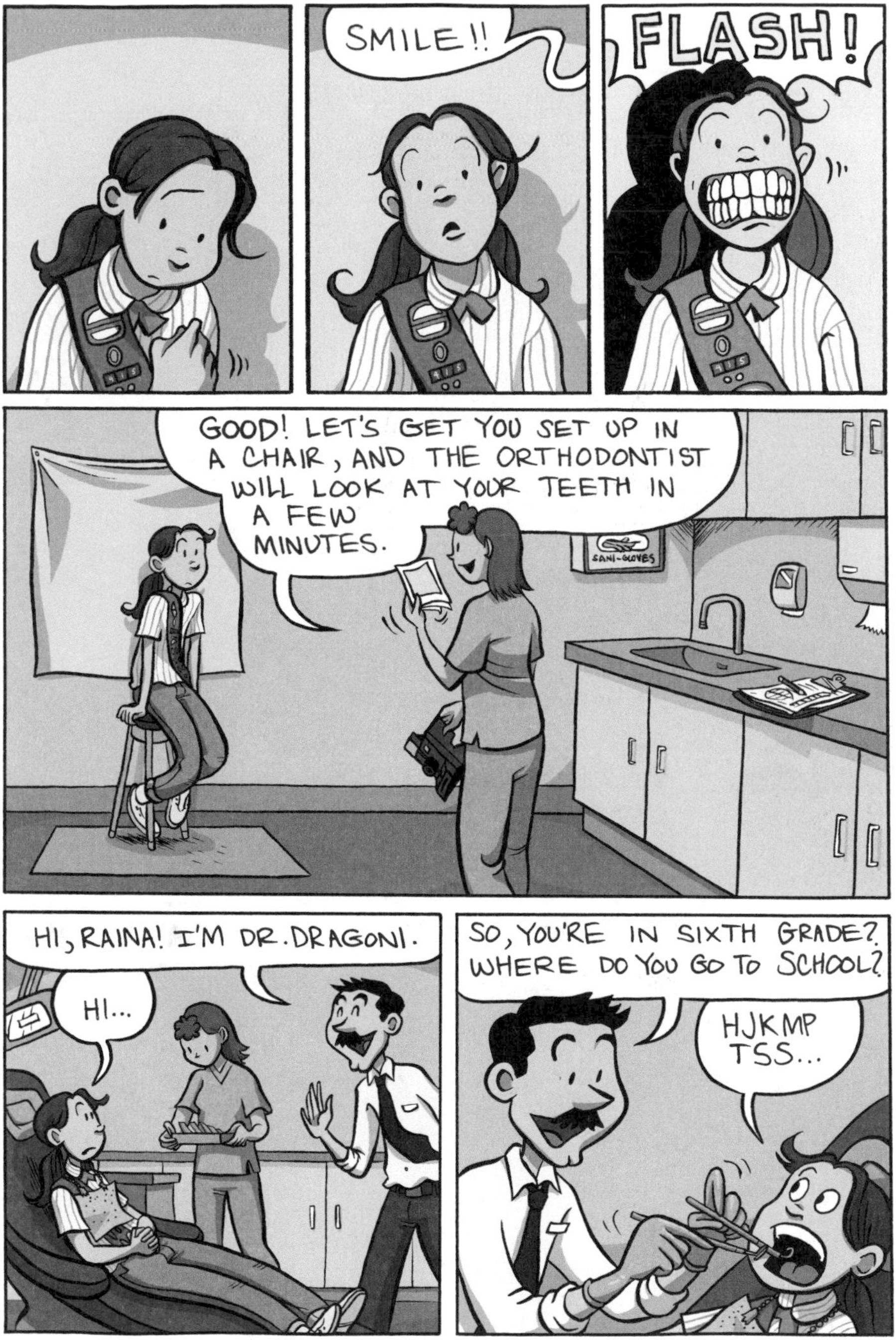
SMILE!!
FLASH!
GOOD! LET'S GET YOU SET UP IN A CHAIR, AND THE ORTHODONTIST WILL LOOK AT YOUR TEETH IN A FEW MINUTES.
SANI-GLOVES
HI, RAINA! I'M DR. DRAGONI.
HI...
SO, YOU'RE IN SIXTH GRADE? WHERE DO YOU GO TO SCHOOL?
HJKMP TSS...

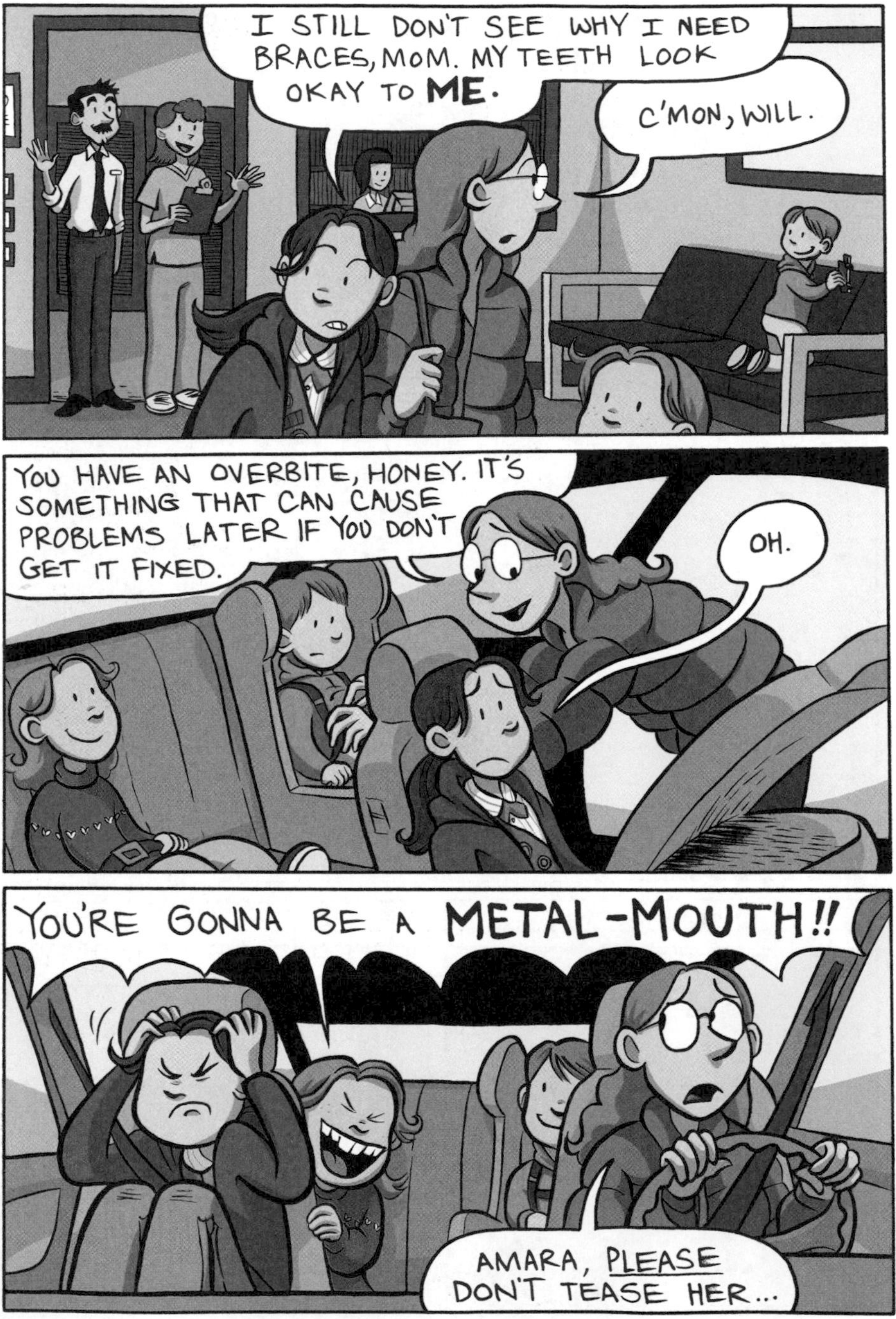
I STILL DON'T SEE WHY I NEED BRACES, MOM. MY TEETH LOOK OKAY TO ME.
C'MON, WILL.
YOU HAVE AN OVERBITE, HONEY. IT'S SOMETHING THAT CAN CAUSE PROBLEMS LATER IF YOU DON'T GET IT FIXED.
OH.
YOU'RE GONNA BE A METAL-MOUTH!!
AMARA, PLEASE DON'T TEASE HER...

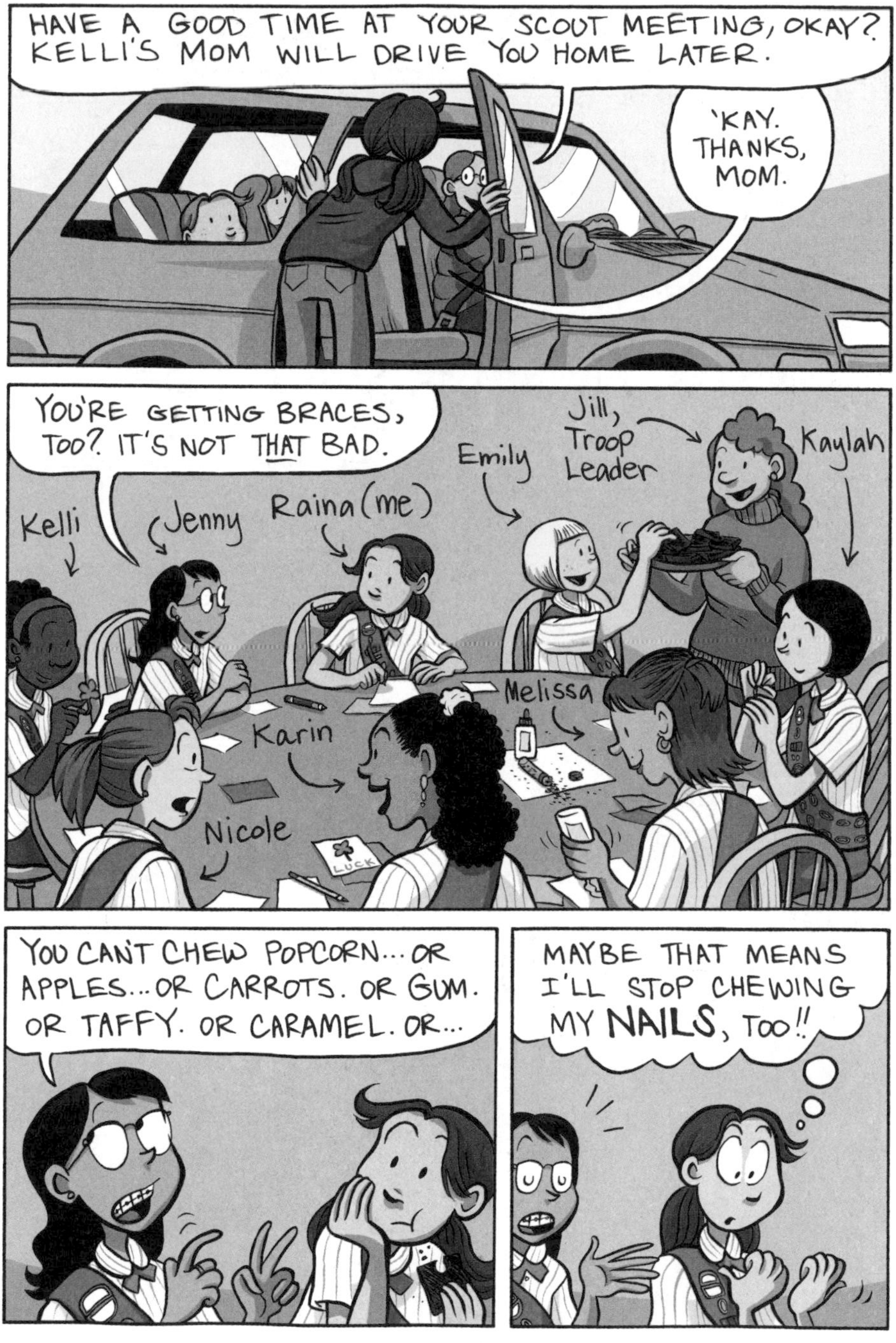
HAVE A GOOD TIME AT YOUR SCOUT MEETING, OKAY? KELLI'S MOM WILL DRIVE YOU HOME LATER.
'KAY. THANKS, MOM.
YOU'RE GETTING BRACES, TOO? IT'S NOT THAT BAD.
Jill, Troop Leader
Kaylah
Emily
Raina (me)
Jenny
Kelli
Melissa
Karin
Nicole
LUCK
YOU CAN'T CHEW POPCORN... OR APPLES... OR CARROTS. OR GUM. OR TAFFY. OR CARAMEL. OR...
MAYBE THAT MEANS I'LL STOP CHEWING MY NAILS, TOO!!

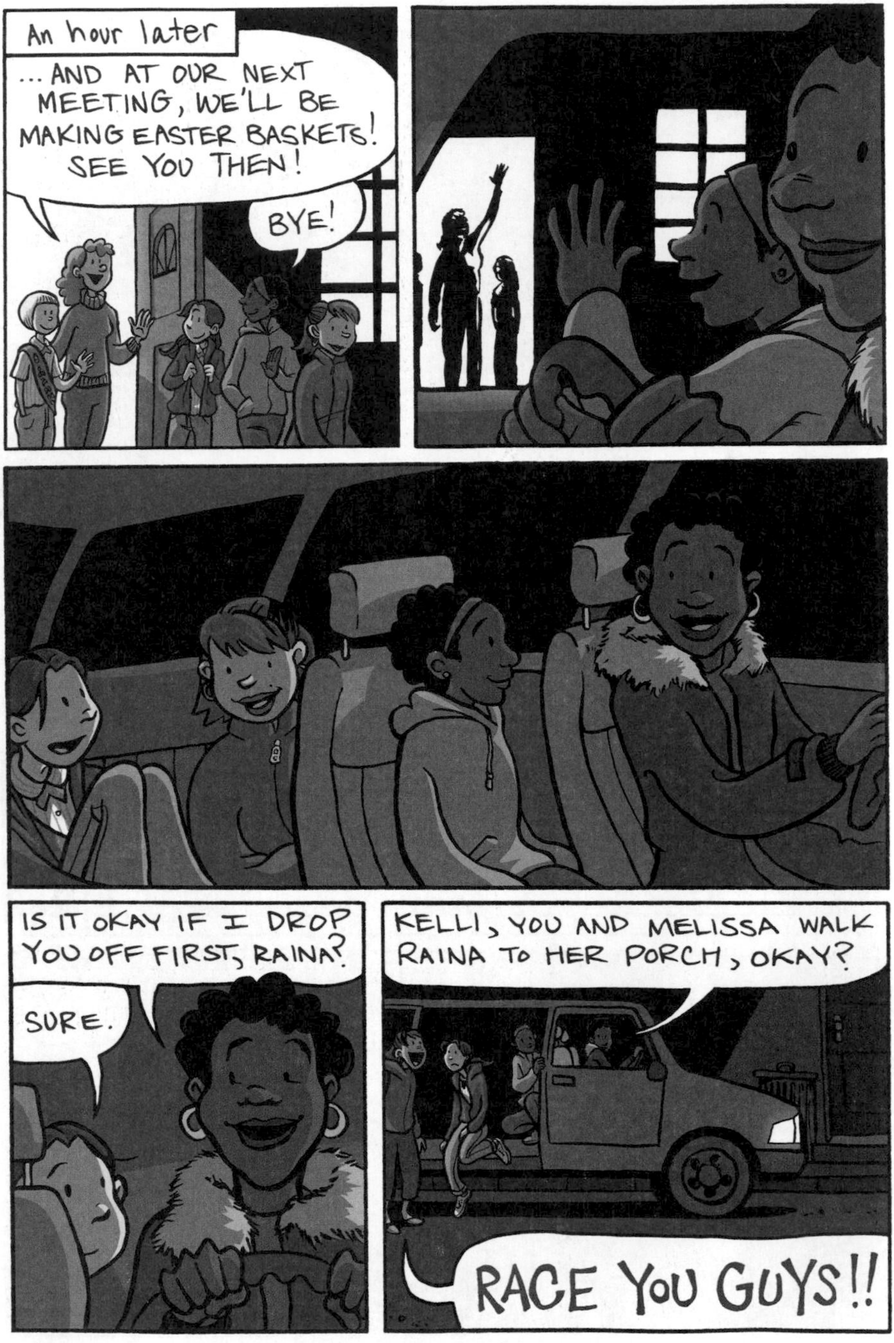
An hour later
...AND AT OUR NEXT MEETING, WE'LL BE MAKING EASTER BASKETS! SEE YOU THEN!
BYE!
IS IT OKAY IF I DROP YOU OFF FIRST, RAINA?
SURE.
KELLI, YOU AND MELISSA WALK RAINA TO HER PORCH, OKAY?
RACE YOU GUYS!!

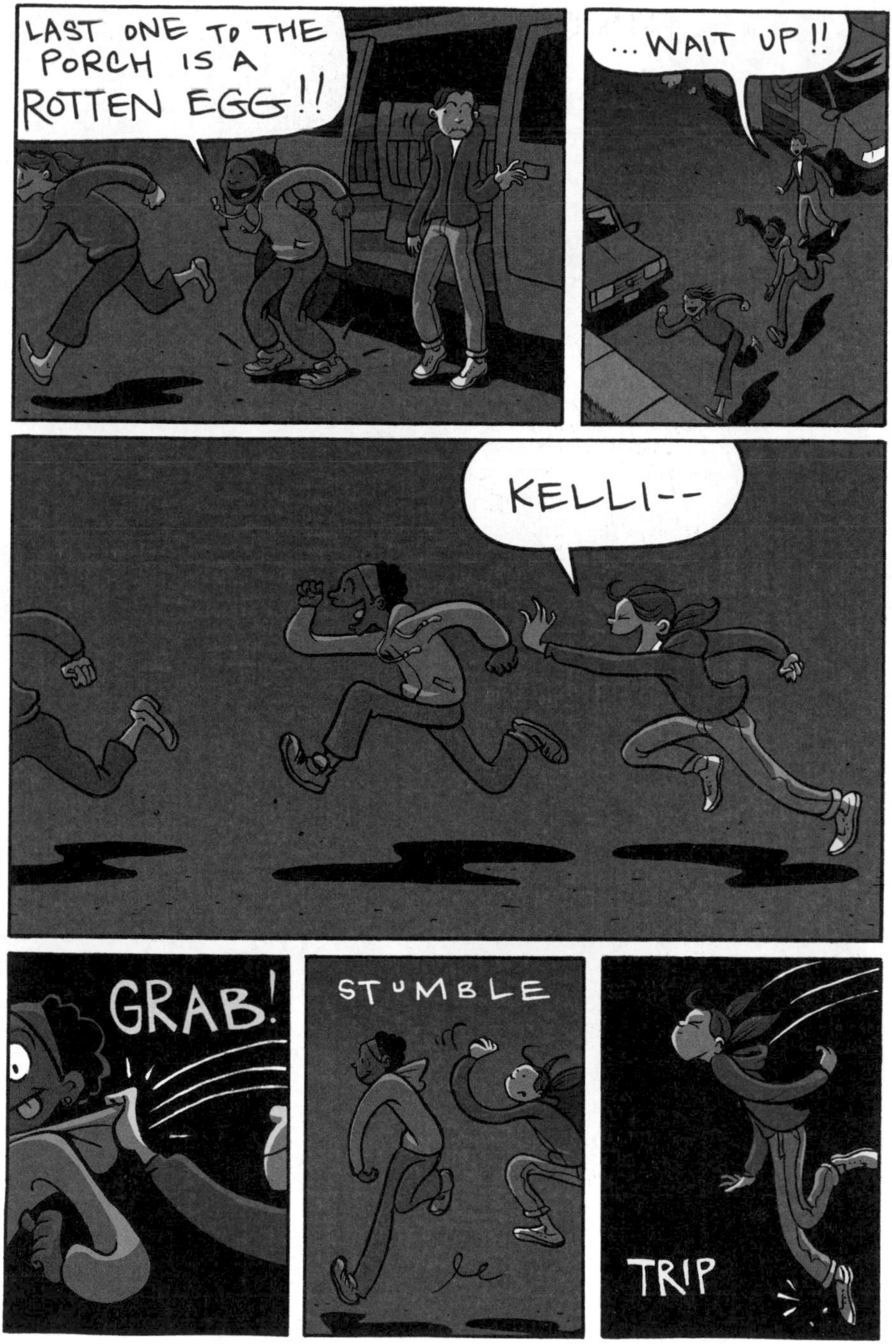
LAST ONE TO THE PORCH IS A ROTTEN EGG!!
...WAIT UP!!
KELLI--
GRAB!
STUMBLE
TRIP

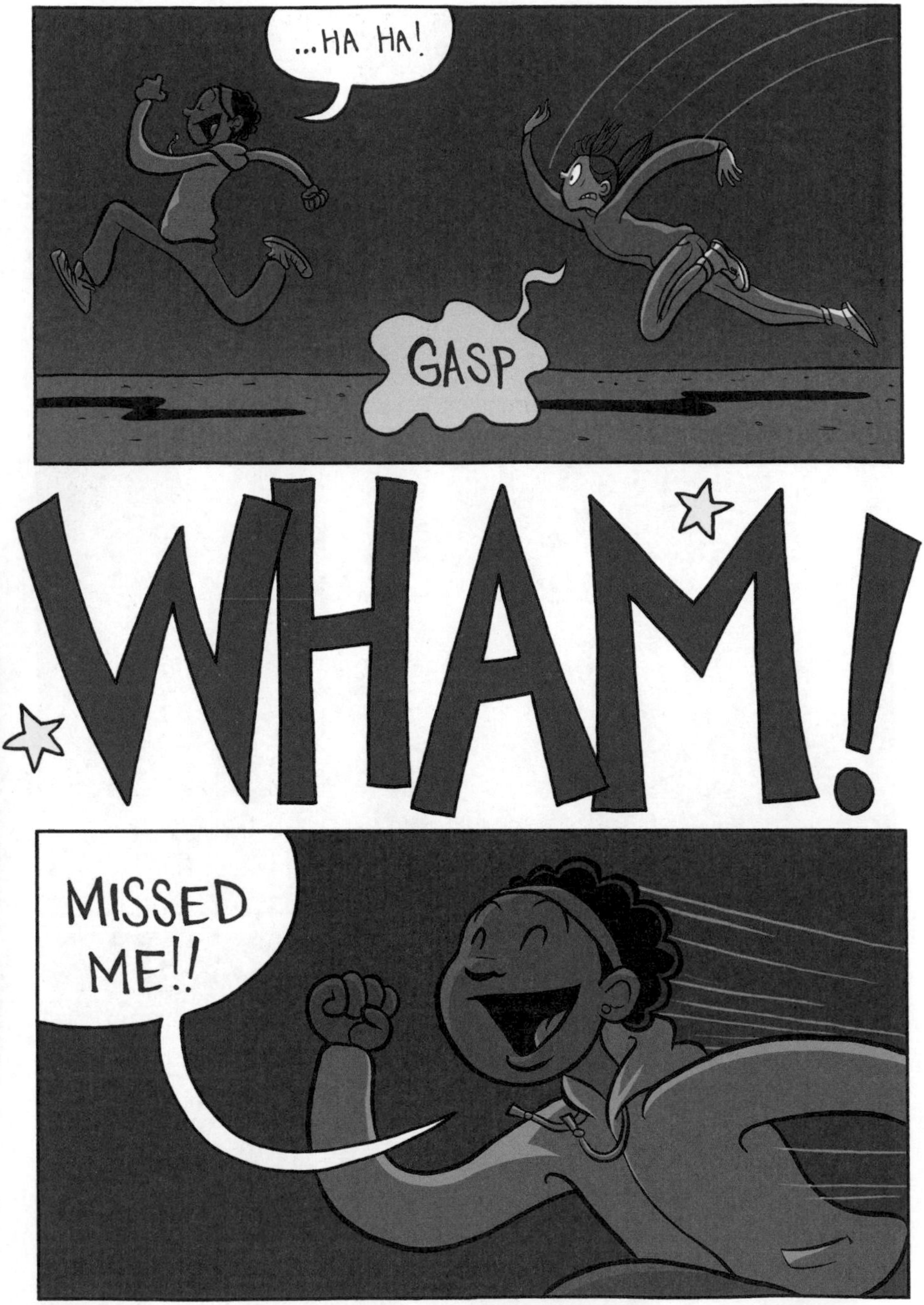
...HA HA!
GASP
WHAM!
MISSED ME!!

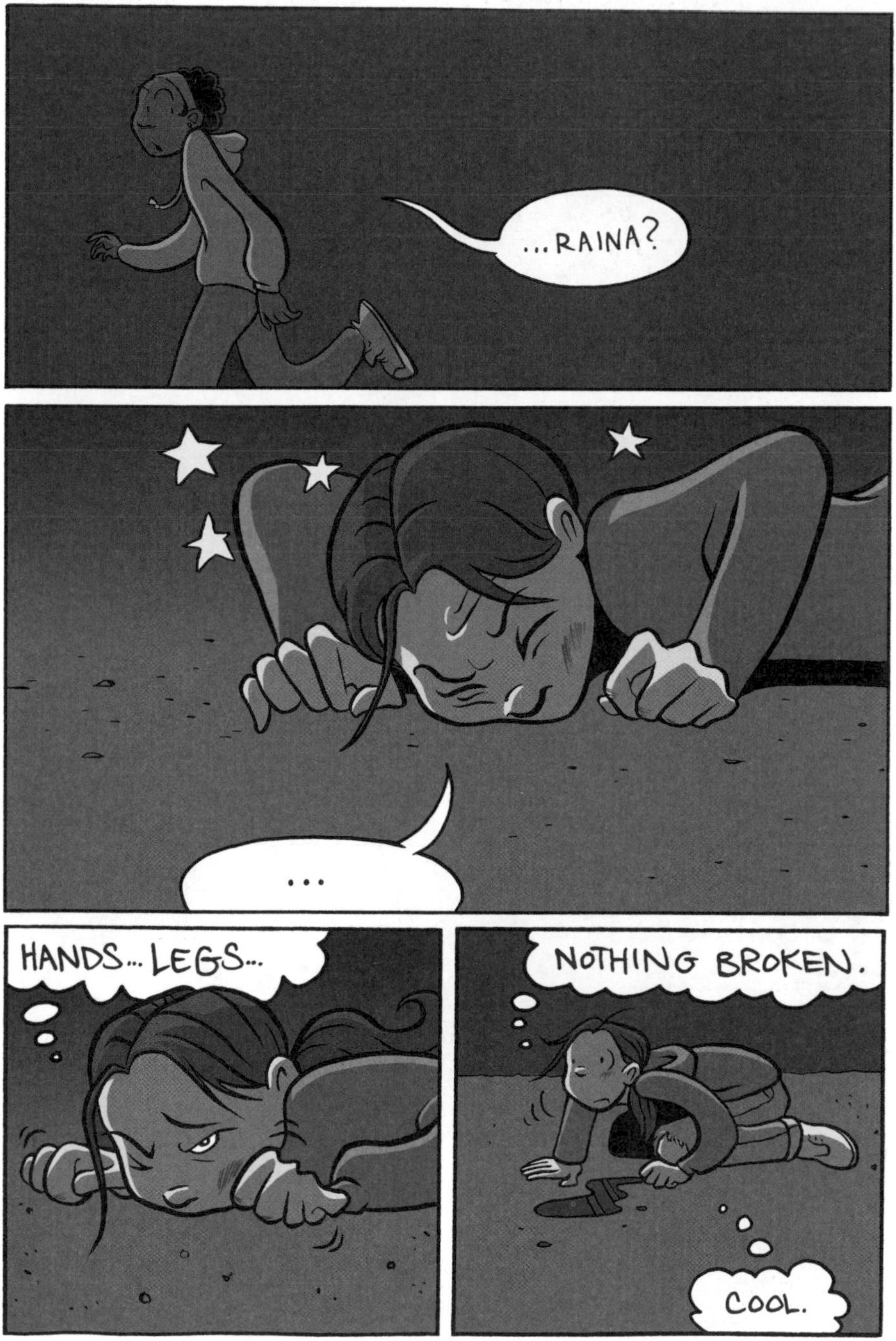
...RAINA?
...
HANDS... LEGS...
NOTHING BROKEN.
COOL.

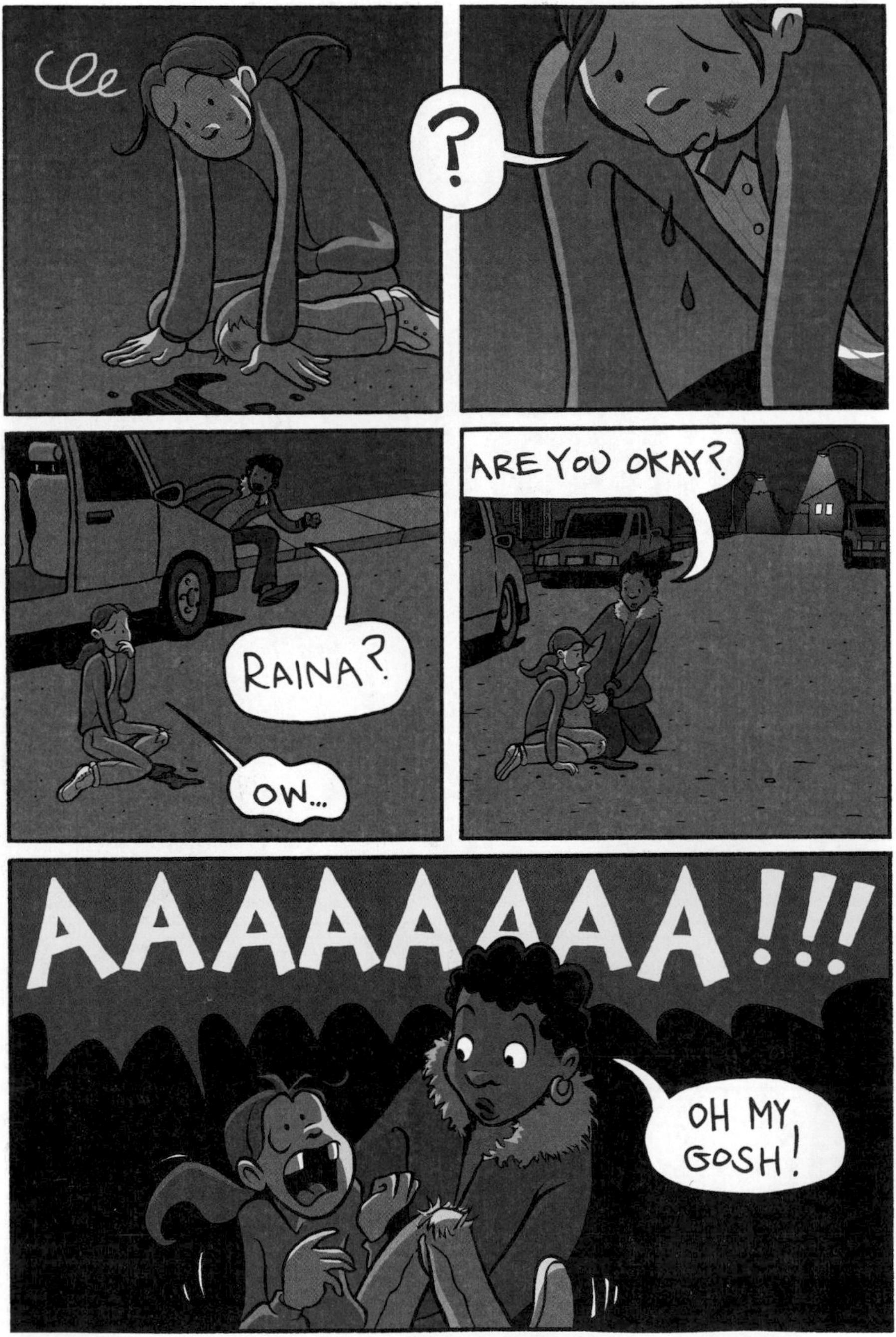
?
RAINA?
OW...
ARE YOU OKAY?
AAAAAAA!!!
OH MY GOSH!

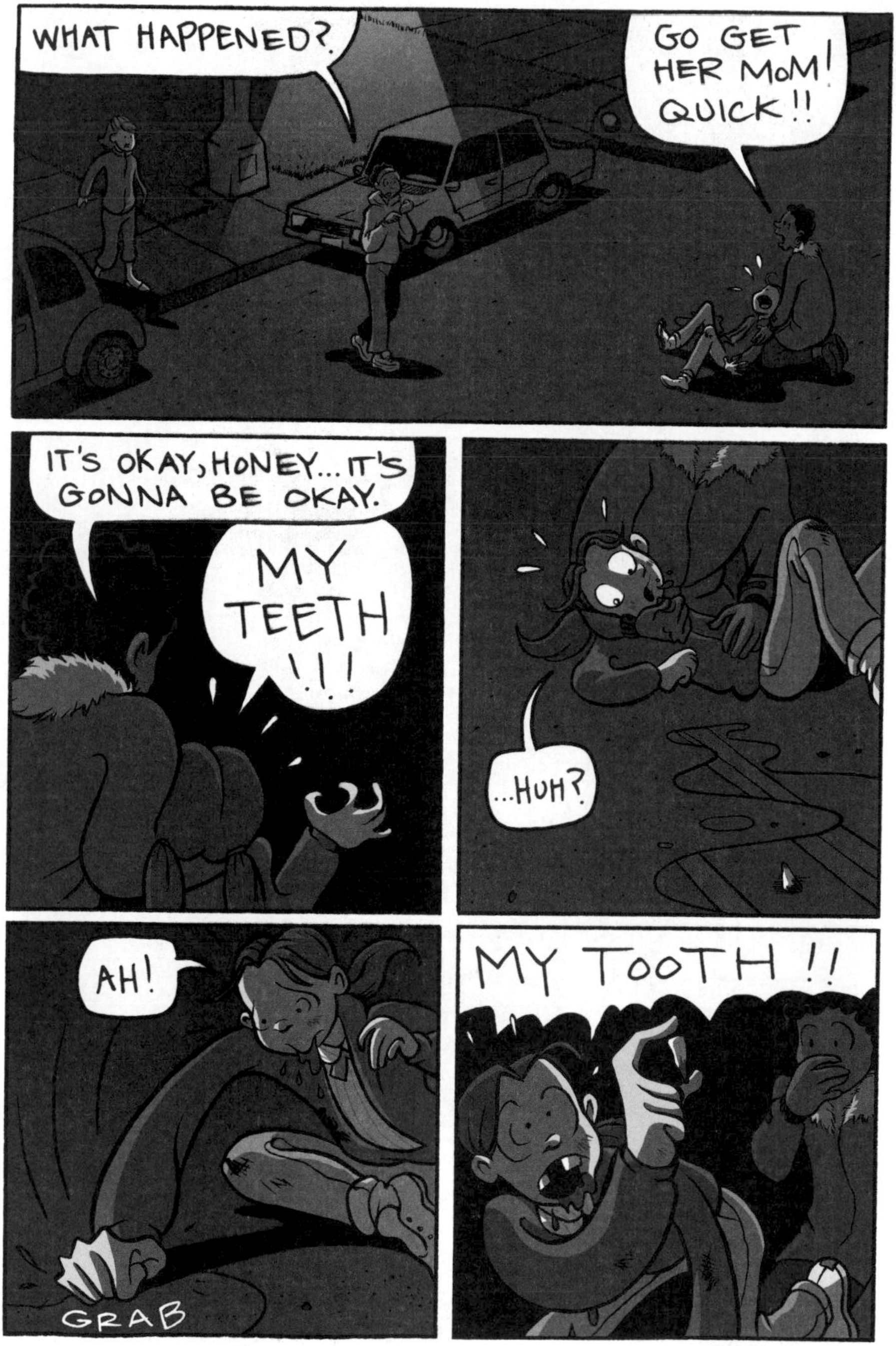
WHAT HAPPENED?
GO GET HER MOM! QUICK!!
IT'S OKAY, HONEY... IT'S GONNA BE OKAY.
MY TEETH !!!
...HUH?
AH!
GRAB
MY TOOTH !!

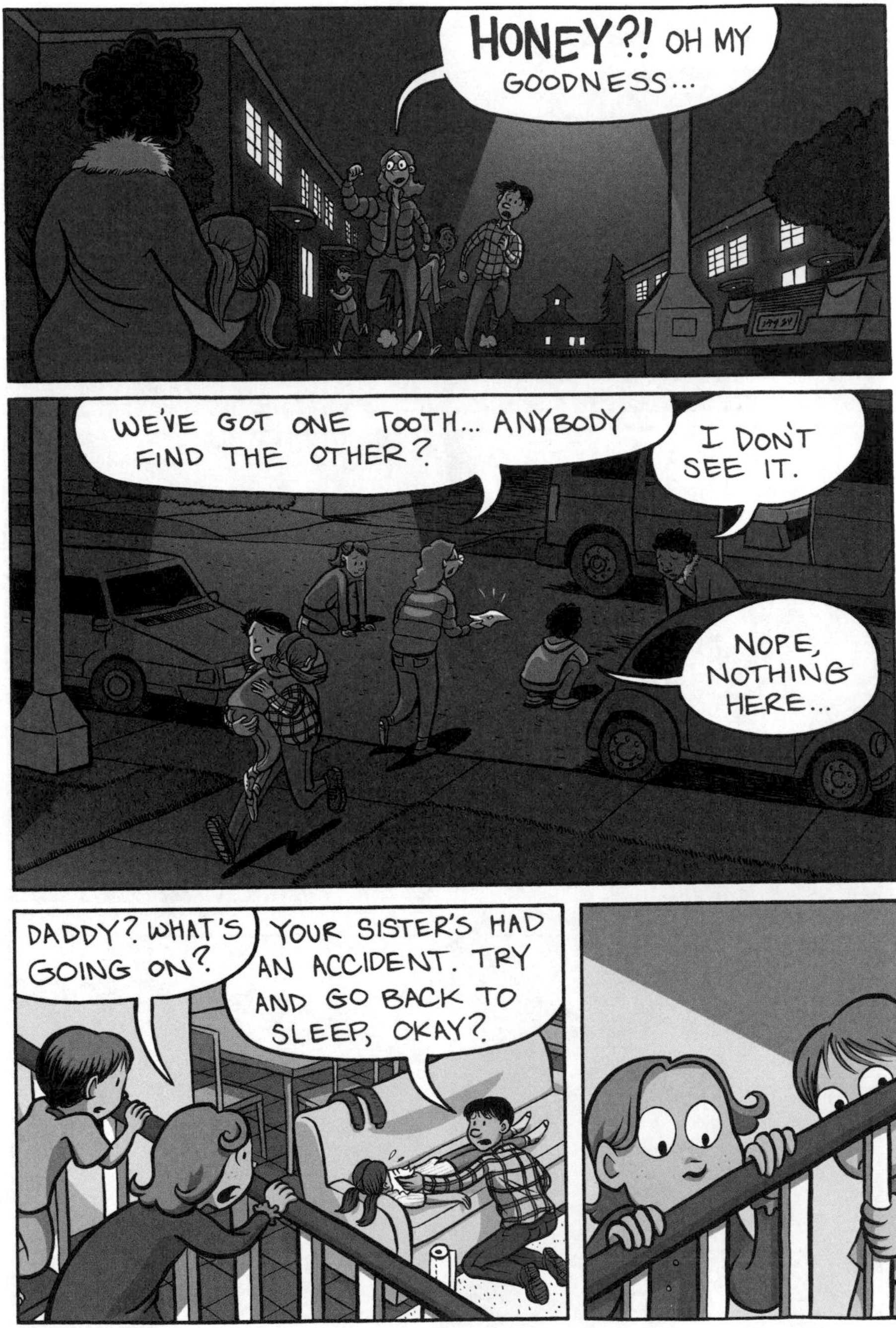
HONEY?! OH MY GOODNESS...
WE'VE GOT ONE TOOTH... ANYBODY FIND THE OTHER?
I DON'T SEE IT.
NOPE, NOTHING HERE...
DADDY? WHAT'S GOING ON?
YOUR SISTER'S HAD AN ACCIDENT. TRY AND GO BACK TO SLEEP, OKAY?

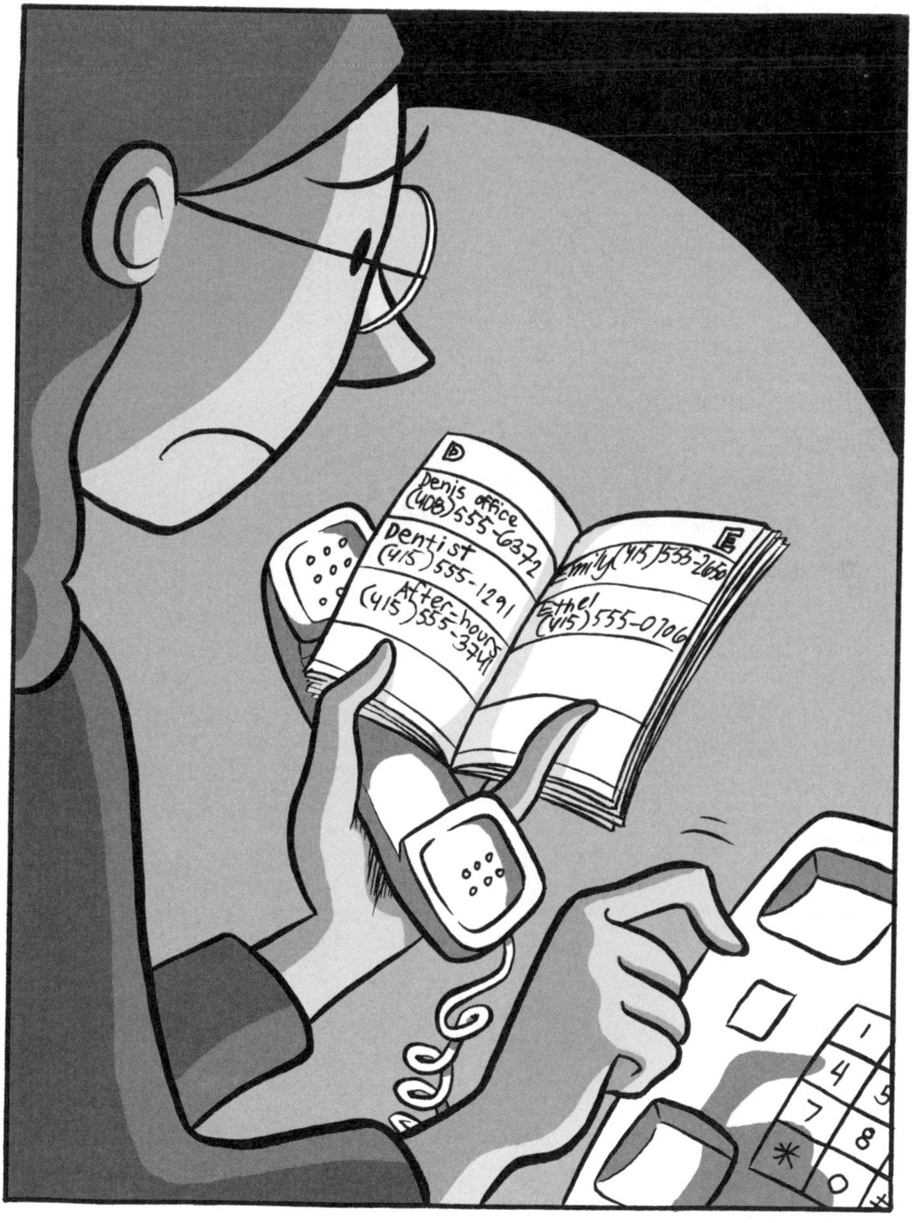
D
Denis office
(408)555-6372
Dentist
(415)555-1291
After-hours
(415)555-3741
E
Emily (415)555-2650
Ethel
(415)555-0706

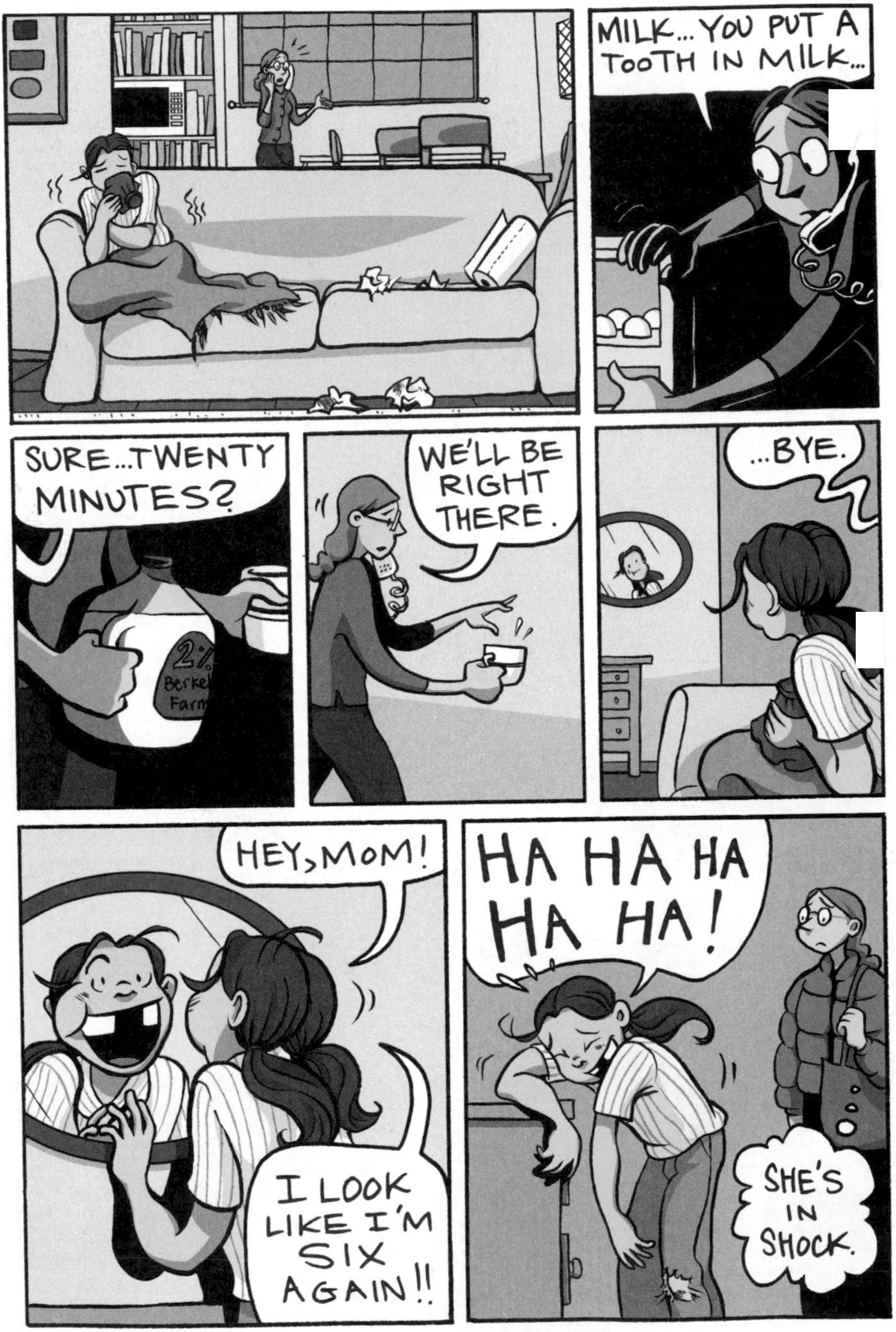
MILK... YOU PUT A TOOTH IN MILK...
SURE...TWENTY MINUTES?
WE'LL BE RIGHT THERE.
...BYE.
HEY, MOM!
I LOOK LIKE I'M SIX AGAIN!!
HA HA HA HA HA!
SHE'S IN SHOCK.

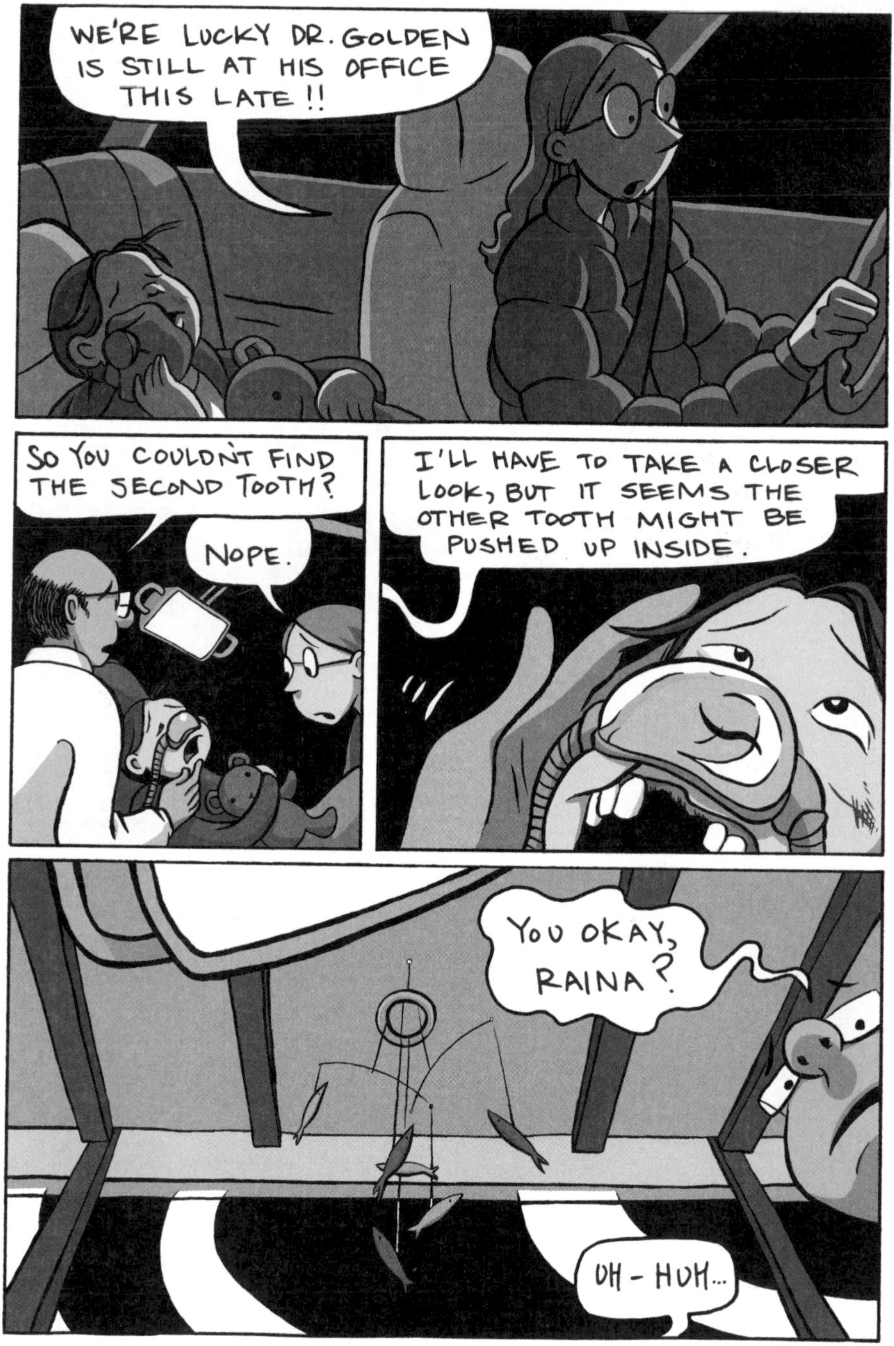
WE'RE LUCKY DR. GOLDEN IS STILL AT HIS OFFICE THIS LATE!!
SO YOU COULDN'T FIND THE SECOND TOOTH?
NOPE.
I'LL HAVE TO TAKE A CLOSER LOOK, BUT IT SEEMS THE OTHER TOOTH MIGHT BE PUSHED UP INSIDE.
YOU OKAY, RAINA?
UH-HUH...

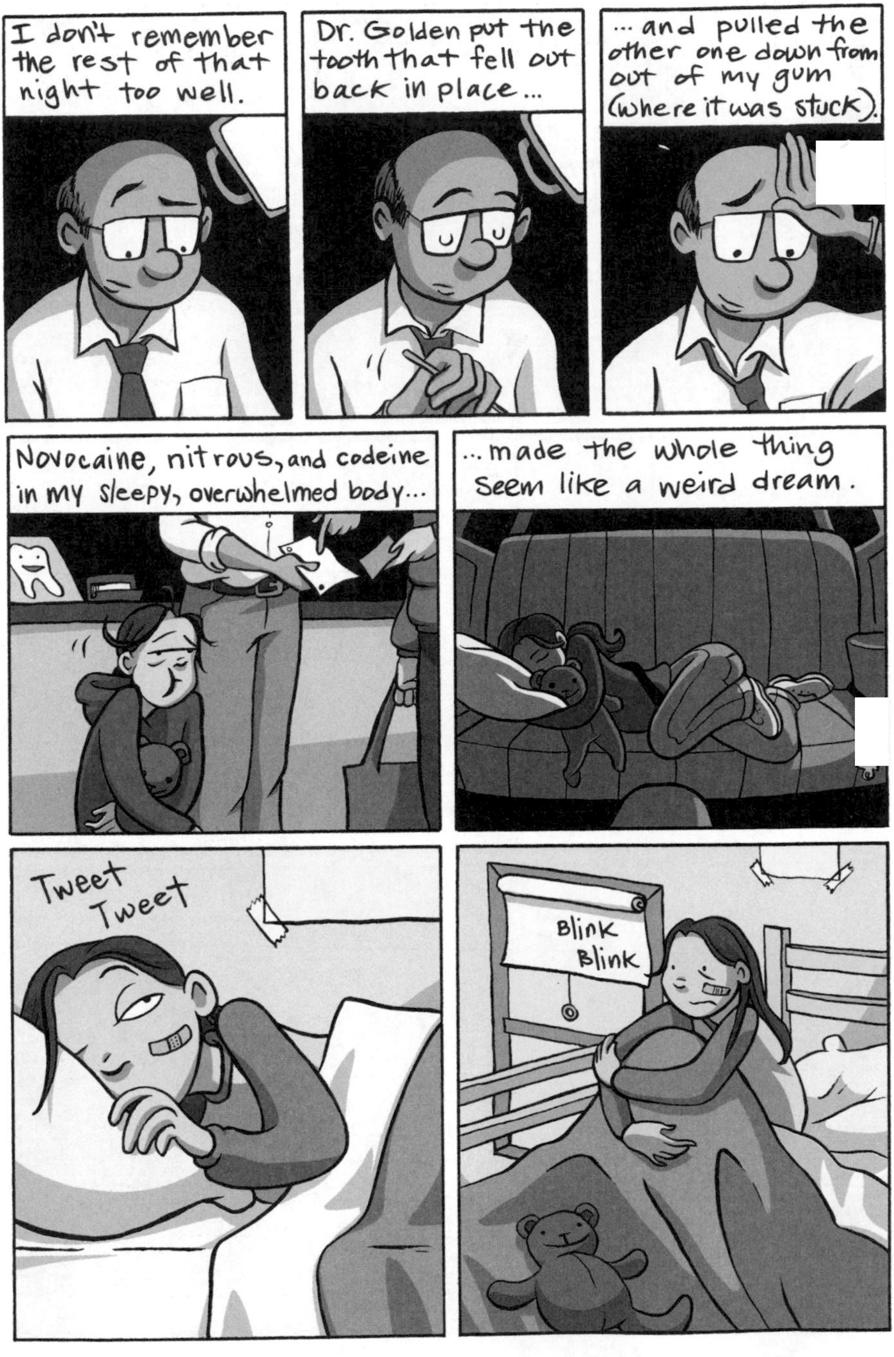
I don't remember the rest of that night too well.
Dr. Golden put the tooth that fell out back in place...
...and pulled the other one down from out of my gum (where it was stuck).
Novocaine, nitrous, and codeine in my sleepy, overwhelmed body...
...made the whole thing seem like a weird dream.
Tweet Tweet
Blink Blink

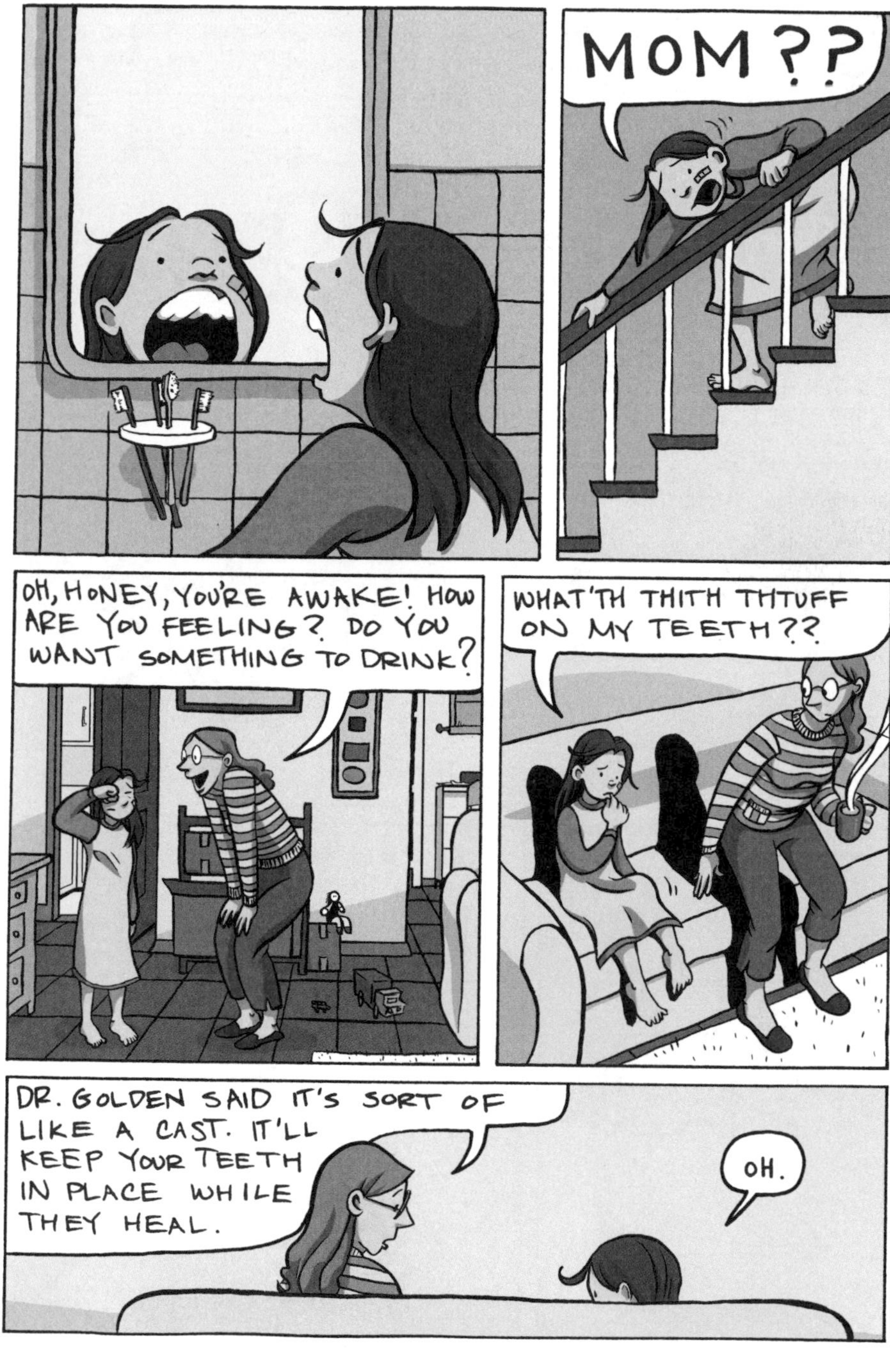
MOM??
OH, HONEY, YOU'RE AWAKE! HOW ARE YOU FEELING? DO YOU WANT SOMETHING TO DRINK?
WHAT'TH THITH THTUFF ON MY TEETH??
DR. GOLDEN SAID IT'S SORT OF LIKE A CAST. IT'LL KEEP YOUR TEETH IN PLACE WHILE THEY HEAL.
OH.

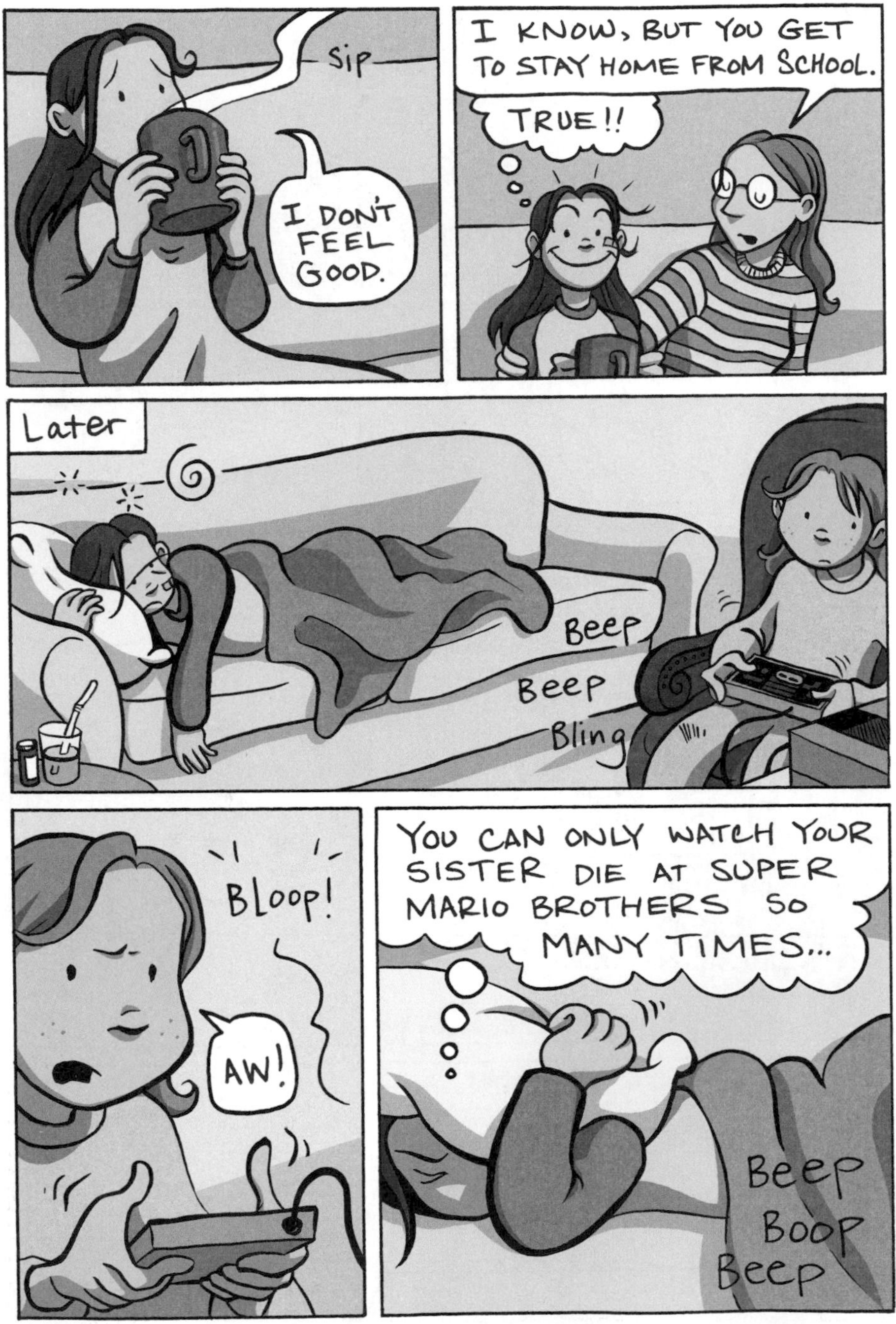
Sip
I DON'T FEEL GOOD.
I KNOW, BUT YOU GET TO STAY HOME FROM SCHOOL.
TRUE!!
Later
Beep
Beep
Bling
BLoop!
AW!
YOU CAN ONLY WATCH YOUR SISTER DIE AT SUPER MARIO BROTHERS SO MANY TIMES...
Beep
Boop
Beep

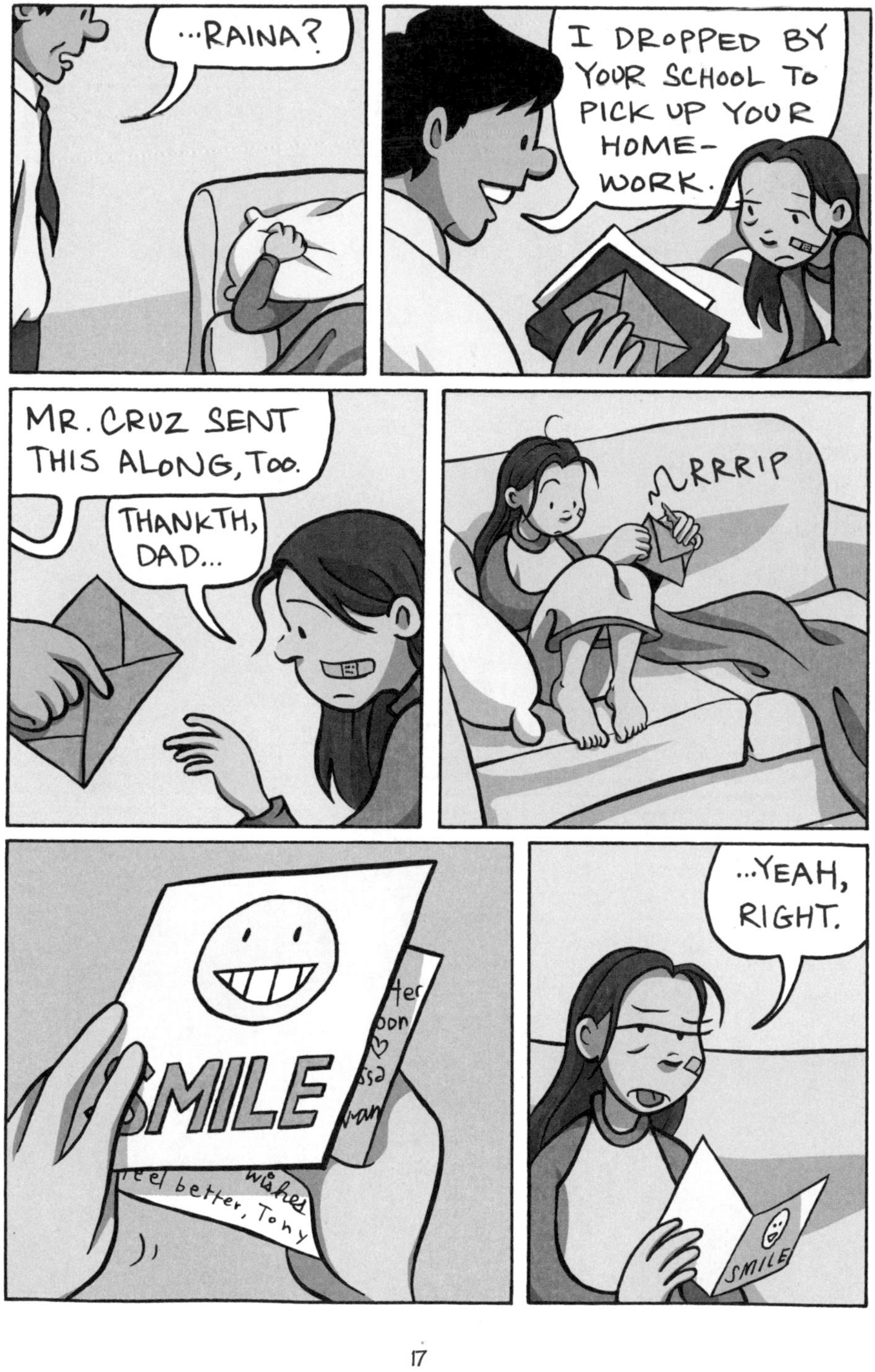
...RAINA?
I DROPPED BY YOUR SCHOOL TO PICK UP YOUR HOME-WORK.
MR. CRUZ SENT THIS ALONG, TOO.
THANKTH, DAD...
RRRIP
SMILE
wishes
better, Tony
...YEAH, RIGHT.
SMILE

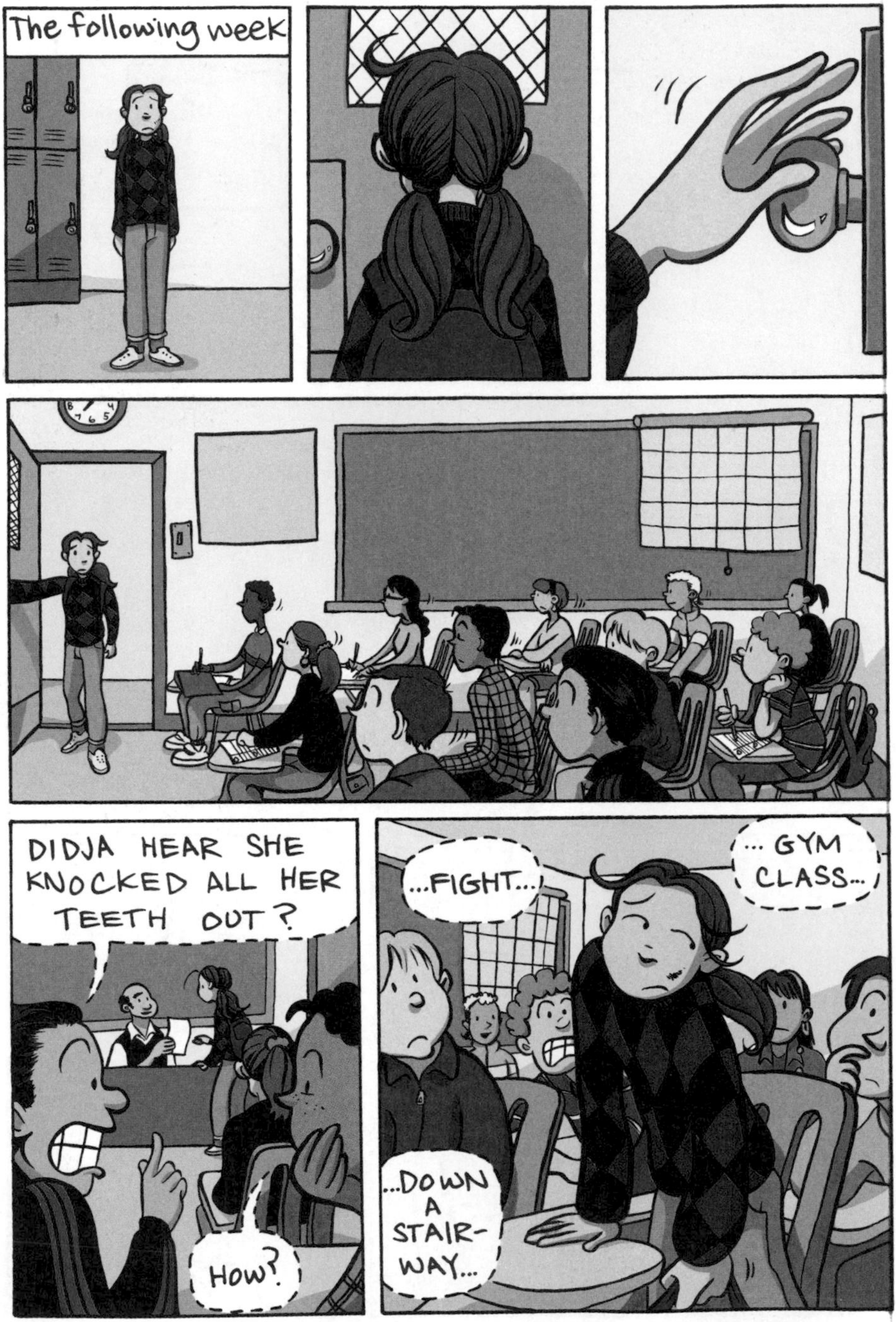
The following week
DIDJA HEAR SHE KNOCKED ALL HER TEETH OUT?
HOW?
...FIGHT...
... GYM CLASS...
...DOWN A STAIR-WAY...

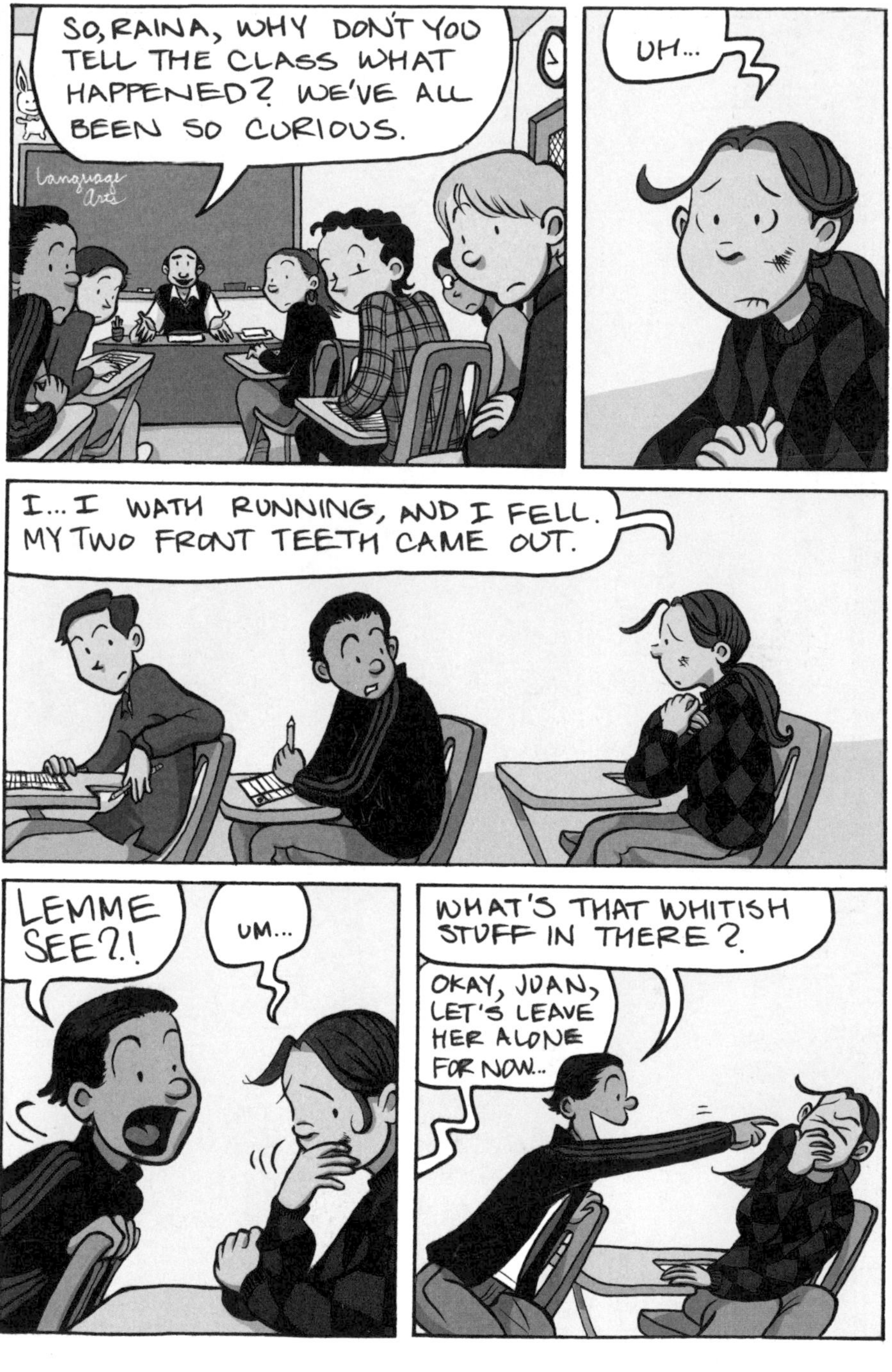
SO, RAINA, WHY DON'T YOU TELL THE CLASS WHAT HAPPENED? WE'VE ALL BEEN SO CURIOUS.
Language Arts
UH...
I... I WATH RUNNING, AND I FELL. MY TWO FRONT TEETH CAME OUT.
LEMME SEE?!
UM...
WHAT'S THAT WHITISH STUFF IN THERE?
OKAY, JUAN, LET'S LEAVE HER ALONE FOR NOW...

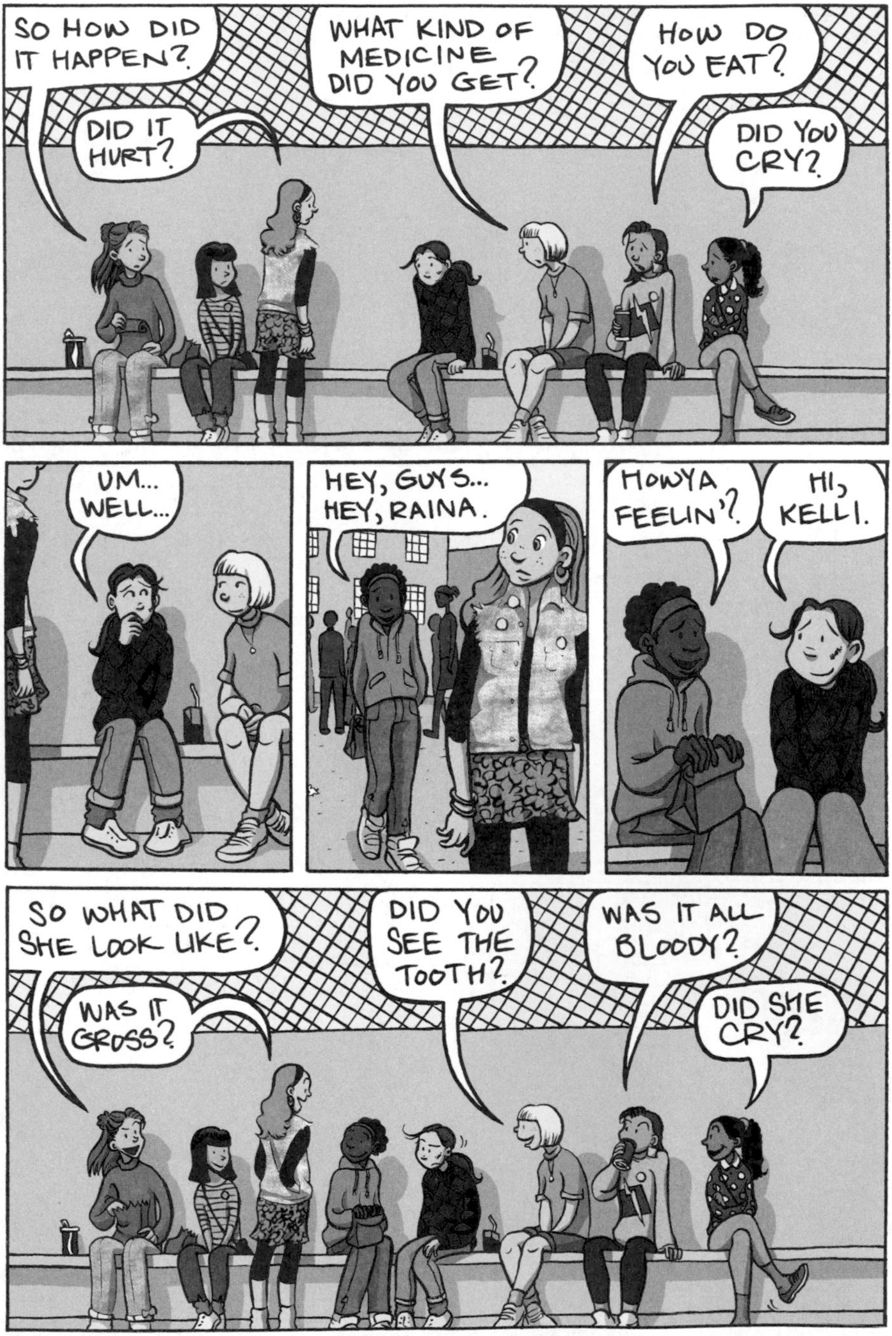
SO HOW DID IT HAPPEN?
DID IT HURT?
WHAT KIND OF MEDICINE DID YOU GET?
HOW DO YOU EAT?
DID YOU CRY?
UM... WELL...
HEY, GUYS... HEY, RAINA.
HOWYA FEELIN'?
HI, KELLI.
SO WHAT DID SHE LOOK LIKE?
WAS IT GROSS?
DID YOU SEE THE TOOTH?
WAS IT ALL BLOODY?
DID SHE CRY?

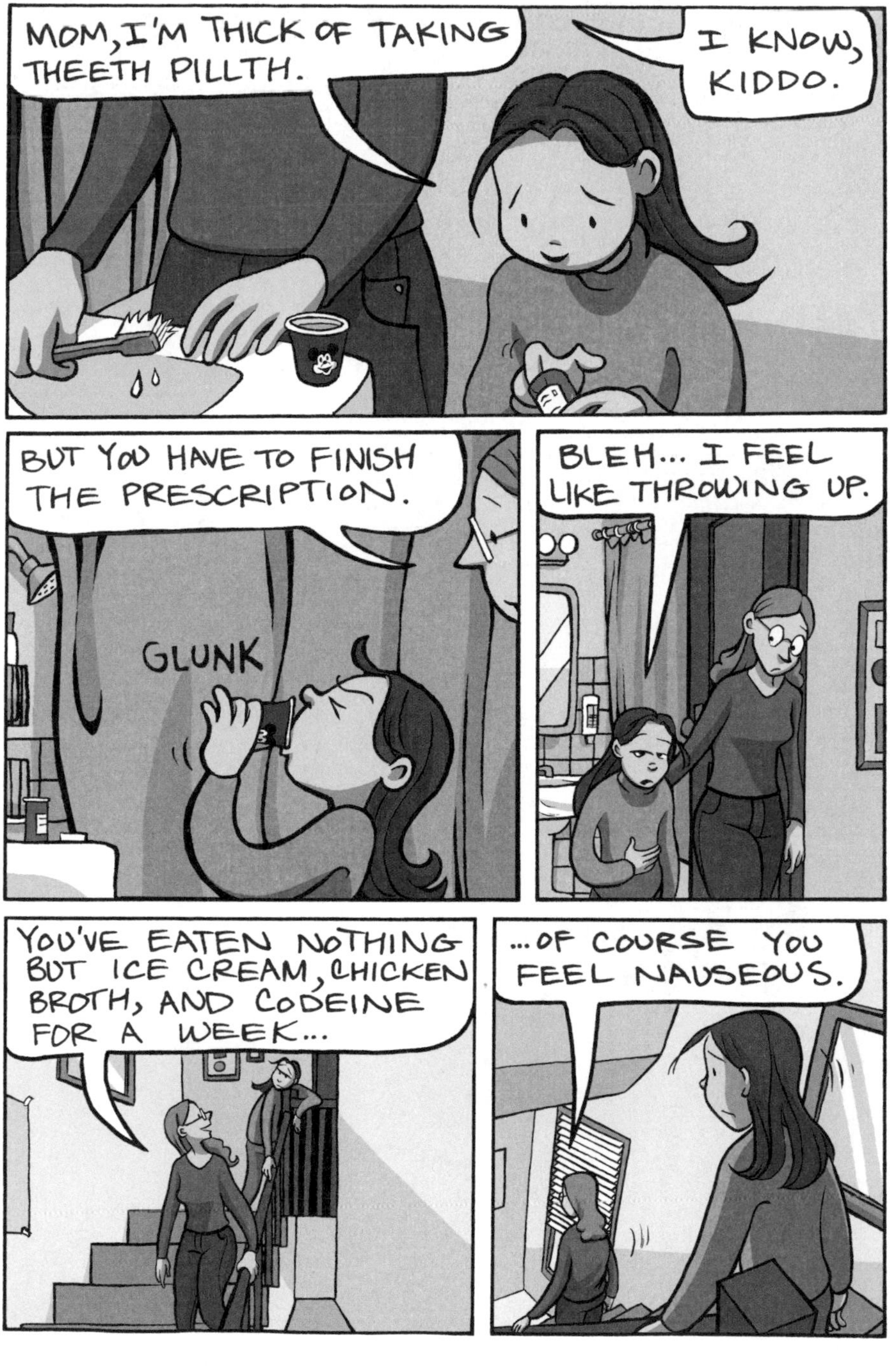
MOM, I'M THICK OF TAKING THEETH PILLTH.
I KNOW, KIDDO.
BUT YOU HAVE TO FINISH THE PRESCRIPTION.
GLUNK
BLEH... I FEEL LIKE THROWING UP.
YOU'VE EATEN NOTHING BUT ICE CREAM, CHICKEN BROTH, AND CODEINE FOR A WEEK...
...OF COURSE YOU FEEL NAUSEOUS.

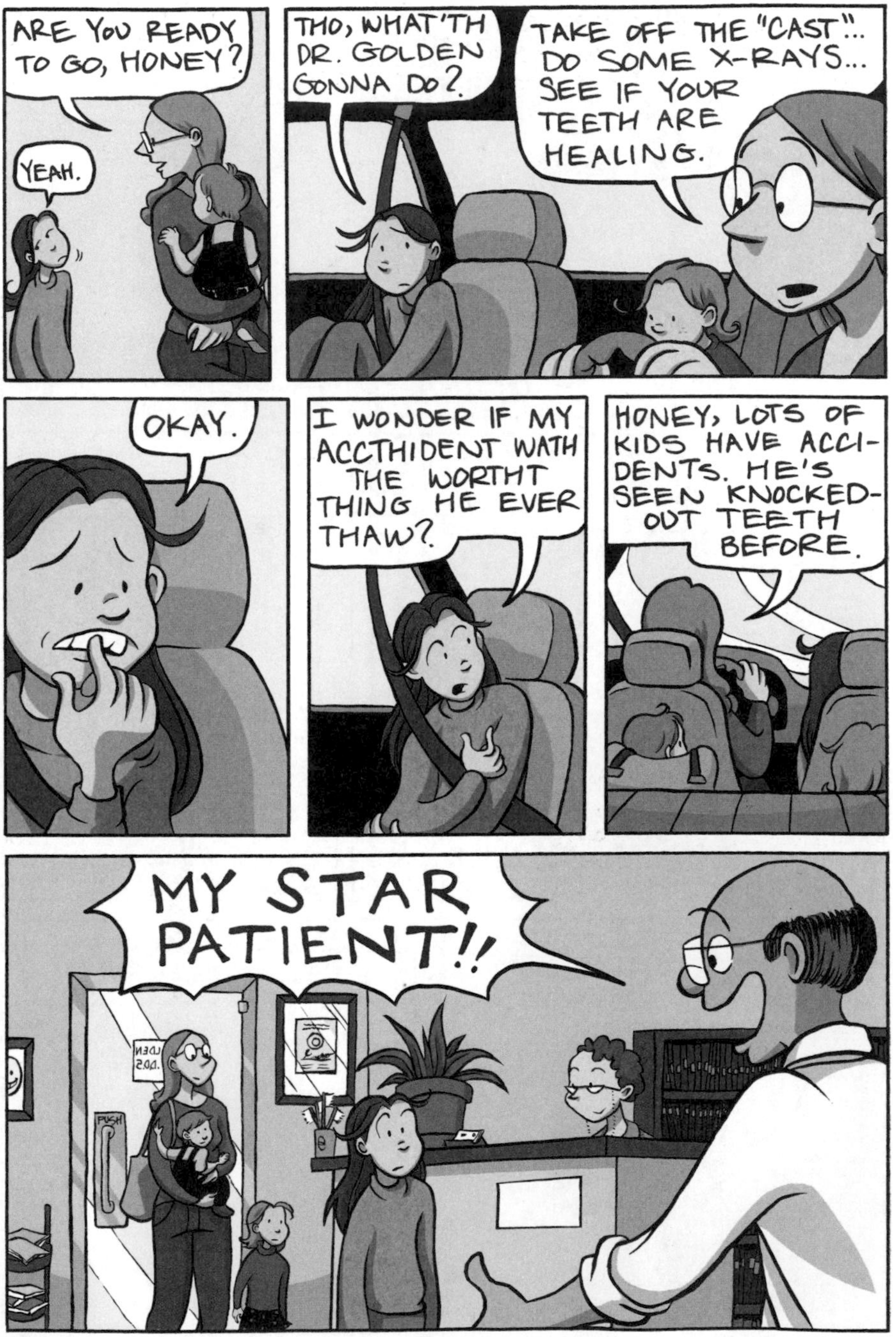
ARE YOU READY TO GO, HONEY?
YEAH.
THO, WHAT'TH DR. GOLDEN GONNA DO?
TAKE OFF THE "CAST"... DO SOME X-RAYS... SEE IF YOUR TEETH ARE HEALING.
OKAY.
I WONDER IF MY ACCTHIDENT WATH THE WORTHT THING HE EVER THAW?
HONEY, LOTS OF KIDS HAVE ACCI-DENTS. HE'S SEEN KNOCKED-OUT TEETH BEFORE.
MY STAR PATIENT!!
PUSH

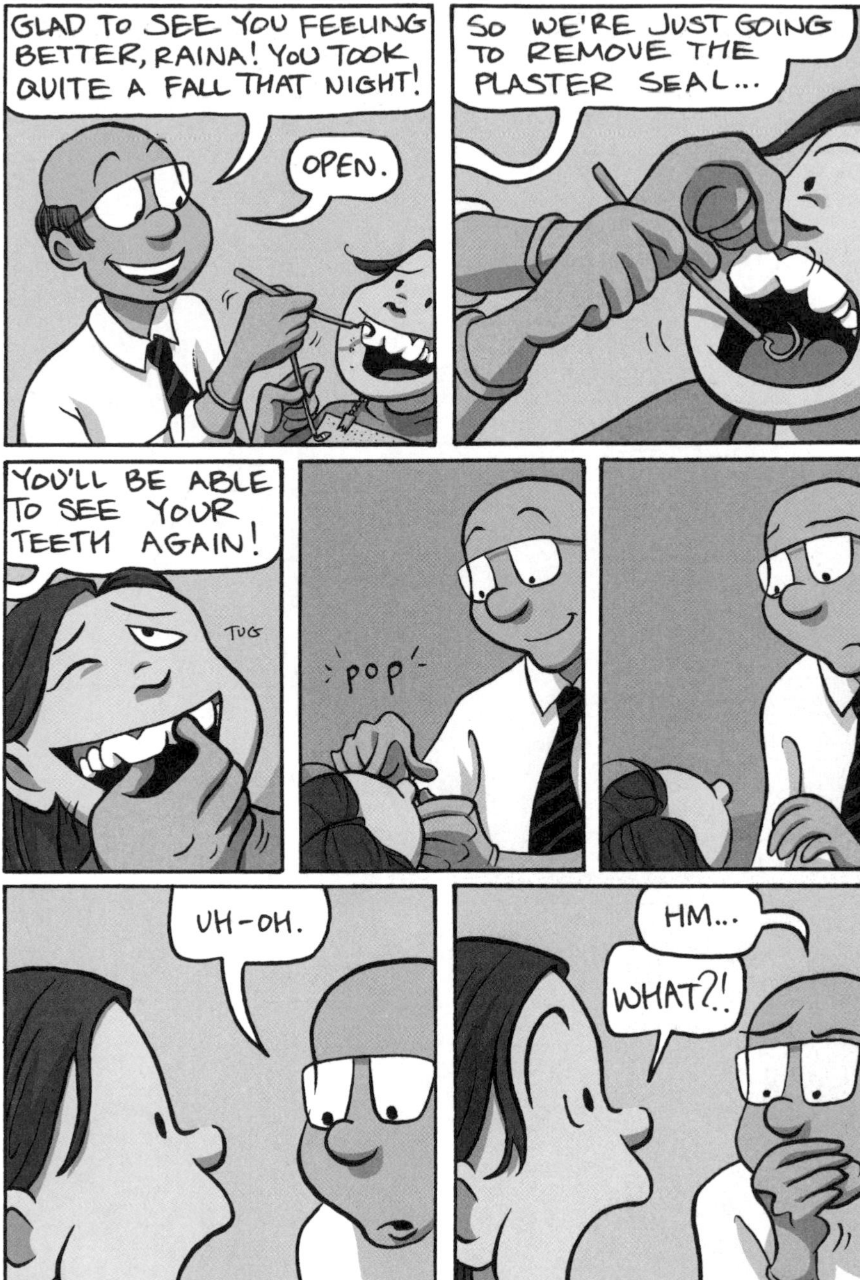
GLAD TO SEE YOU FEELING BETTER, RAINA! YOU TOOK QUITE A FALL THAT NIGHT!
OPEN.
SO WE'RE JUST GOING TO REMOVE THE PLASTER SEAL...
YOU'LL BE ABLE TO SEE YOUR TEETH AGAIN!
TUG
pop
UH-OH.
HM...
WHAT?!

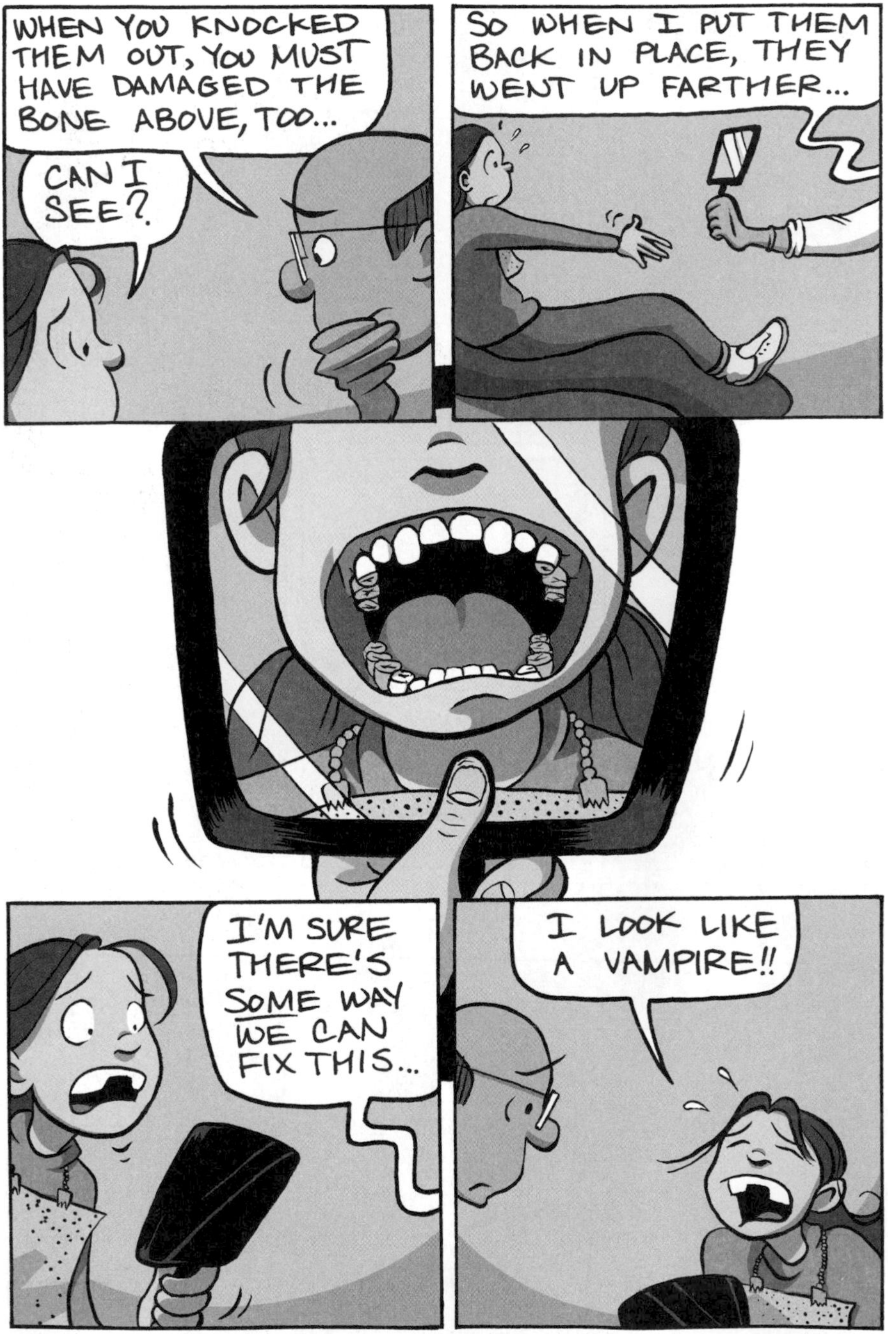
WHEN YOU KNOCKED THEM OUT, YOU MUST HAVE DAMAGED THE BONE ABOVE, TOO...
CAN I SEE?
SO WHEN I PUT THEM BACK IN PLACE, THEY WENT UP FARTHER...
I'M SURE THERE'S SOME WAY WE CAN FIX THIS...
I LOOK LIKE A VAMPIRE!!

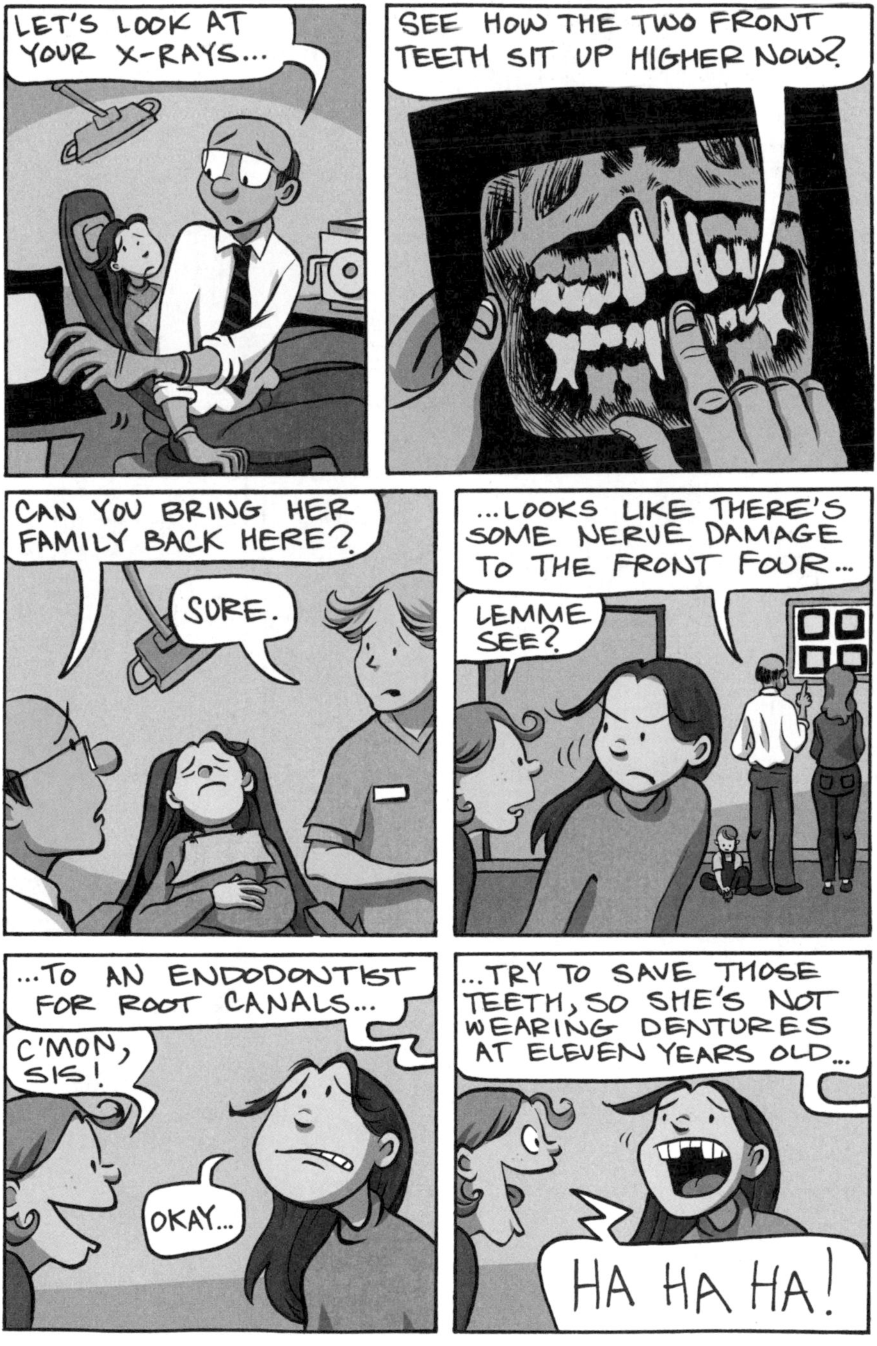
LET'S LOOK AT YOUR X-RAYS...
SEE HOW THE TWO FRONT TEETH SIT UP HIGHER NOW?
CAN YOU BRING HER FAMILY BACK HERE?
SURE.
...LOOKS LIKE THERE'S SOME NERVE DAMAGE TO THE FRONT FOUR...
LEMME SEE?
...TO AN ENDODONTIST FOR ROOT CANALS...
C'MON, SIS!
OKAY...
...TRY TO SAVE THOSE TEETH, SO SHE'S NOT WEARING DENTURES AT ELEVEN YEARS OLD...
HA HA HA!

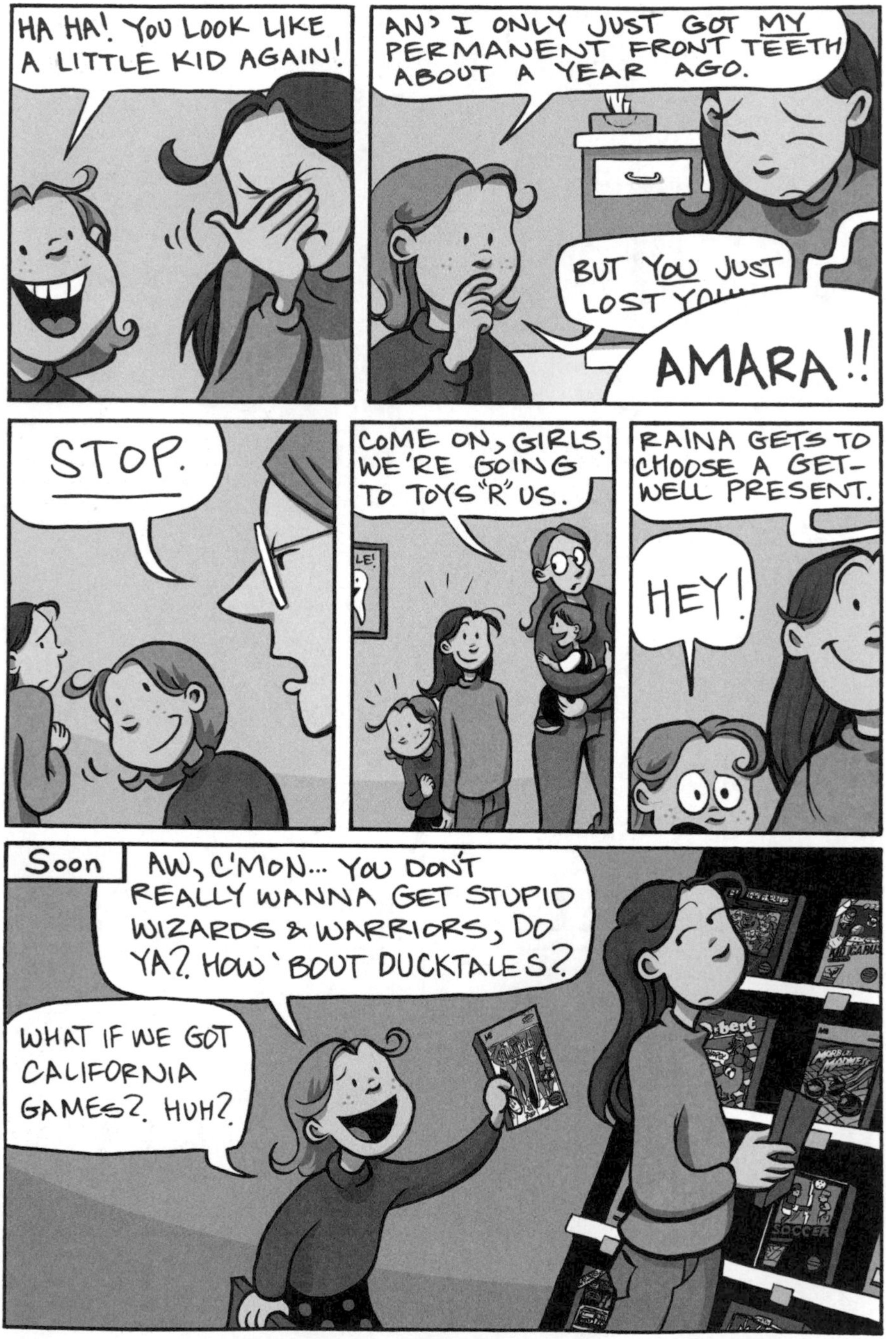
HA HA! YOU LOOK LIKE A LITTLE KID AGAIN!
AN' I ONLY JUST GOT MY PERMANENT FRONT TEETH ABOUT A YEAR AGO.
BUT YOU JUST LOST YOU
AMARA!!
STOP.
COME ON, GIRLS. WE'RE GOING TO TOYS"R"US.
RAINA GETS TO CHOOSE A GET-WELL PRESENT.
HEY!
Soon
AW, C'MON... YOU DON'T REALLY WANNA GET STUPID WIZARDS & WARRIORS, DO YA? HOW 'BOUT DUCKTALES?
WHAT IF WE GOT CALIFORNIA GAMES? HUH?

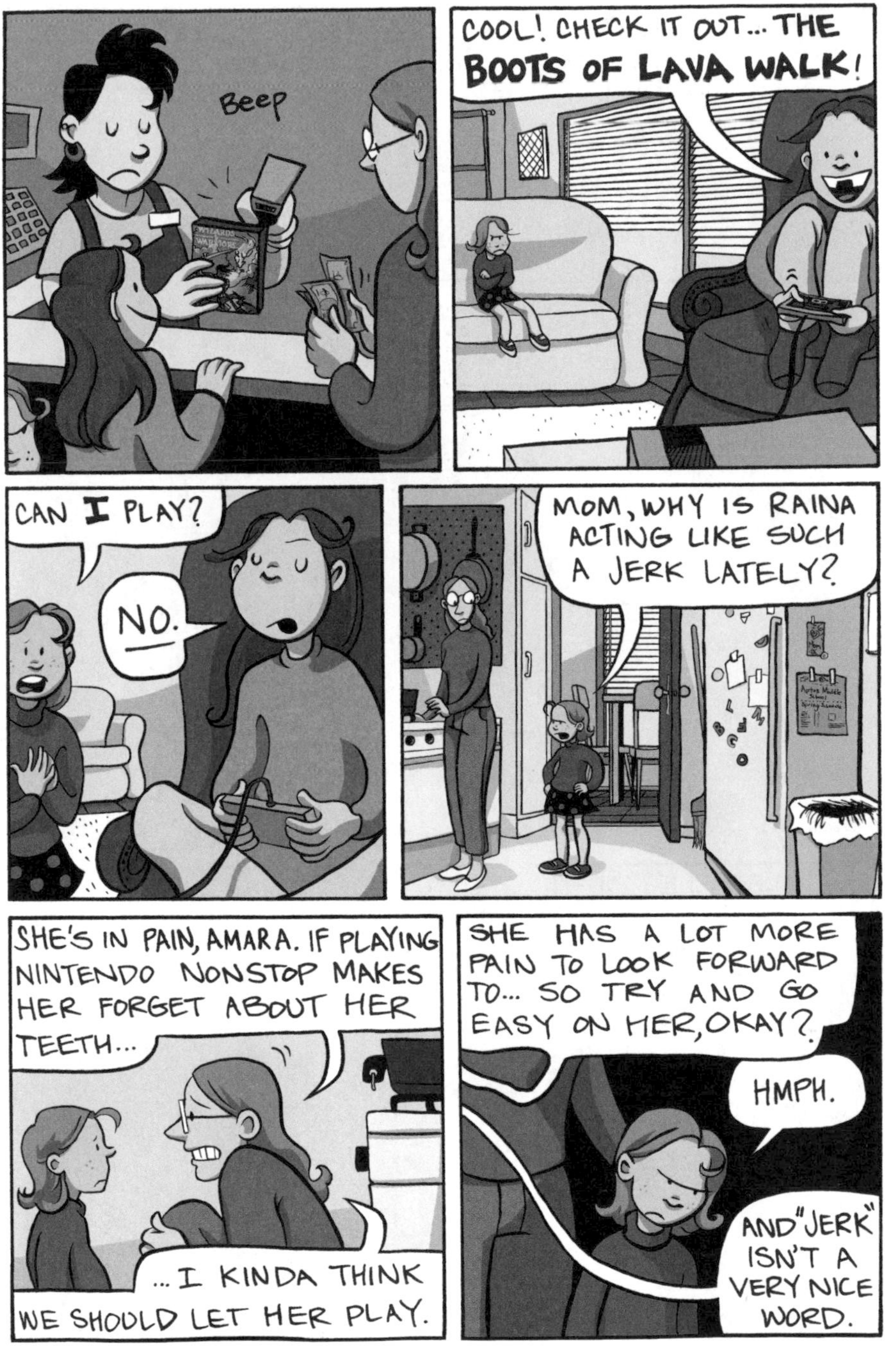
Beep
COOL! CHECK IT OUT... THE BOOTS OF LAVA WALK!
CAN I PLAY?
NO.
MOM, WHY IS RAINA ACTING LIKE SUCH A JERK LATELY?
SHE'S IN PAIN, AMARA. IF PLAYING NINTENDO NONSTOP MAKES HER FORGET ABOUT HER TEETH...
...I KINDA THINK WE SHOULD LET HER PLAY.
SHE HAS A LOT MORE PAIN TO LOOK FORWARD TO... SO TRY AND GO EASY ON HER, OKAY?
HMPH.
AND "JERK" ISN'T A VERY NICE WORD.

CHAPTER TWO

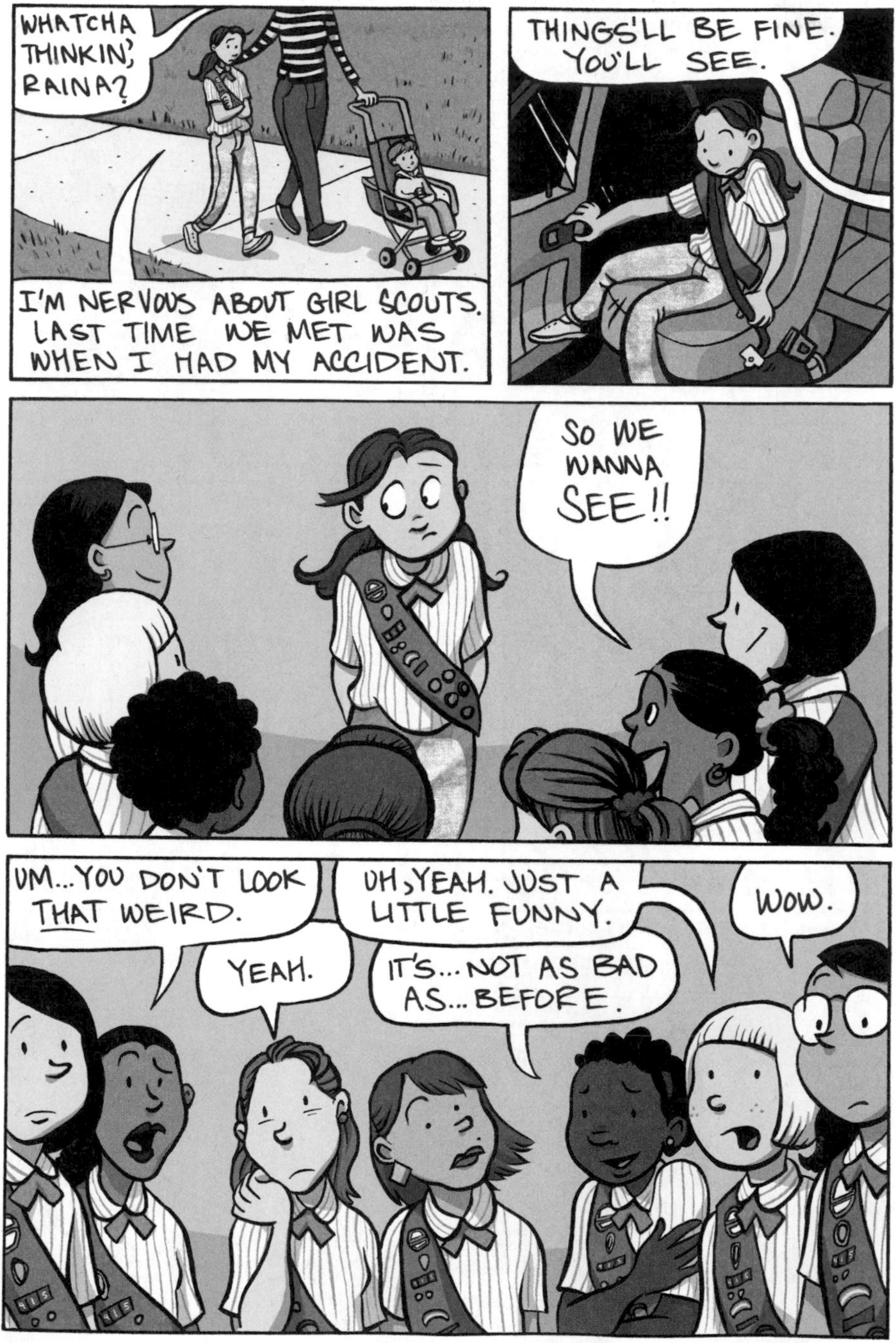
WHATCHA THINKIN', RAINA?
I'M NERVOUS ABOUT GIRL SCOUTS. LAST TIME WE MET WAS WHEN I HAD MY ACCIDENT.
THINGS'LL BE FINE. YOU'LL SEE.
SO WE WANNA SEE!!
UM... YOU DON'T LOOK THAT WEIRD.
YEAH.
UH, YEAH. JUST A LITTLE FUNNY.
IT'S... NOT AS BAD AS... BEFORE.
WOW.

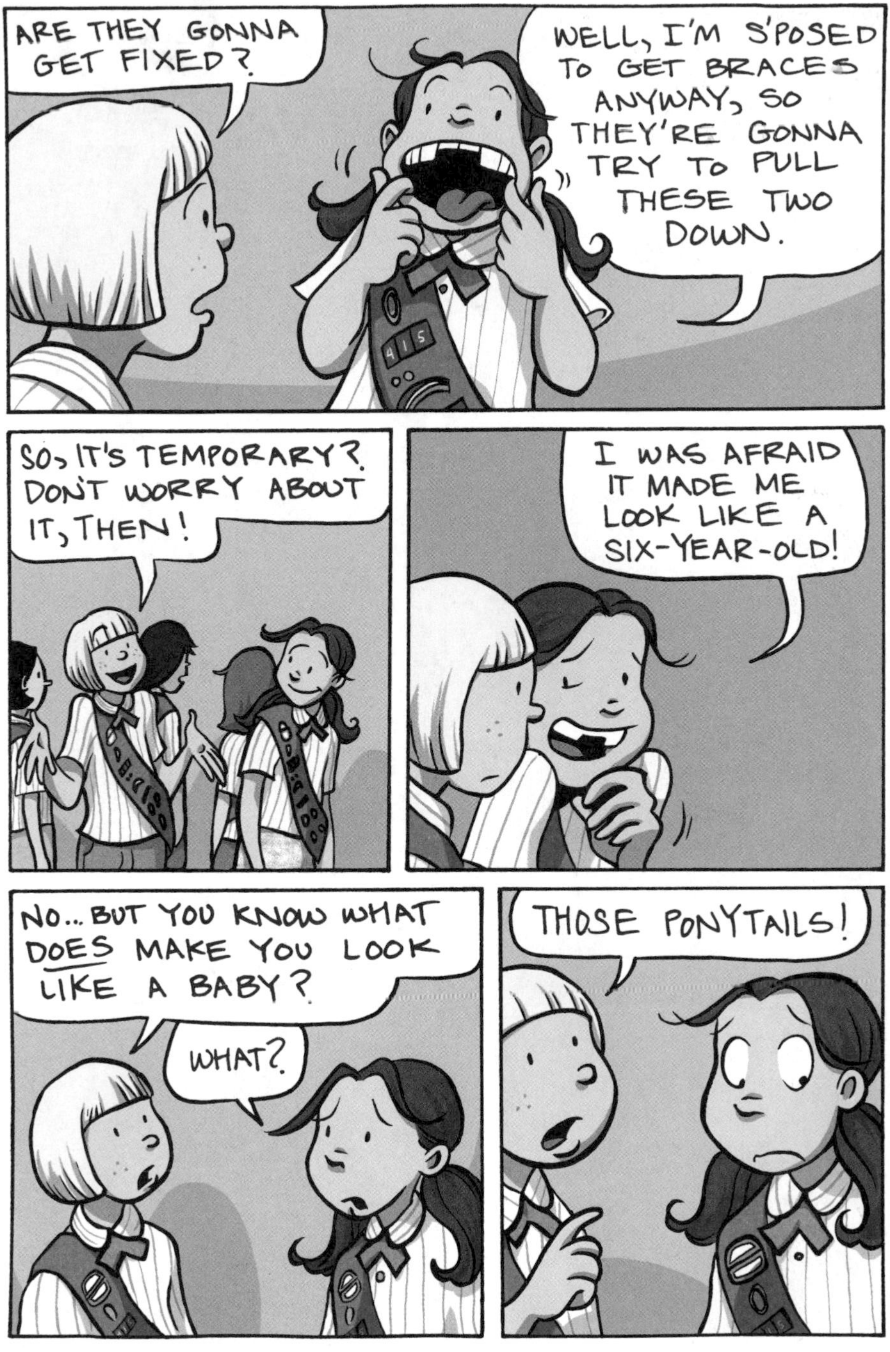
ARE THEY GONNA GET FIXED?
WELL, I'M S'POSED TO GET BRACES ANYWAY, SO THEY'RE GONNA TRY TO PULL THESE TWO DOWN.
SO, IT'S TEMPORARY? DON'T WORRY ABOUT IT, THEN!
I WAS AFRAID IT MADE ME LOOK LIKE A SIX-YEAR-OLD!
NO... BUT YOU KNOW WHAT DOES MAKE YOU LOOK LIKE A BABY?
WHAT?
THOSE PONYTAILS!

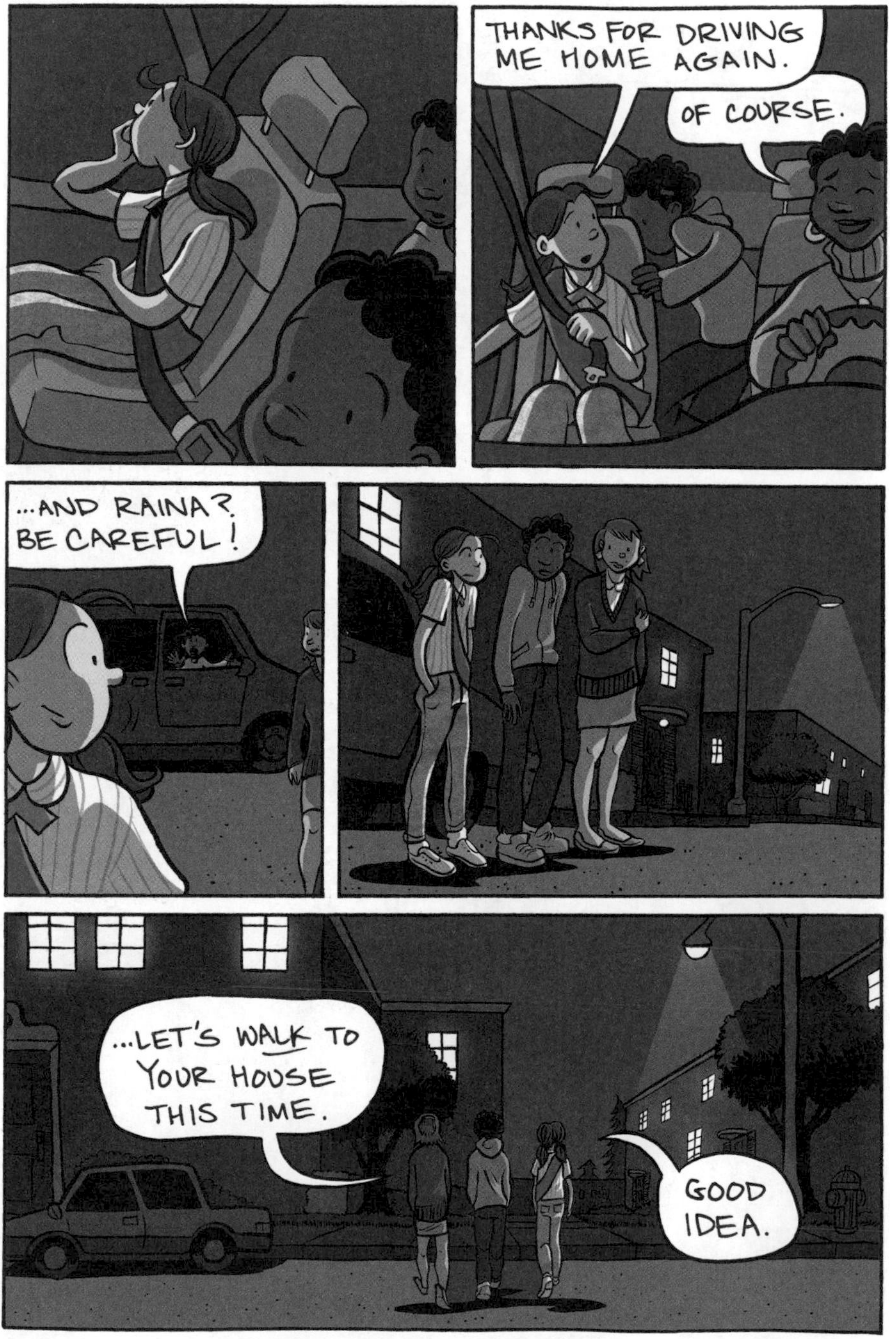
THANKS FOR DRIVING ME HOME AGAIN.
OF COURSE.
...AND RAINA? BE CAREFUL!
...LET'S WALK TO YOUR HOUSE THIS TIME.
GOOD IDEA.

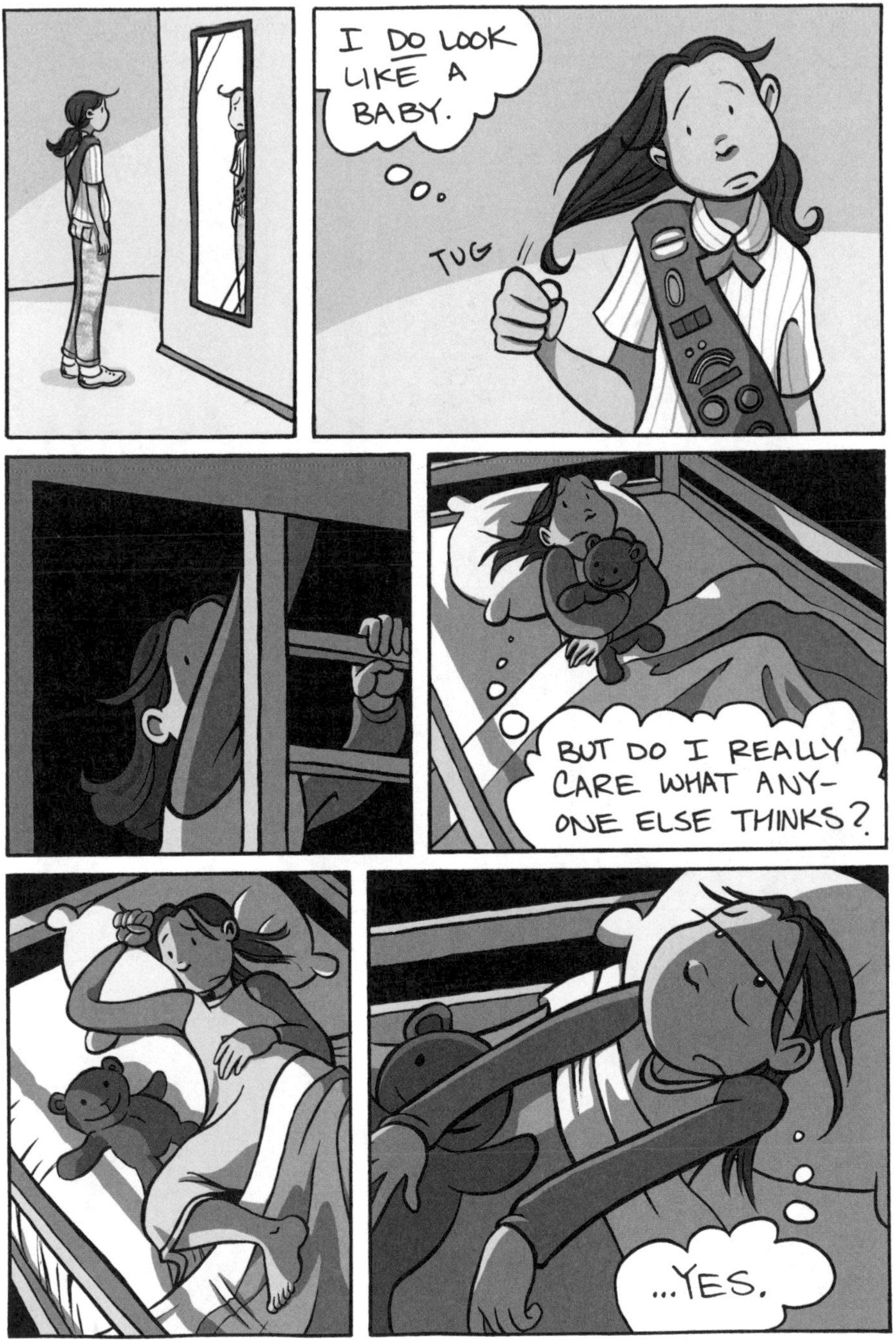
I DO LOOK LIKE A BABY.
TUG
BUT DO I REALLY CARE WHAT ANY-ONE ELSE THINKS?
...YES.

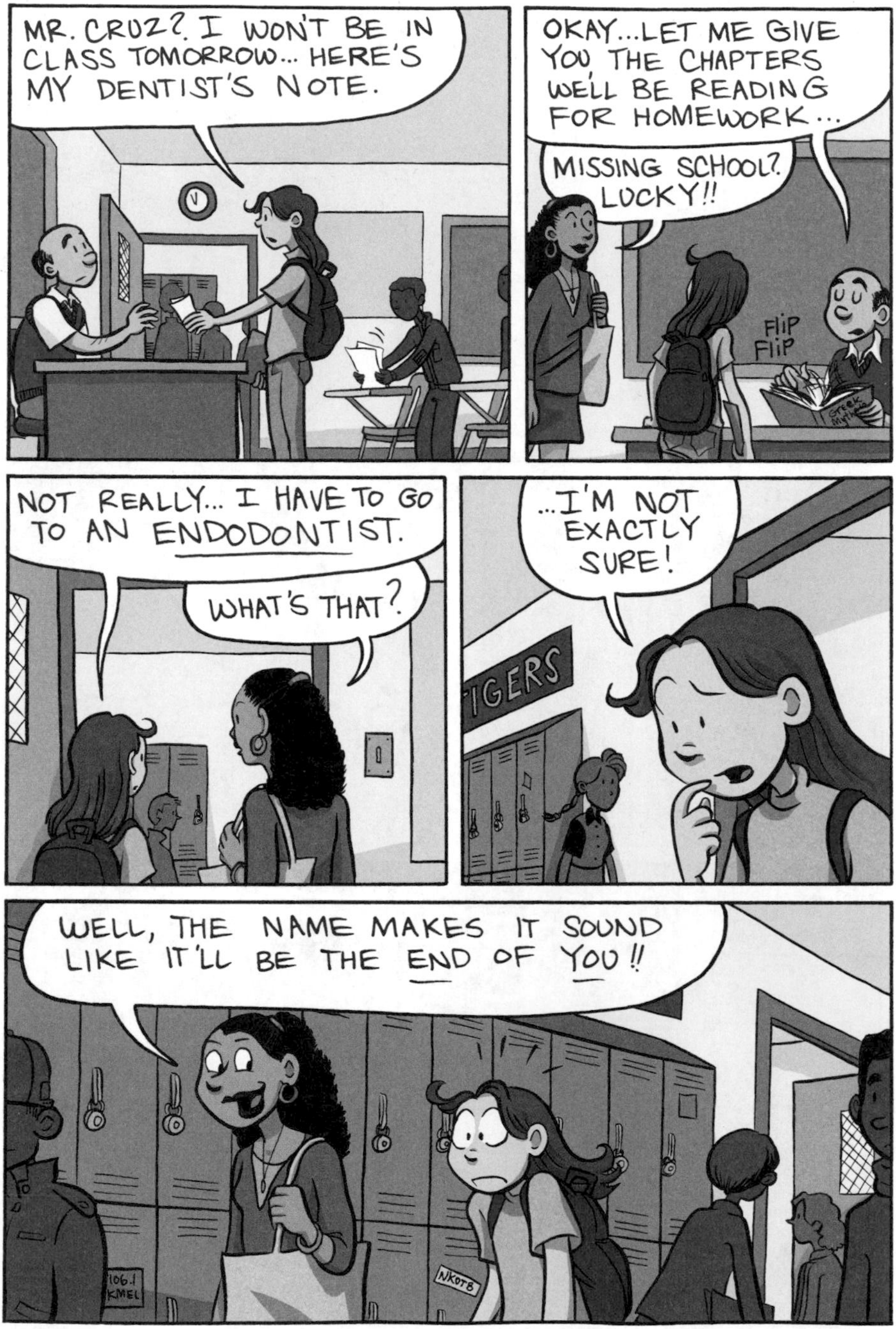
MR. CRUZ? I WON'T BE IN CLASS TOMORROW... HERE'S MY DENTIST'S NOTE.
OKAY... LET ME GIVE YOU THE CHAPTERS WE'LL BE READING FOR HOMEWORK...
MISSING SCHOOL? LUCKY!!
FLIP FLIP
Greek Myths
NOT REALLY... I HAVE TO GO TO AN ENDODONTIST.
WHAT'S THAT?
...I'M NOT EXACTLY SURE!
TIGERS
WELL, THE NAME MAKES IT SOUND LIKE IT'LL BE THE END OF YOU!!
106.1 KMEL
NKOTB

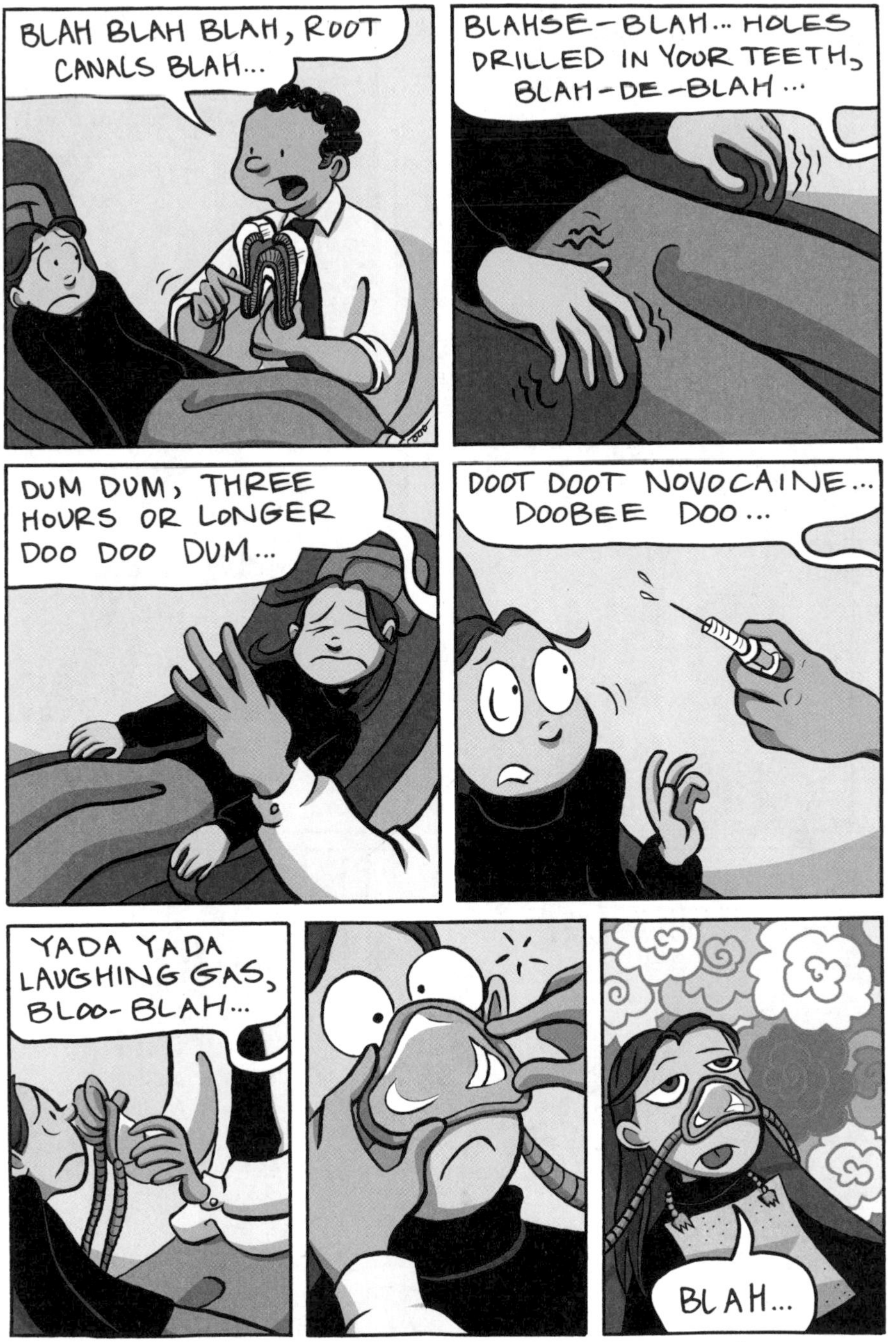
BLAH BLAH BLAH, ROOT CANALS BLAH...
BLAHSE-BLAH... HOLES DRILLED IN YOUR TEETH, BLAH-DE-BLAH...
DUM DUM, THREE HOURS OR LONGER DOO DOO DUM...
DOOT DOOT NOVOCAINE... DOOBEE DOO...
YADA YADA LAUGHING GAS, BLOO-BLAH...
BLAH...

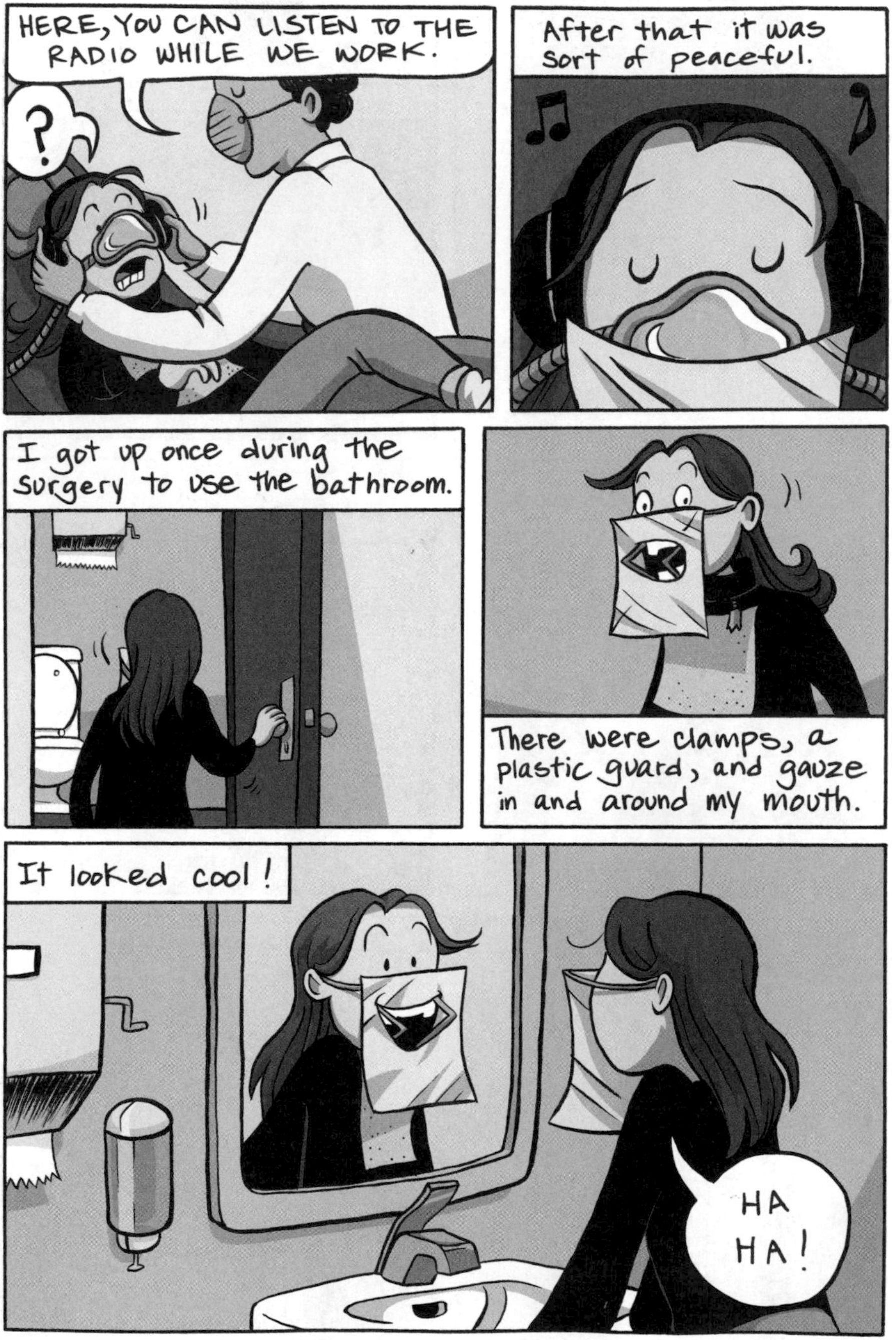
HERE, YOU CAN LISTEN TO THE RADIO WHILE WE WORK.
?
After that it was sort of peaceful.
I got up once during the surgery to use the bathroom.
There were clamps, a plastic guard, and gauze in and around my mouth.
It looked cool!
HA HA!

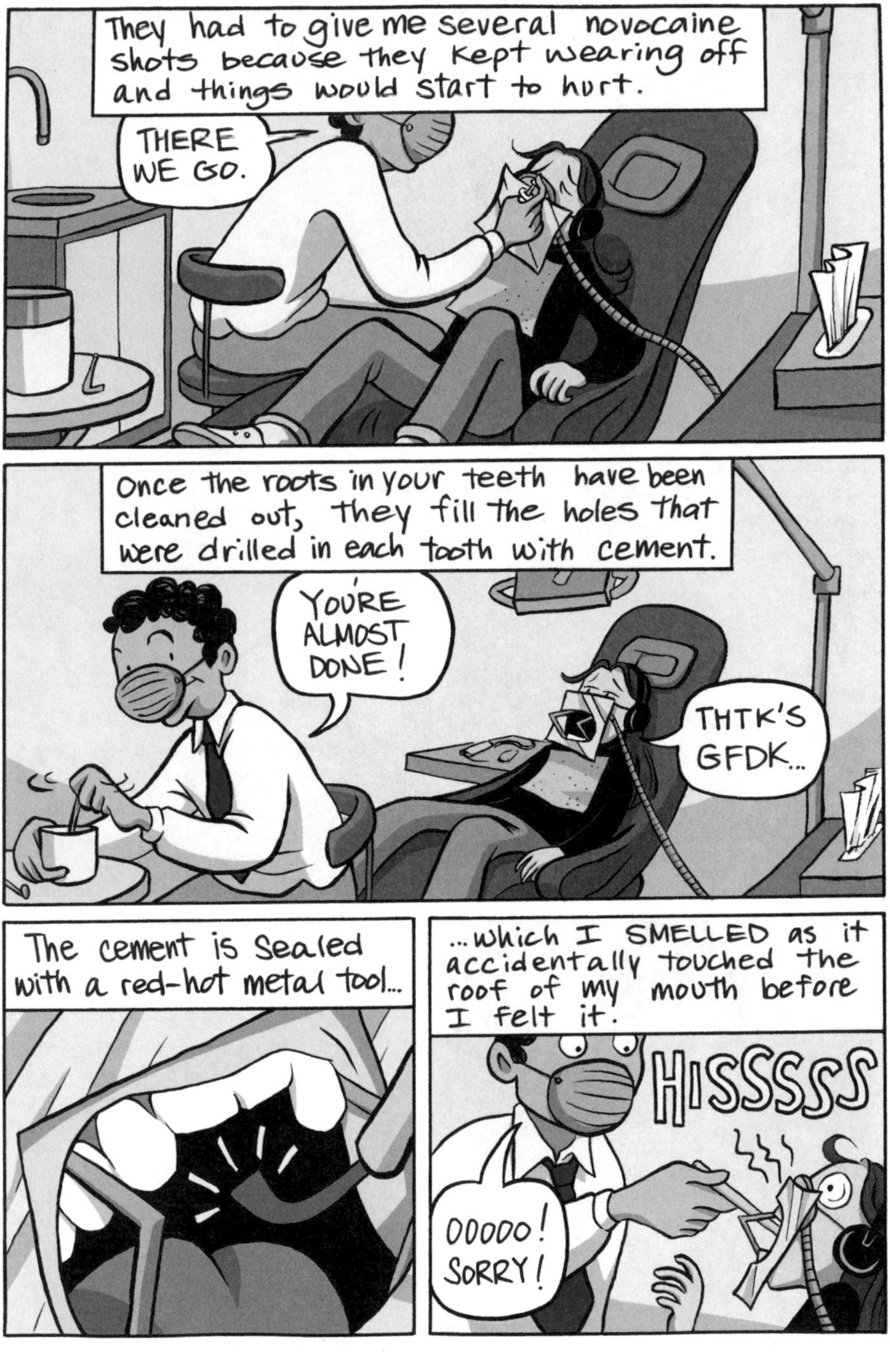
They had to give me several novocaine shots because they kept wearing off and things would start to hurt.
THERE WE GO.
Once the roots in your teeth have been cleaned out, they fill the holes that were drilled in each tooth with cement.
YOU'RE ALMOST DONE!
THTK'S GFDK...
The cement is sealed with a red-hot metal tool...
...which I SMELLED as it accidentally touched the roof of my mouth before I felt it.
HISSSSS
OOOOO! SORRY!

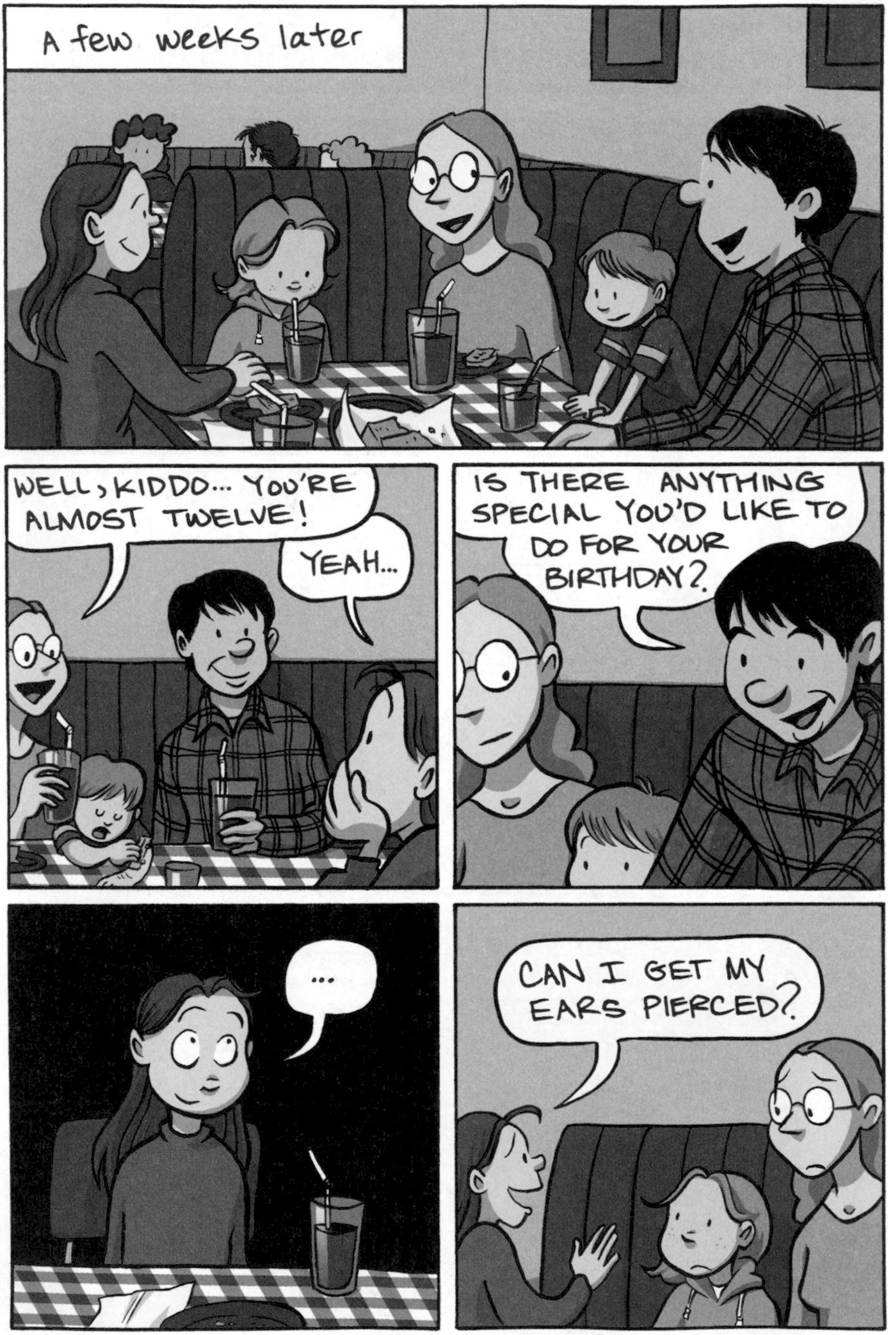
A few weeks later
WELL, KIDDO... YOU'RE ALMOST TWELVE!
YEAH...
IS THERE ANYTHING SPECIAL YOU'D LIKE TO DO FOR YOUR BIRTHDAY?
...
CAN I GET MY EARS PIERCED?

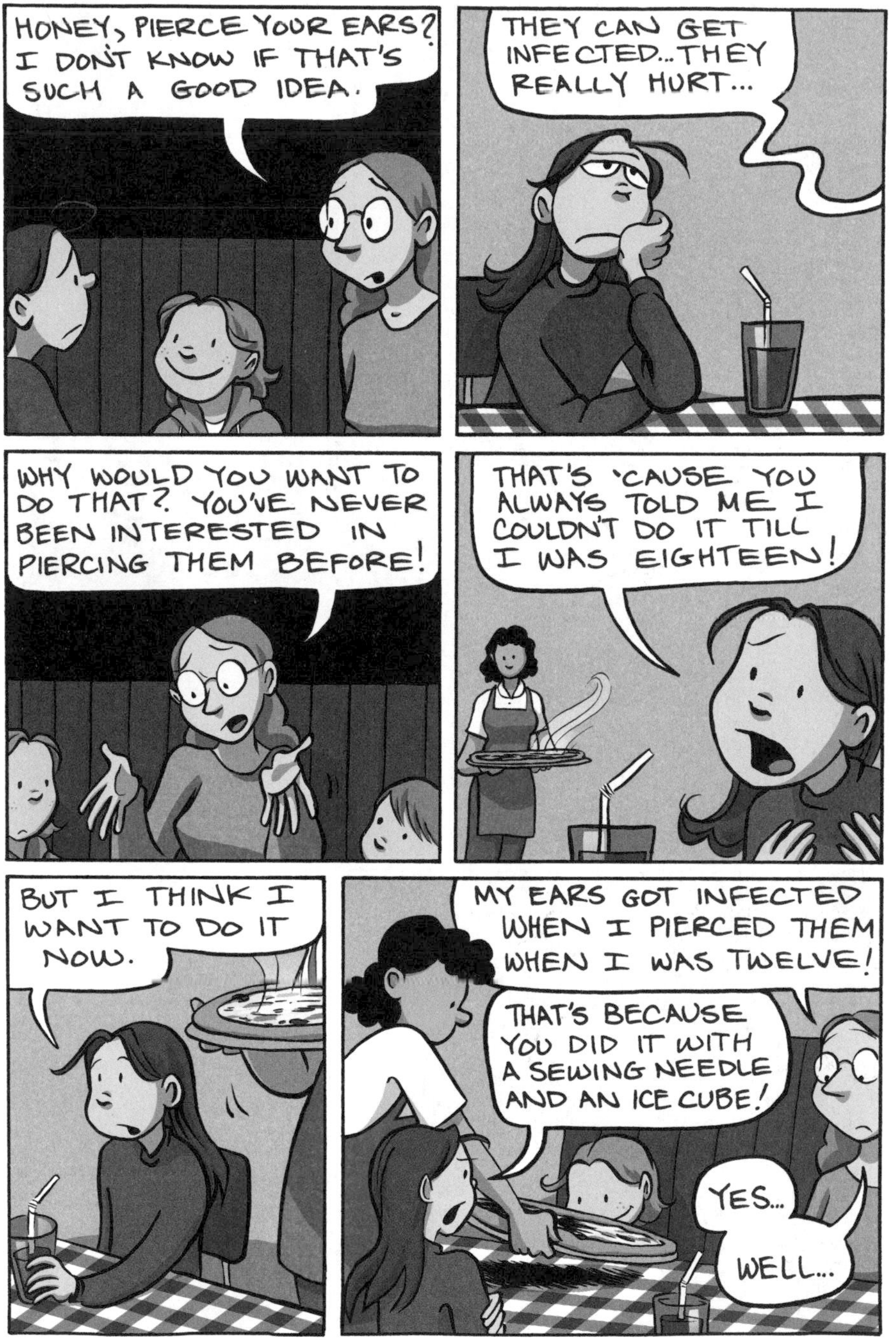
HONEY, PIERCE YOUR EARS? I DON'T KNOW IF THAT'S SUCH A GOOD IDEA.
THEY CAN GET INFECTED... THEY REALLY HURT...
WHY WOULD YOU WANT TO DO THAT? YOU'VE NEVER BEEN INTERESTED IN PIERCING THEM BEFORE!
THAT'S 'CAUSE YOU ALWAYS TOLD ME I COULDN'T DO IT TILL I WAS EIGHTEEN!
BUT I THINK I WANT TO DO IT NOW.
MY EARS GOT INFECTED WHEN I PIERCED THEM WHEN I WAS TWELVE!
THAT'S BECAUSE YOU DID IT WITH A SEWING NEEDLE AND AN ICE CUBE!
YES...
WELL...

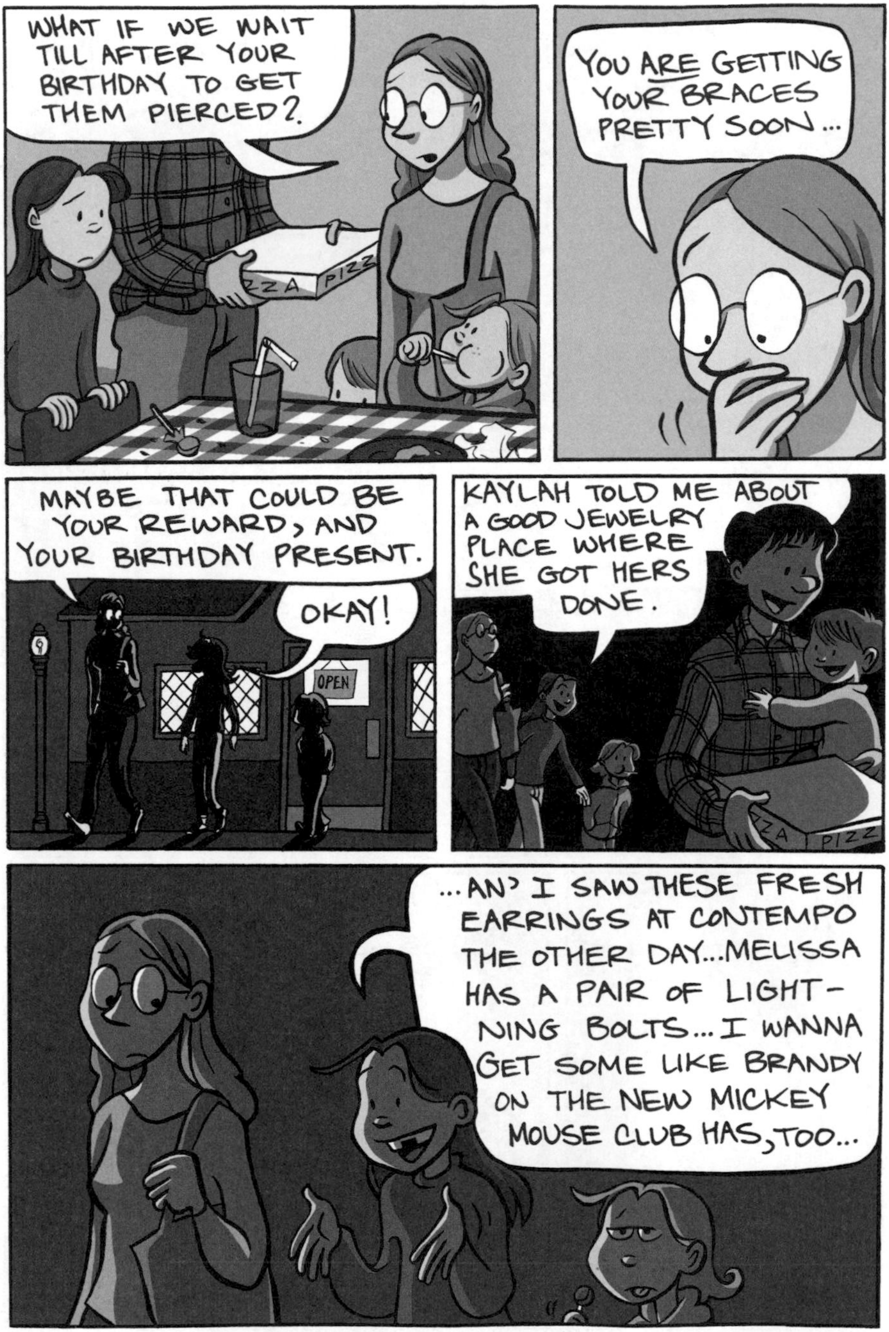
WHAT IF WE WAIT TILL AFTER YOUR BIRTHDAY TO GET THEM PIERCED?
PIZZA PIZZ
YOU ARE GETTING YOUR BRACES PRETTY SOON...
MAYBE THAT COULD BE YOUR REWARD, AND YOUR BIRTHDAY PRESENT.
OKAY!
OPEN
KAYLAH TOLD ME ABOUT A GOOD JEWELRY PLACE WHERE SHE GOT HERS DONE.
ZZA PIZZ
...AN' I SAW THESE FRESH EARRINGS AT CONTEMPO THE OTHER DAY...MELISSA HAS A PAIR OF LIGHT-NING BOLTS...I WANNA GET SOME LIKE BRANDY ON THE NEW MICKEY MOUSE CLUB HAS, TOO...

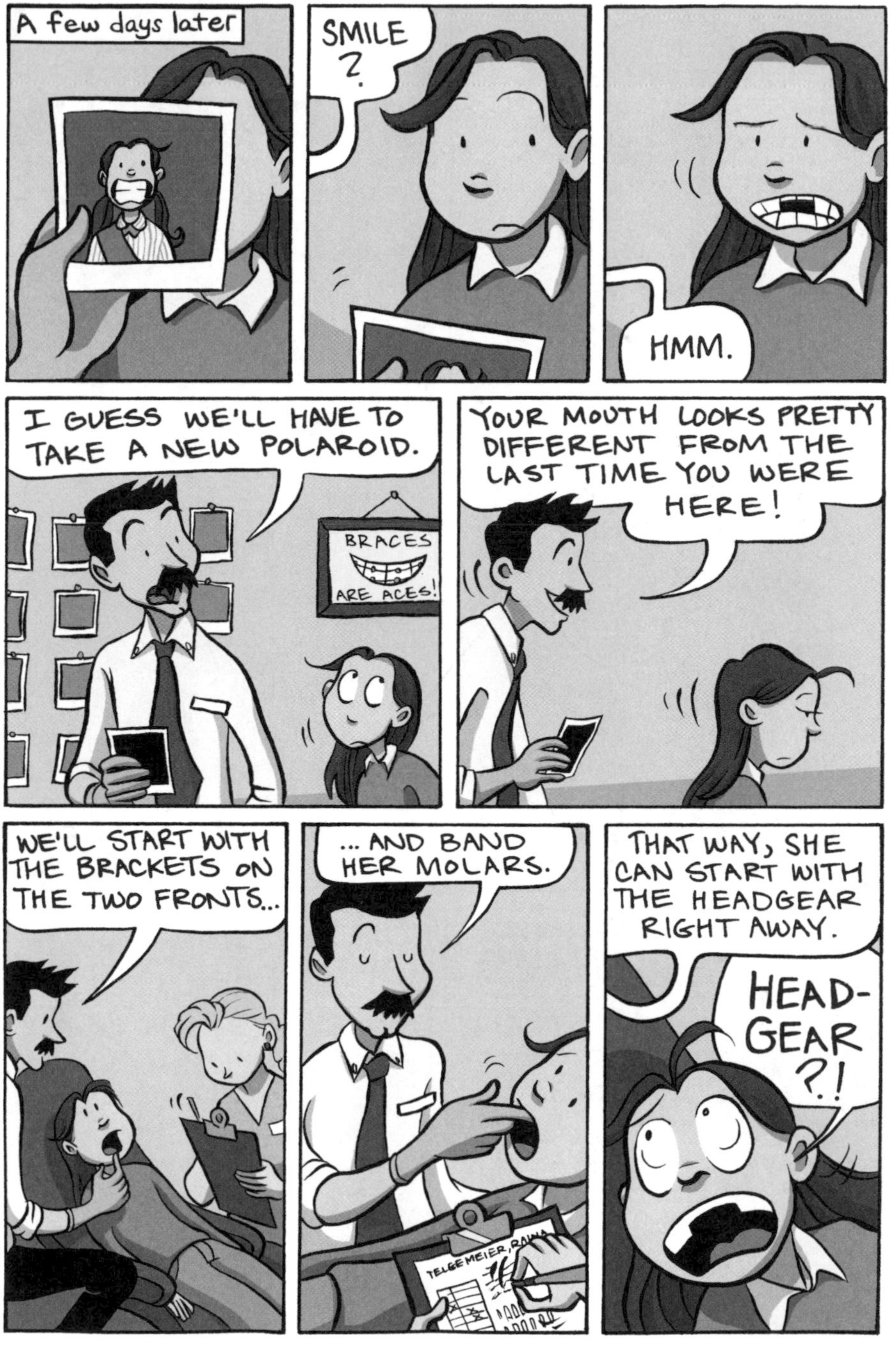
A few days later
SMILE ?
HMM.
I GUESS WE'LL HAVE TO TAKE A NEW POLAROID.
BRACES
ARE ACES!
YOUR MOUTH LOOKS PRETTY DIFFERENT FROM THE LAST TIME YOU WERE HERE!
WE'LL START WITH THE BRACKETS ON THE TWO FRONTS...
... AND BAND HER MOLARS.
TELGEMEIER,
THAT WAY, SHE CAN START WITH THE HEADGEAR RIGHT AWAY.
HEAD-GEAR ?!

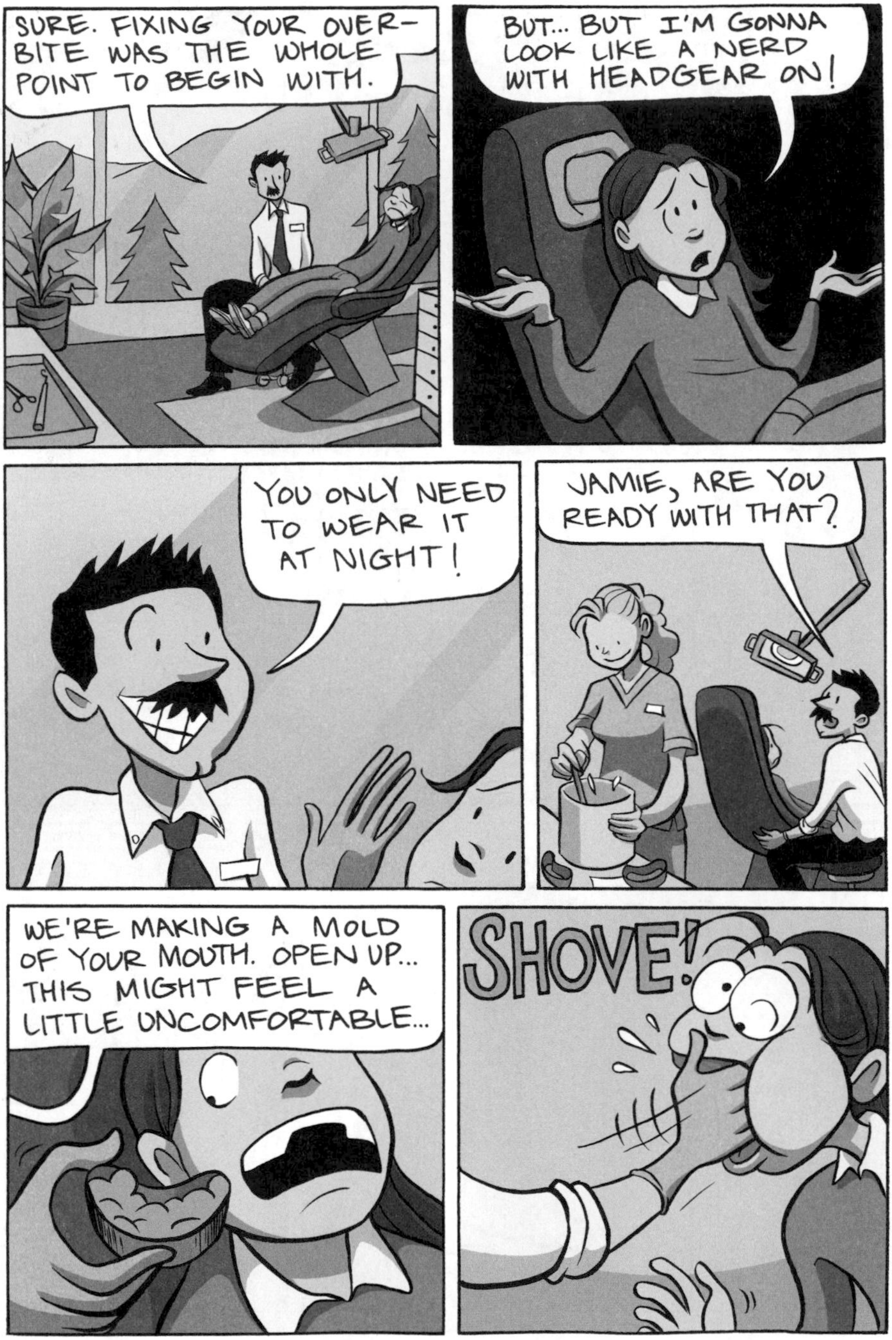
SURE. FIXING YOUR OVER-BITE WAS THE WHOLE POINT TO BEGIN WITH.
BUT... BUT I'M GONNA LOOK LIKE A NERD WITH HEADGEAR ON!
YOU ONLY NEED TO WEAR IT AT NIGHT!
JAMIE, ARE YOU READY WITH THAT?
WE'RE MAKING A MOLD OF YOUR MOUTH. OPEN UP... THIS MIGHT FEEL A LITTLE UNCOMFORTABLE...
SHOVE!

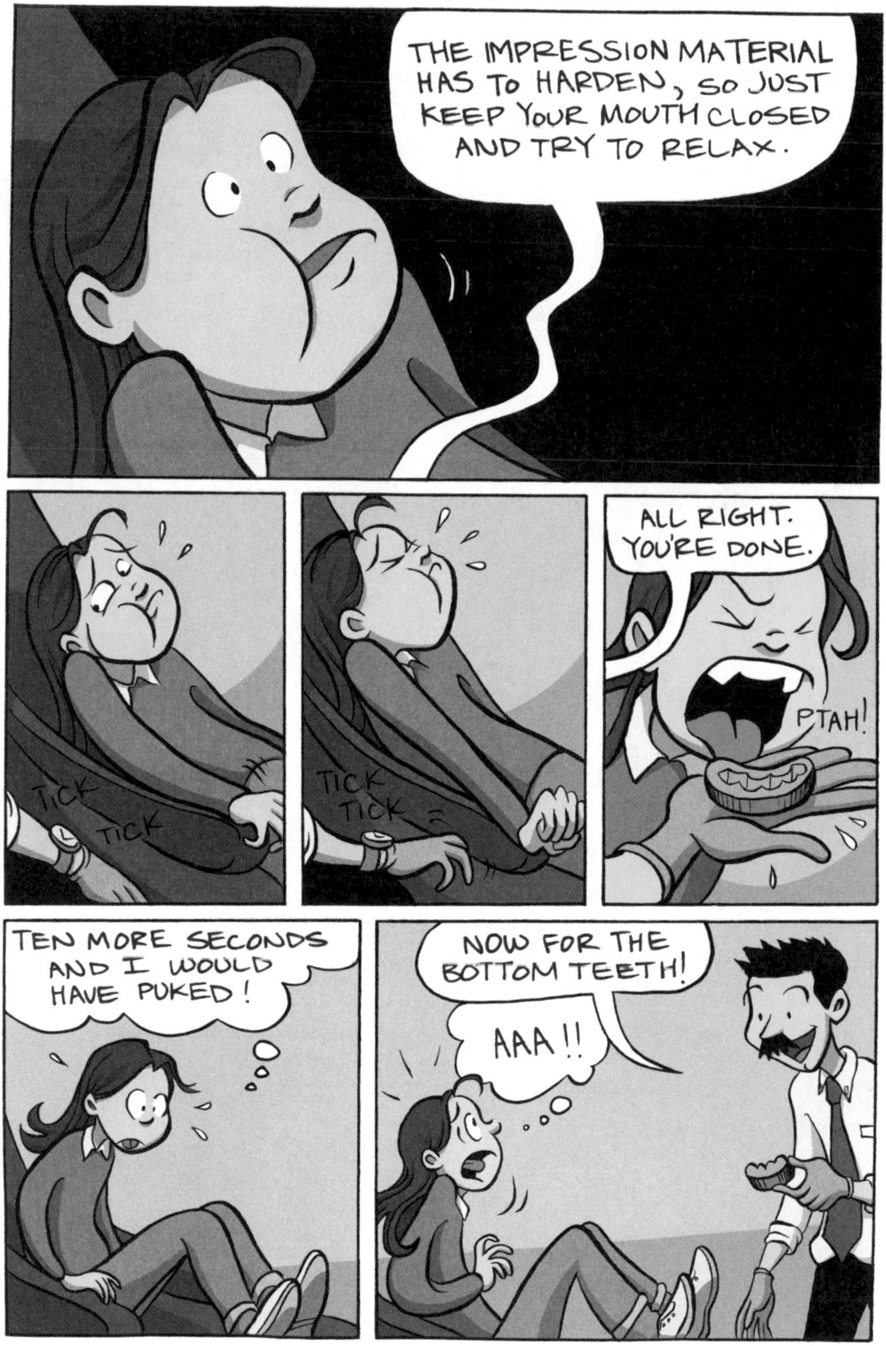
THE IMPRESSION MATERIAL HAS TO HARDEN, SO JUST KEEP YOUR MOUTH CLOSED AND TRY TO RELAX.
TICK TICK
TICK TICK
ALL RIGHT. YOU'RE DONE.
PTAH!
TEN MORE SECONDS AND I WOULD HAVE PUKED!
NOW FOR THE BOTTOM TEETH!
AAA!!

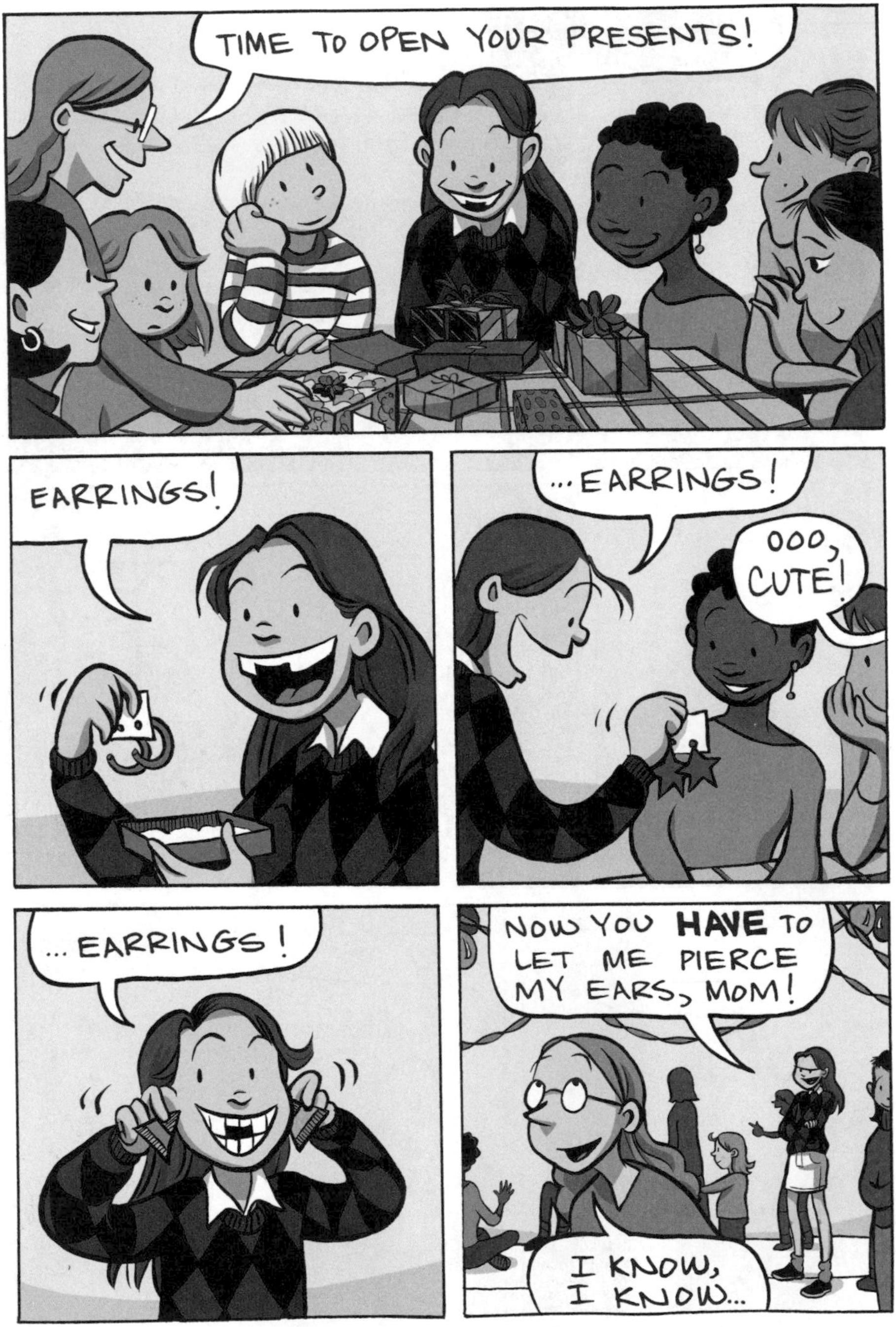
TIME TO OPEN YOUR PRESENTS!
EARRINGS!
...EARRINGS!
OOO, CUTE!
...EARRINGS!
NOW YOU **HAVE** TO LET ME PIERCE MY EARS, MOM!
I KNOW, I KNOW...

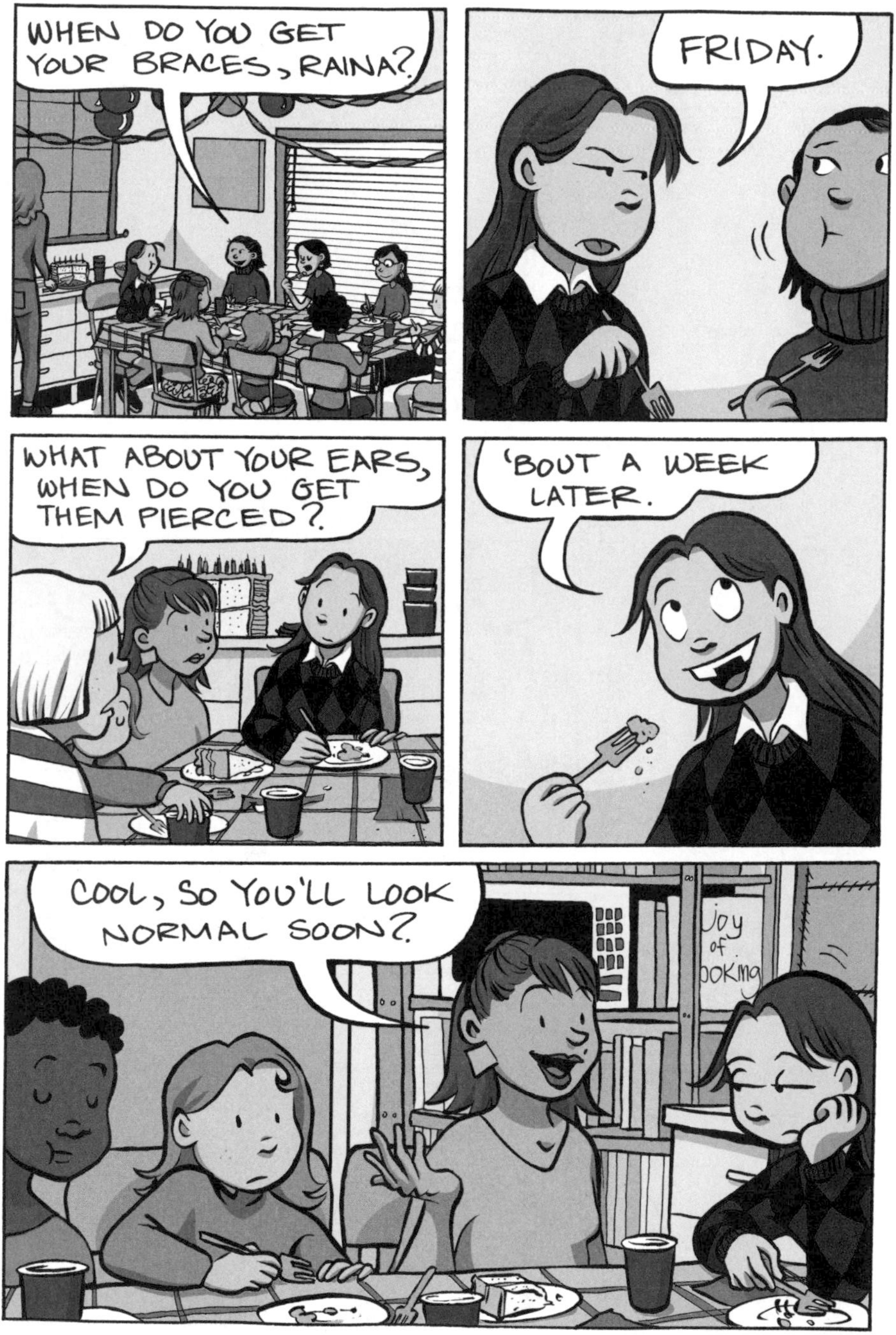
WHEN DO YOU GET YOUR BRACES, RAINA?
FRIDAY.
WHAT ABOUT YOUR EARS, WHEN DO YOU GET THEM PIERCED?
'BOUT A WEEK LATER.
COOL, SO YOU'LL LOOK NORMAL SOON?
joy of ooking

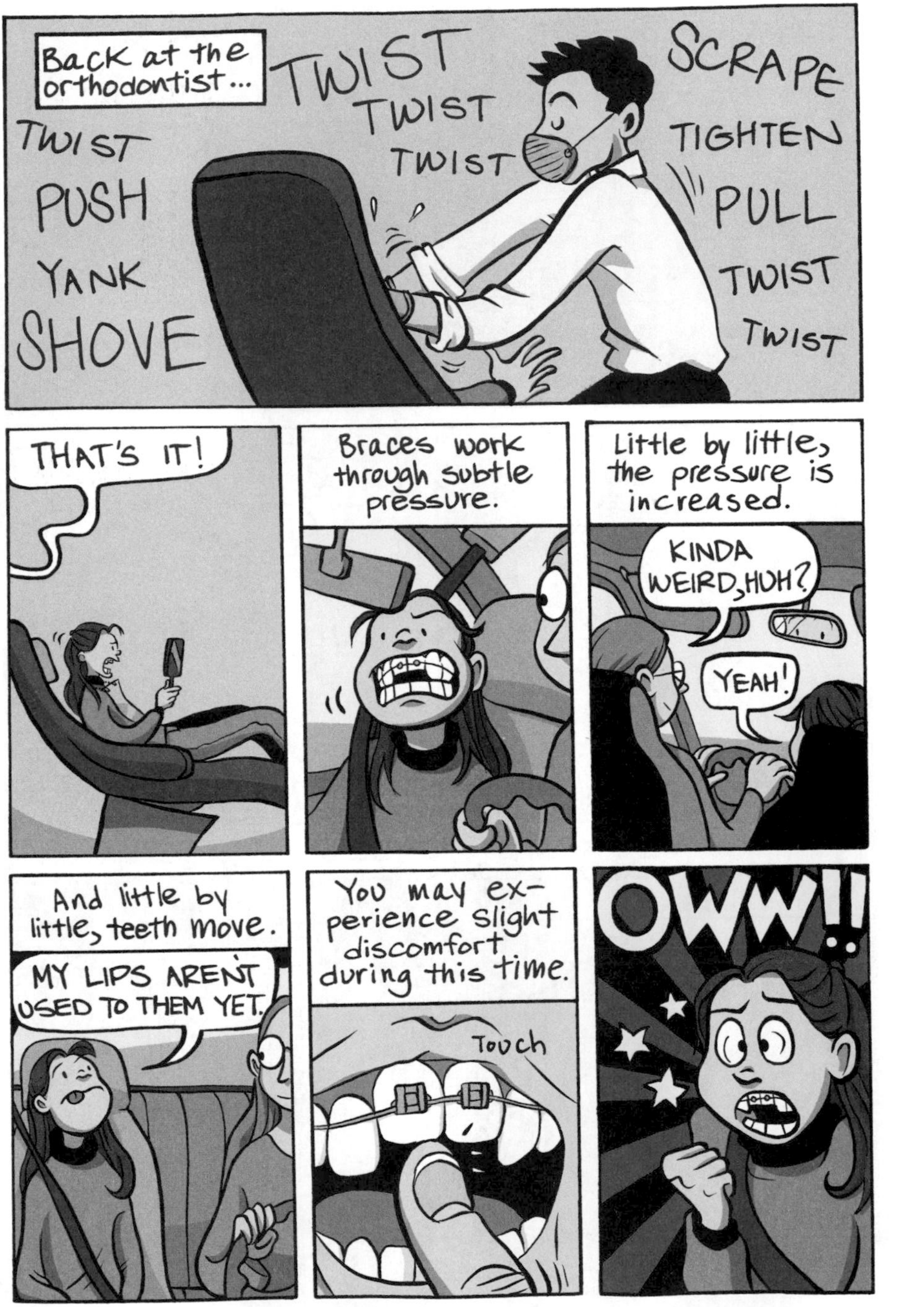
Back at the orthodontist...
TWIST
TWIST
TWIST
SCRAPE
TIGHTEN
TWIST
PUSH
YANK
SHOVE
PULL
TWIST
TWIST
THAT'S IT!
Braces work through subtle pressure.
Little by little, the pressure is increased.
KINDA WEIRD, HUH?
YEAH!
And little by little, teeth move.
MY LIPS AREN'T USED TO THEM YET.
You may experience slight discomfort during this time.
Touch
OWW!!

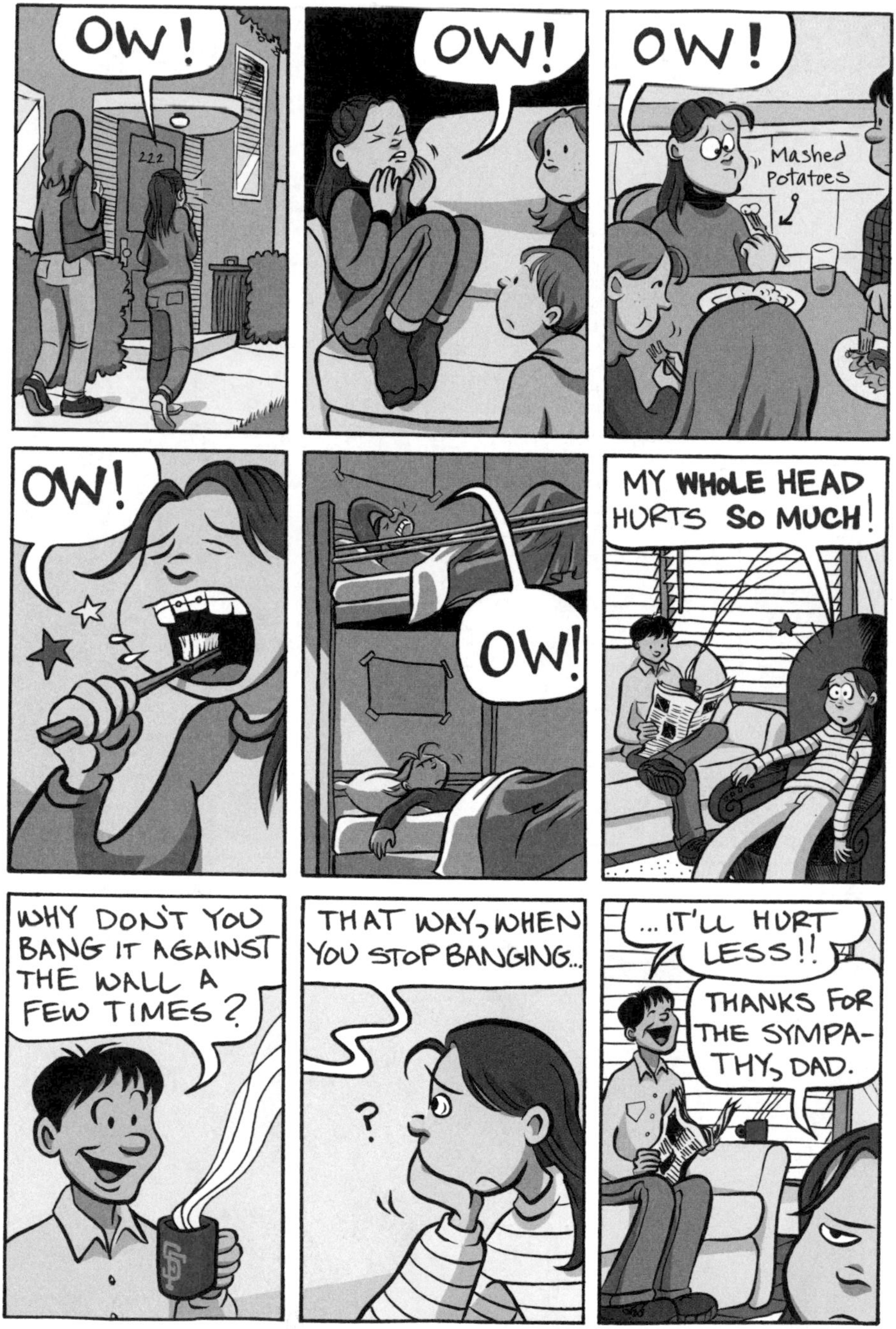
OW!
OW!
OW!
Mashed Potatoes
OW!
OW!
MY WHOLE HEAD HURTS SO MUCH!
WHY DON'T YOU BANG IT AGAINST THE WALL A FEW TIMES?
THAT WAY, WHEN YOU STOP BANGING...
?
...IT'LL HURT LESS!!
THANKS FOR THE SYMPATHY, DAD.

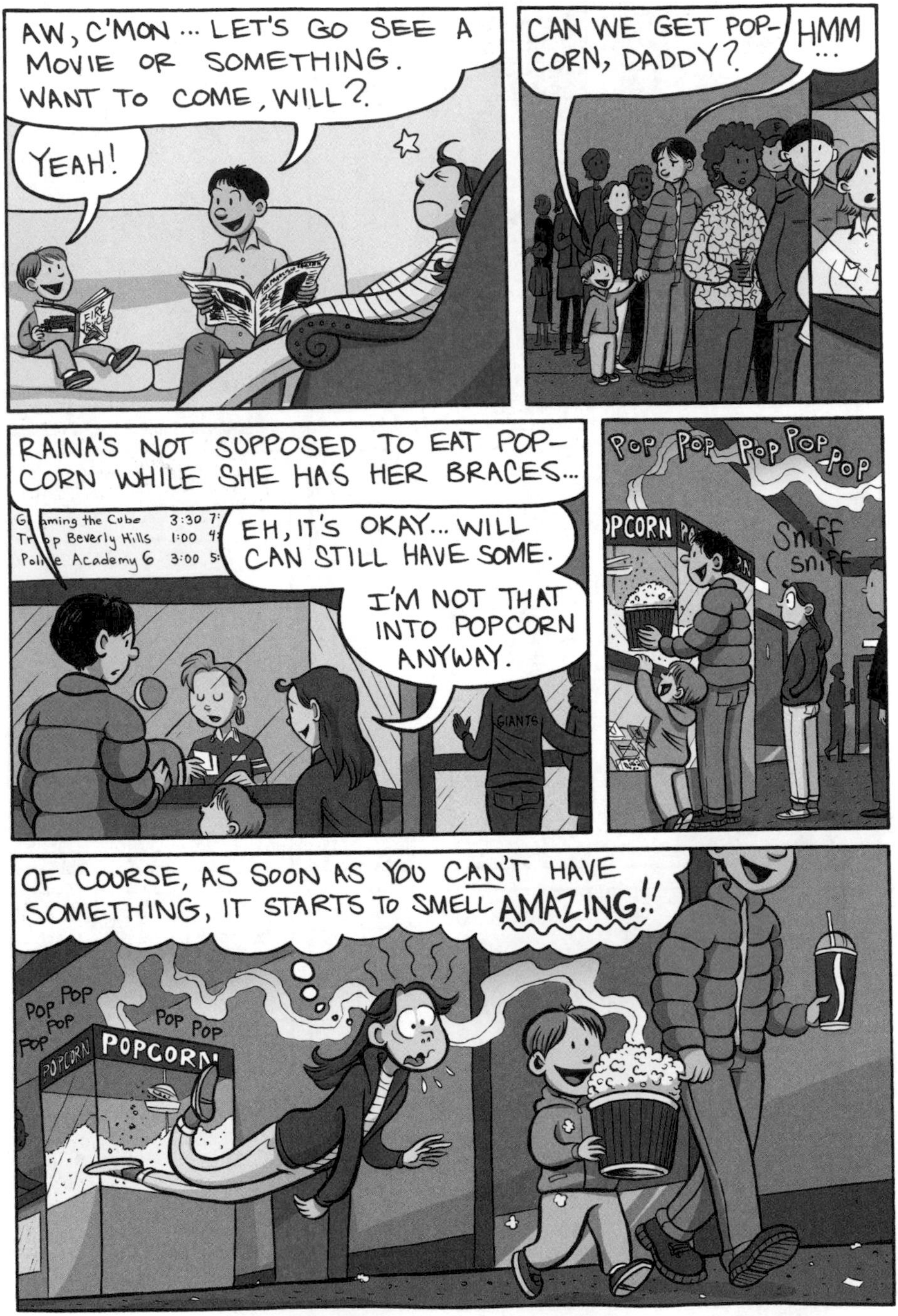
AW, C'MON ... LET'S GO SEE A MOVIE OR SOMETHING. WANT TO COME, WILL?
YEAH!
CAN WE GET POP-CORN, DADDY?
HMM ...
RAINA'S NOT SUPPOSED TO EAT POP-CORN WHILE SHE HAS HER BRACES...
EH, IT'S OKAY... WILL CAN STILL HAVE SOME.
I'M NOT THAT INTO POPCORN ANYWAY.
POP POP POP POP POP
POPCORN
Sniff sniff
OF COURSE, AS SOON AS YOU CAN'T HAVE SOMETHING, IT STARTS TO SMELL AMAZING!!
POP POP POP POP POP POP POP
POPCORN

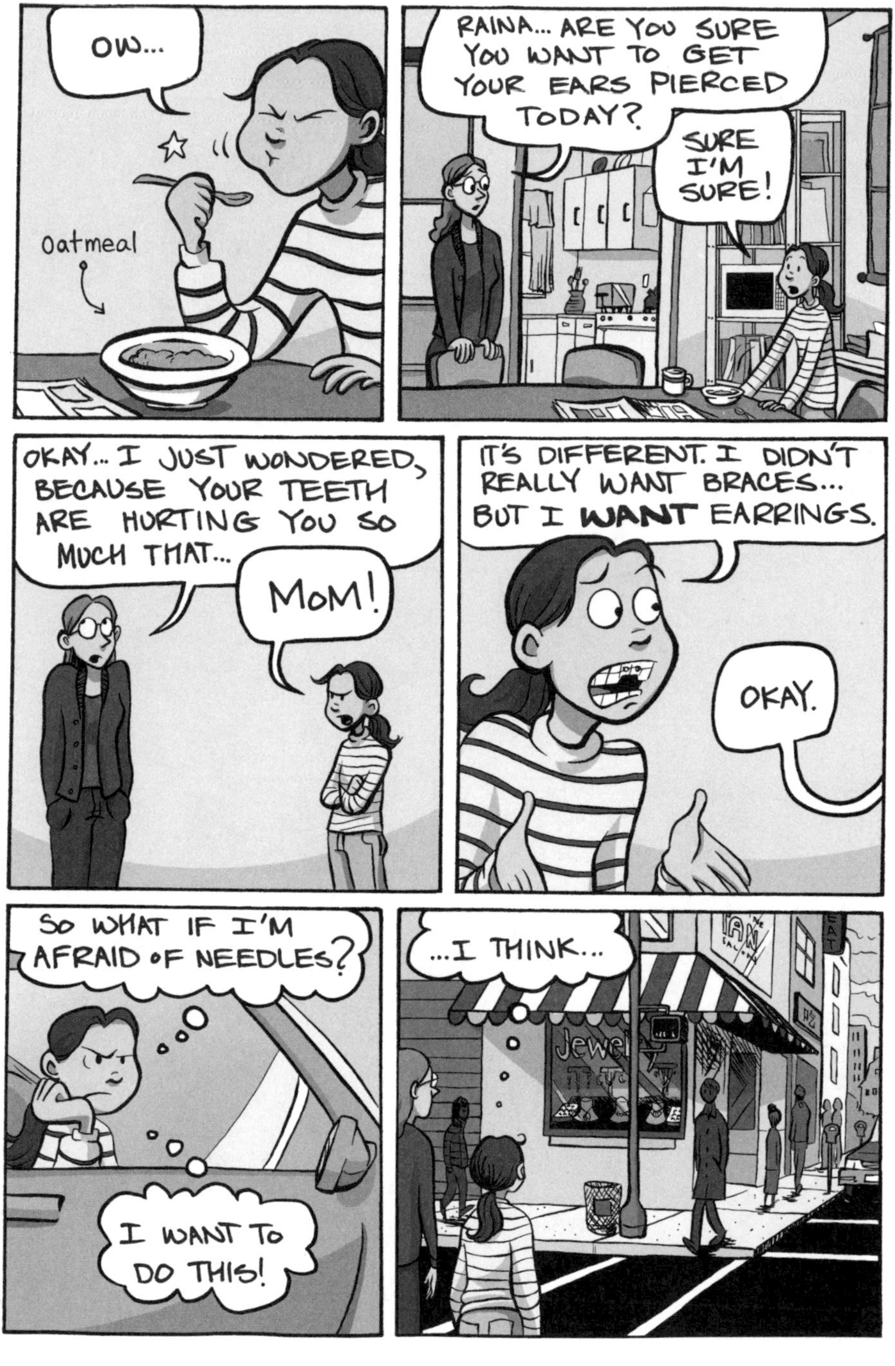
OW...
Oatmeal
RAINA... ARE YOU SURE YOU WANT TO GET YOUR EARS PIERCED TODAY?
SURE I'M SURE!
OKAY... I JUST WONDERED, BECAUSE YOUR TEETH ARE HURTING YOU SO MUCH THAT...
MOM!
IT'S DIFFERENT. I DIDN'T REALLY WANT BRACES... BUT I **WANT** EARRINGS.
OKAY.
SO WHAT IF I'M AFRAID OF NEEDLES?
I WANT TO DO THIS!
...I THINK...
Jewel

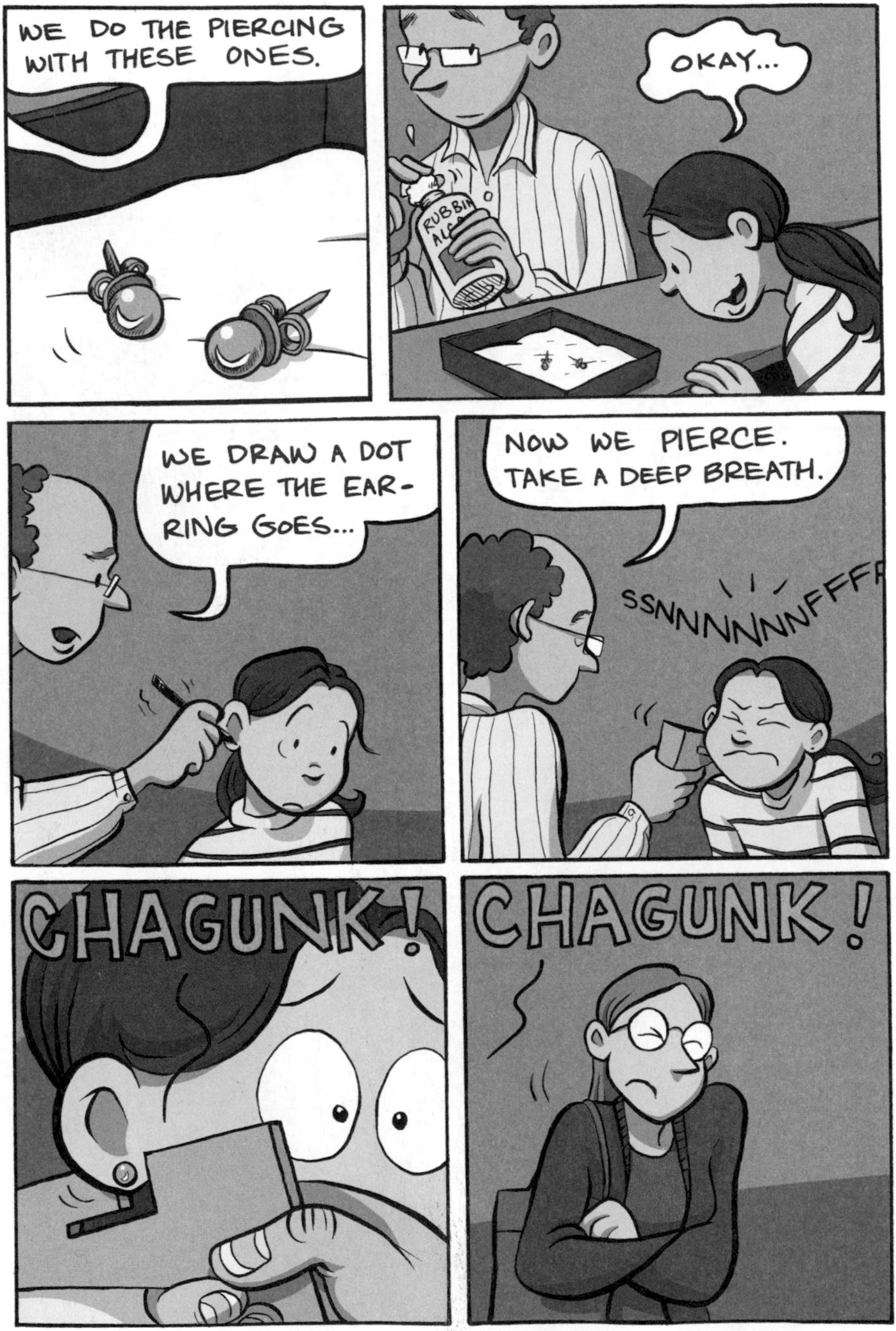
WE DO THE PIERCING WITH THESE ONES.
OKAY...
WE DRAW A DOT WHERE THE EAR-RING GOES...
NOW WE PIERCE. TAKE A DEEP BREATH.
SSNNNNNNFFFF
CHAGUNK!
CHAGUNK!

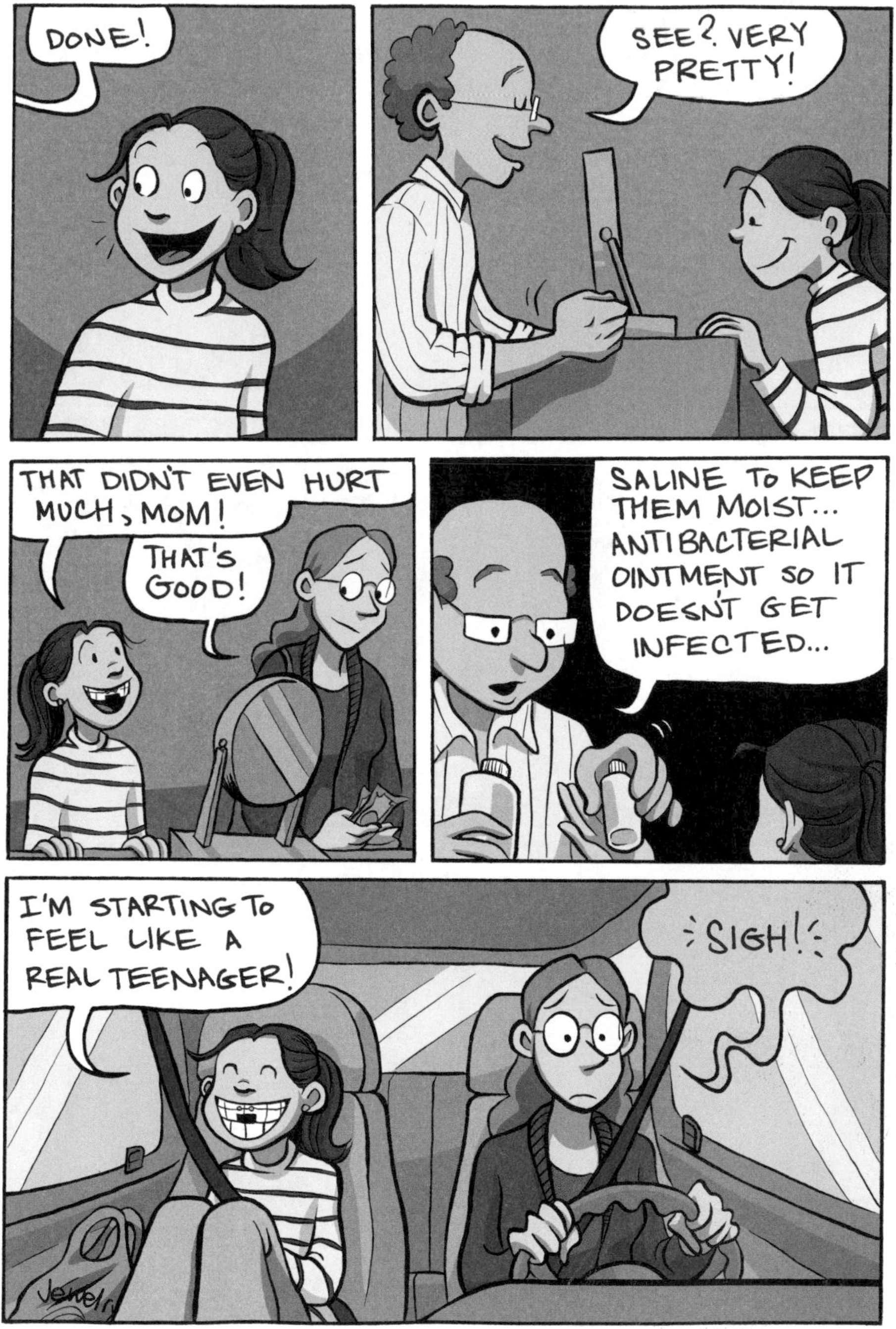
DONE!
SEE? VERY PRETTY!
THAT DIDN'T EVEN HURT MUCH, MOM!
THAT'S GOOD!
SALINE TO KEEP THEM MOIST... ANTIBACTERIAL OINTMENT SO IT DOESN'T GET INFECTED...
I'M STARTING TO FEEL LIKE A REAL TEENAGER!
SIGH!
JEWELRY

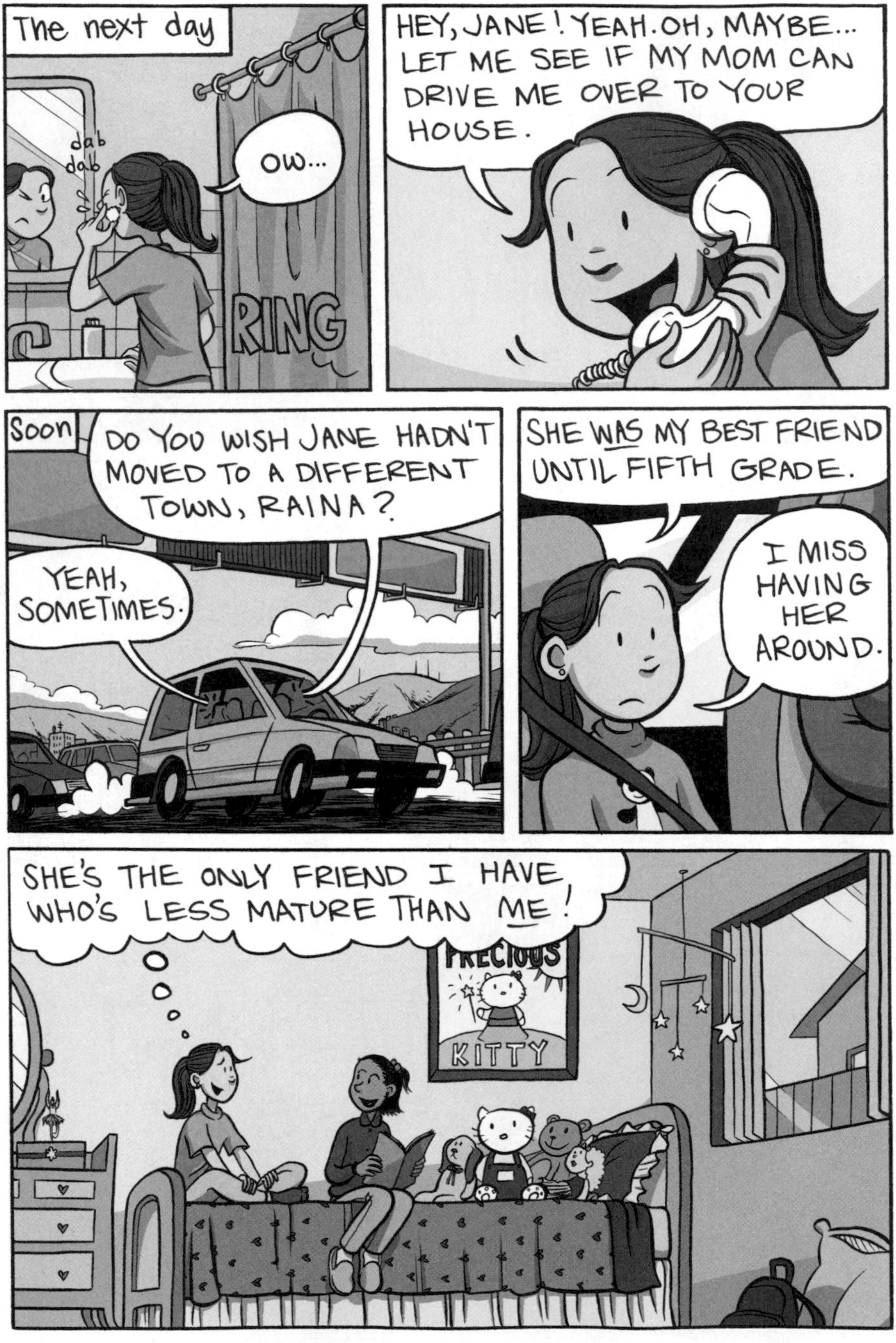
The next day
dab dab
OW...
RING
HEY, JANE! YEAH. OH, MAYBE... LET ME SEE IF MY MOM CAN DRIVE ME OVER TO YOUR HOUSE.
Soon
DO YOU WISH JANE HADN'T MOVED TO A DIFFERENT TOWN, RAINA?
YEAH, SOMETIMES.
SHE WAS MY BEST FRIEND UNTIL FIFTH GRADE.
I MISS HAVING HER AROUND.
SHE'S THE ONLY FRIEND I HAVE WHO'S LESS MATURE THAN ME!
PRECIOUS
KITTY

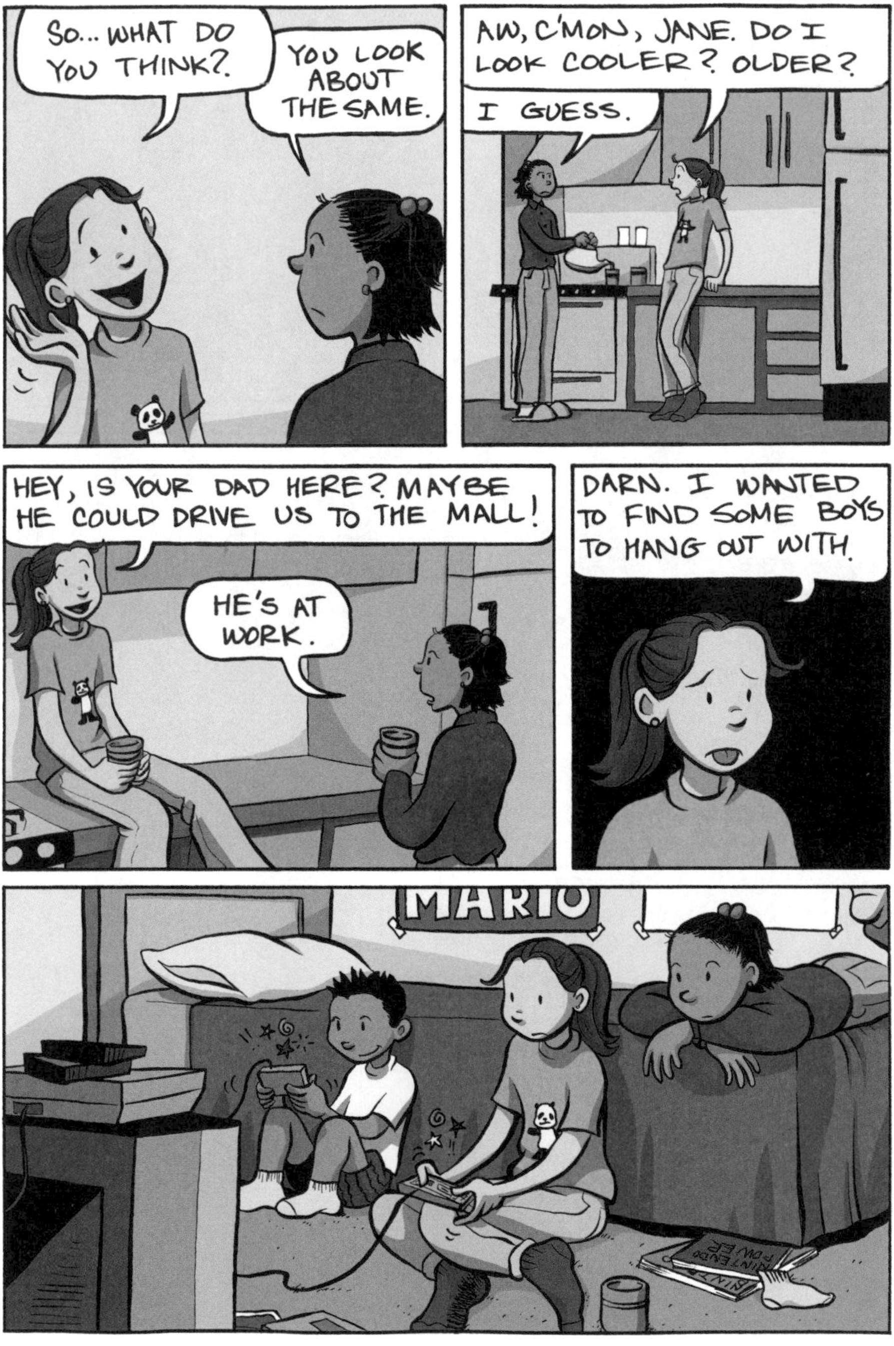
SO... WHAT DO YOU THINK?
YOU LOOK ABOUT THE SAME.
AW, C'MON, JANE. DO I LOOK COOLER? OLDER?
I GUESS.
HEY, IS YOUR DAD HERE? MAYBE HE COULD DRIVE US TO THE MALL!
HE'S AT WORK.
DARN. I WANTED TO FIND SOME BOYS TO HANG OUT WITH.
MARIO
NINTENDO POWER

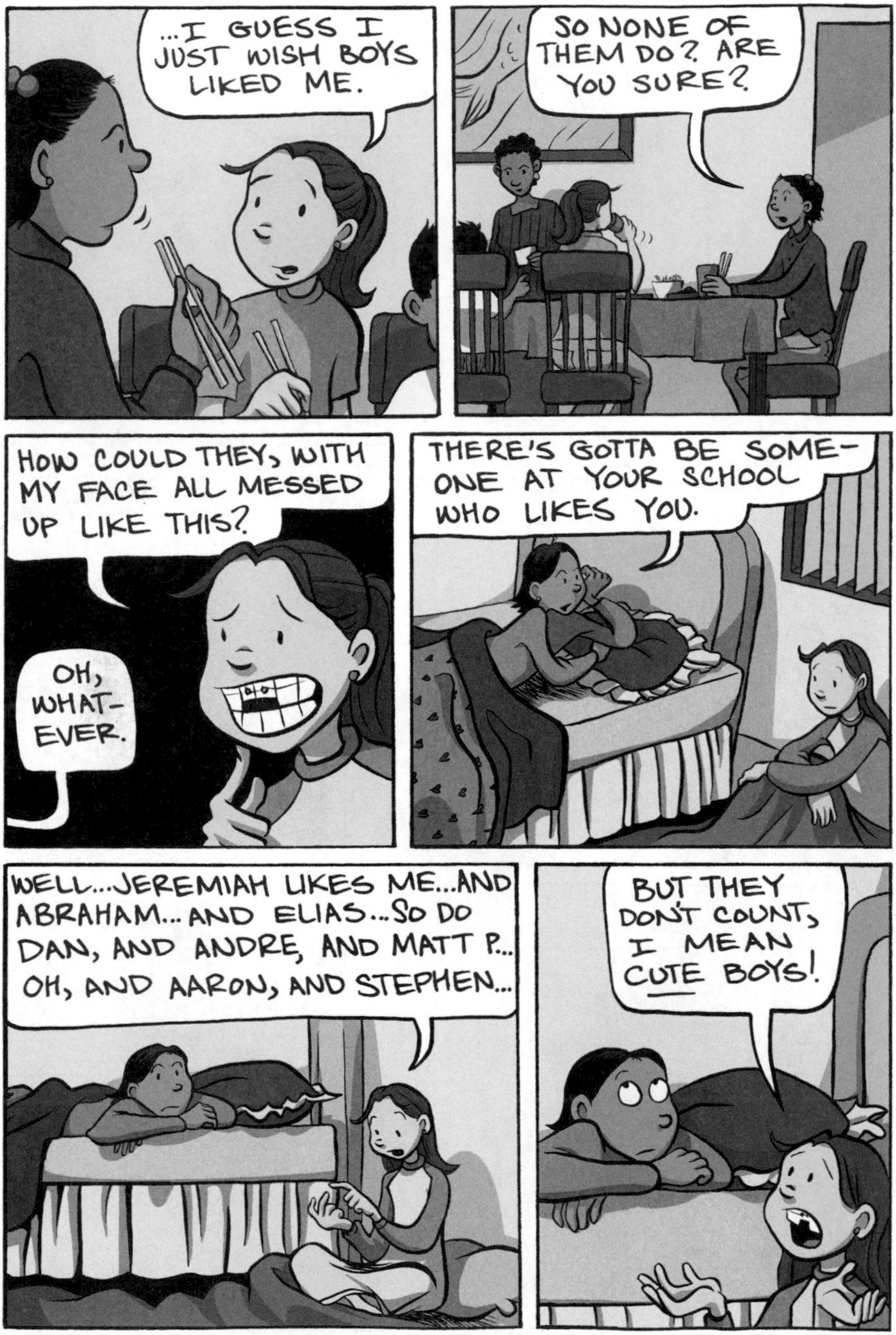
...I GUESS I JUST WISH BOYS LIKED ME.
SO NONE OF THEM DO? ARE YOU SURE?
HOW COULD THEY, WITH MY FACE ALL MESSED UP LIKE THIS?
OH, WHAT-EVER.
THERE'S GOTTA BE SOME-ONE AT YOUR SCHOOL WHO LIKES YOU.
WELL...JEREMIAH LIKES ME...AND ABRAHAM... AND ELIAS...SO DO DAN, AND ANDRE, AND MATT P... OH, AND AARON, AND STEPHEN...
BUT THEY DON'T COUNT, I MEAN CUTE BOYS!

CHAPTER THREE

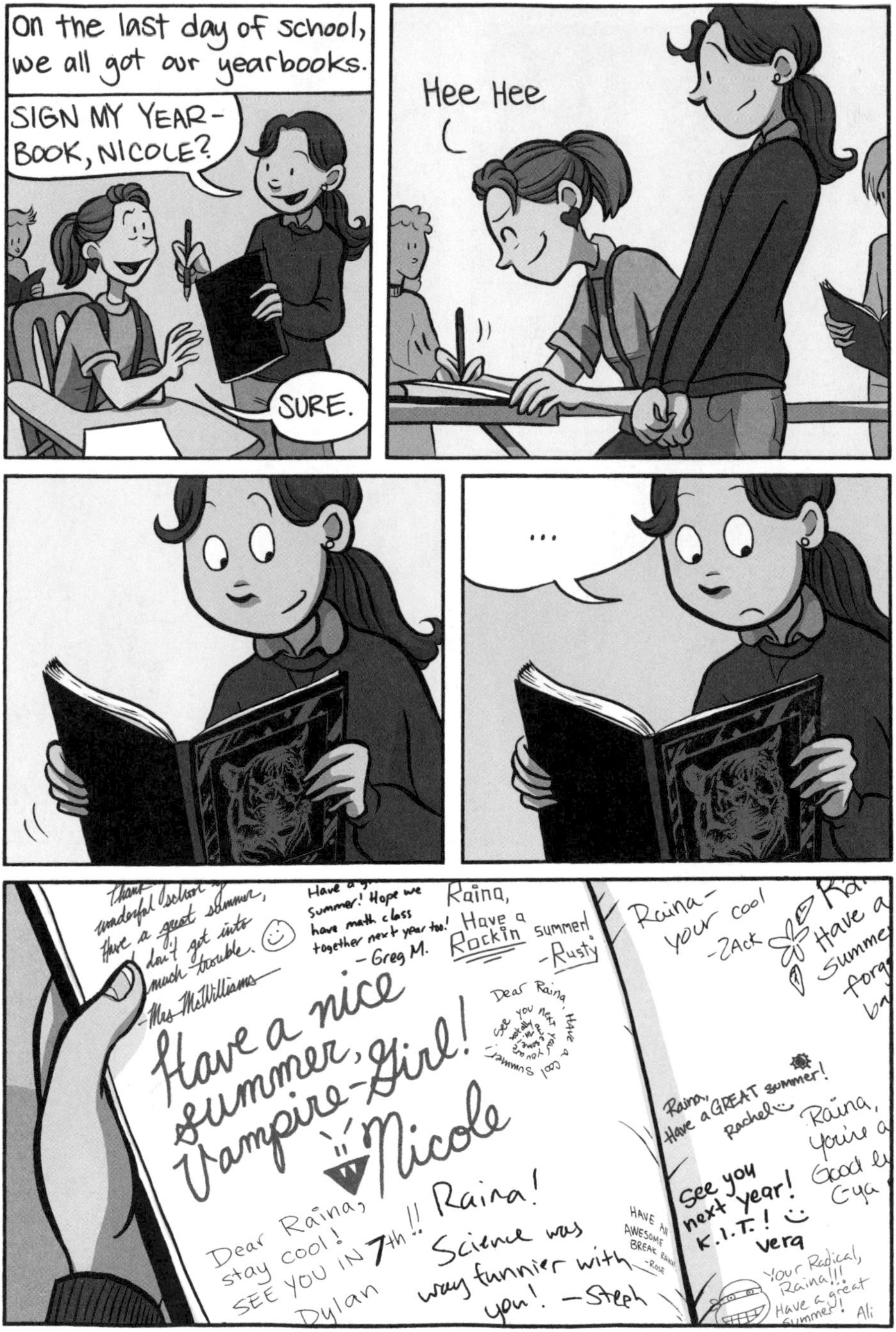
On the last day of school, we all got our yearbooks.
SIGN MY YEAR-BOOK, NICOLE?
SURE.
Hee Hee
...
Have a nice summer, Vampire-Girl! Nicole
Have a great summer, don't get into much trouble. -Mrs McWilliams
summer! Hope we have math class together next year too! -Greg M.
Raina, Have a Rockin summer! -Rusty
Dear Raina, Have a cool summer! See you next year, you are totally awesome!
Dear Raina, stay cool! SEE YOU IN 7th!! Dylan
Raina! Science was way funnier with you! -Steph
HAVE AN AWESOME BREAK RAINA! -ROSE
Raina- your cool -ZAck
Raina, Have a GREAT summer! Rachel
See you next year! K.I.T.! vera
Your Radical, Raina!!! Have a great summer! Ali

That summer was pretty normal, as summers go.

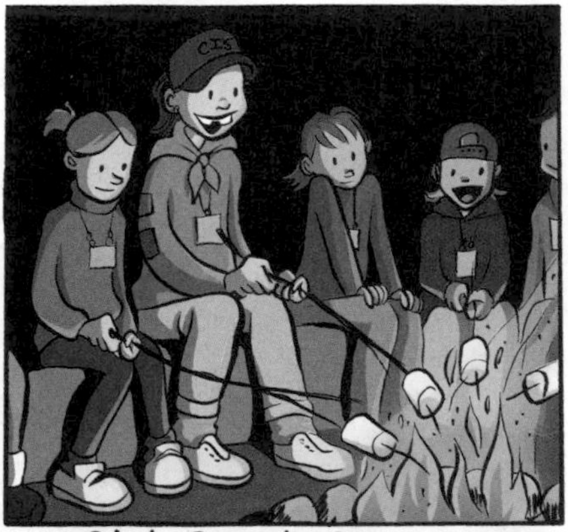
Girl Scout Camp

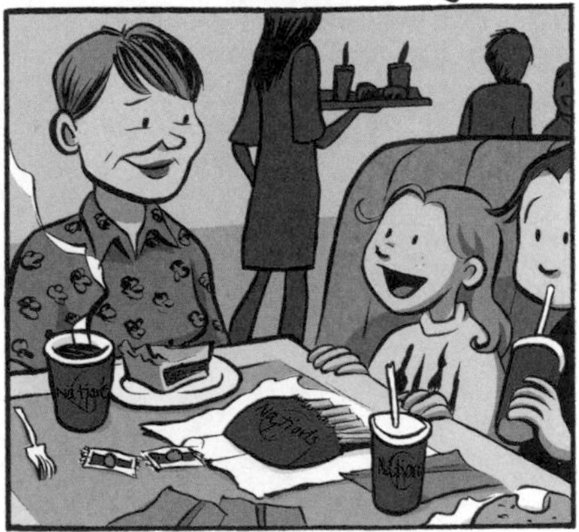
Grandma

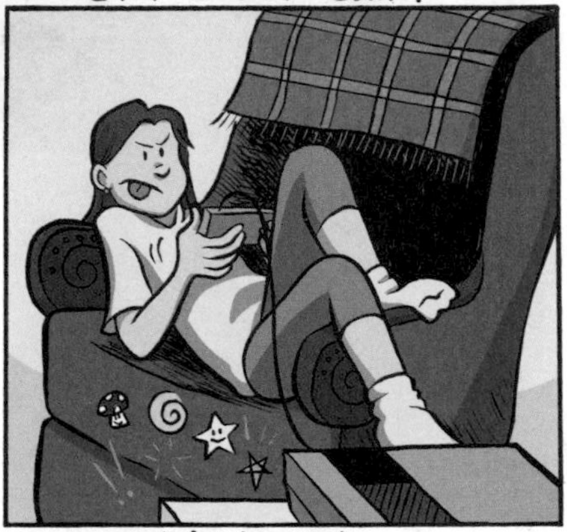
Nintendo

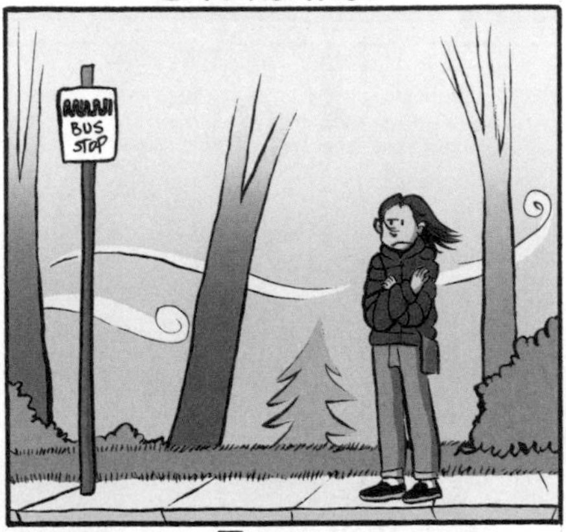
BUS STOP
Fog

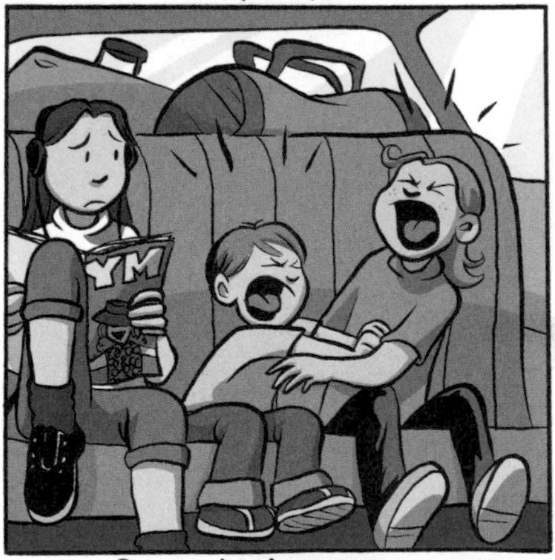
YM
Car trips

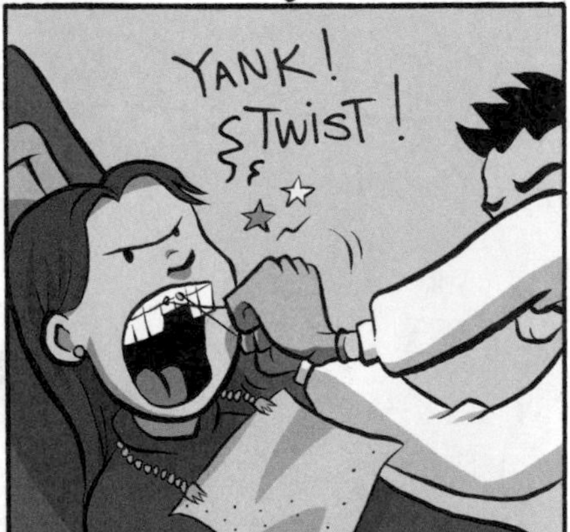
YANK!
TWIST!
Orthodontist

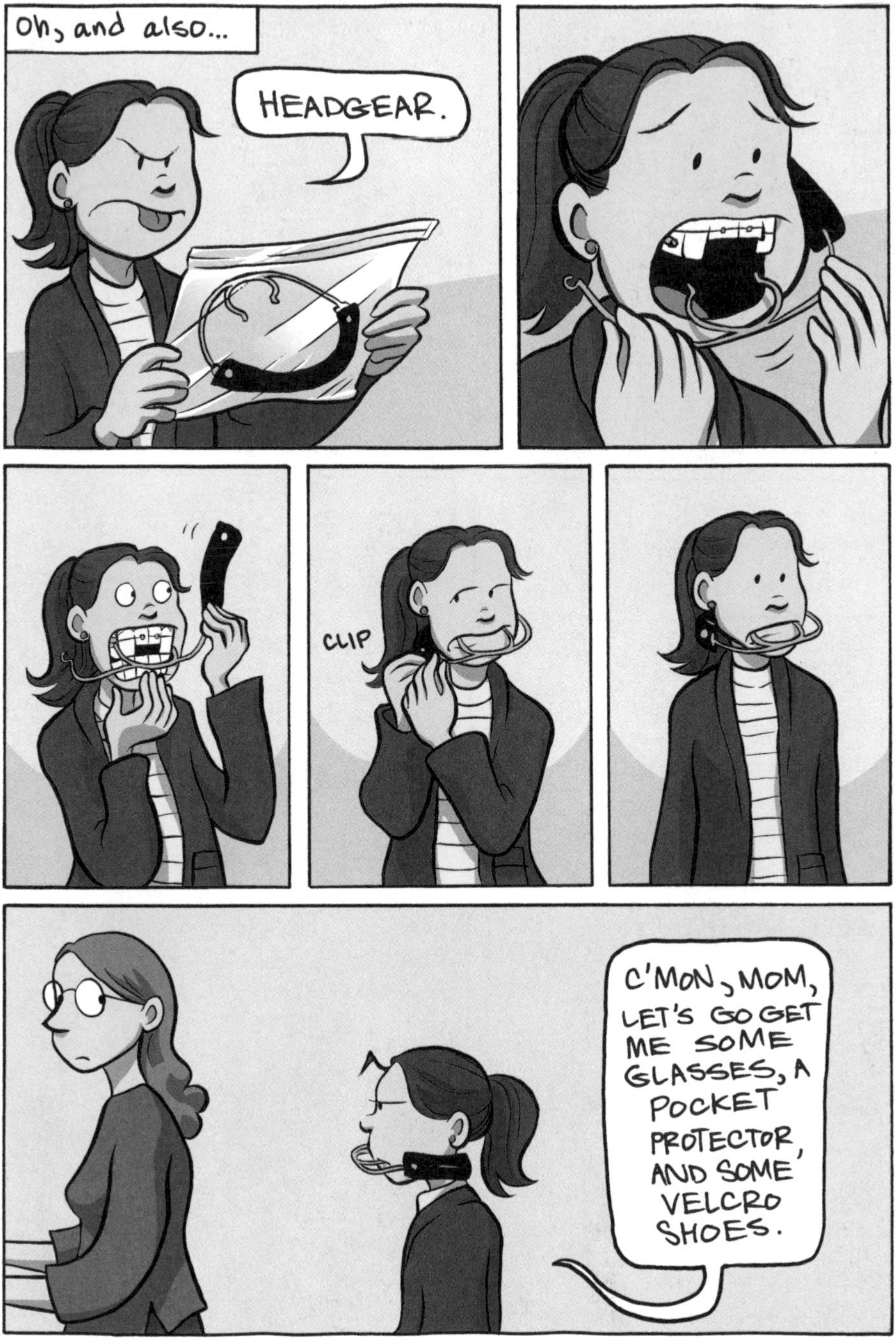
Oh, and also...
HEADGEAR.
CLIP
C'MON, MOM, LET'S GO GET ME SOME GLASSES, A POCKET PROTECTOR, AND SOME VELCRO SHOES.

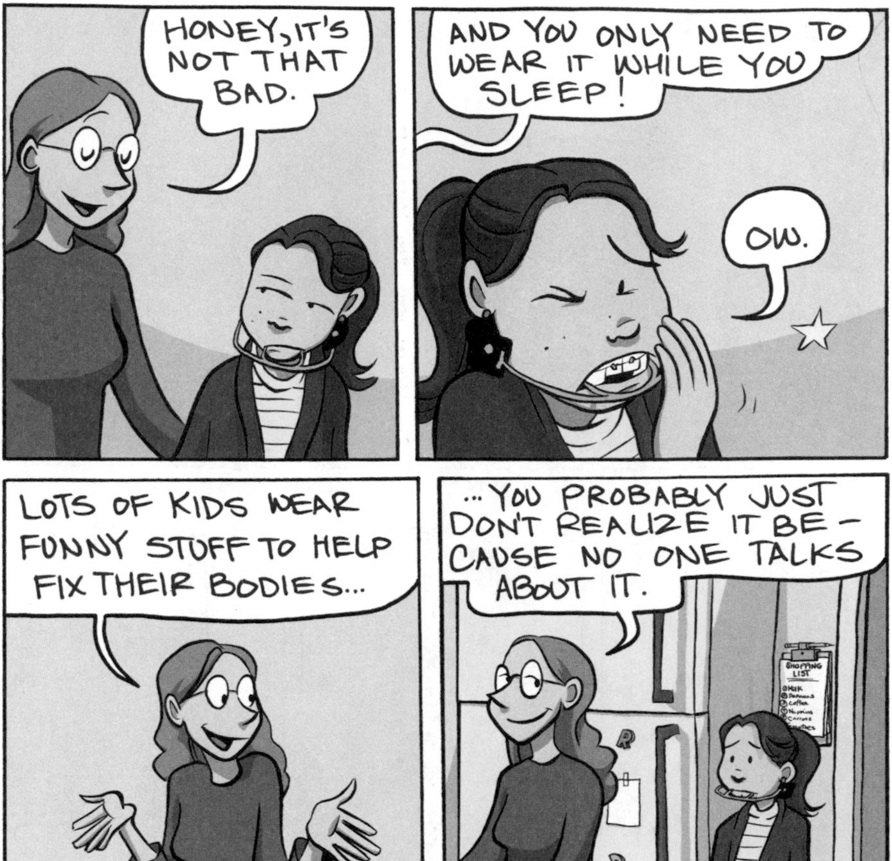
HONEY, IT'S NOT THAT BAD.
AND YOU ONLY NEED TO WEAR IT WHILE YOU SLEEP!
OW.
LOTS OF KIDS WEAR FUNNY STUFF TO HELP FIX THEIR BODIES...
...YOU PROBABLY JUST DON'T REALIZE IT BE-CAUSE NO ONE TALKS ABOUT IT.
SHOPPING LIST
WELL, MAYBE SOMEONE SHOULD START TALKING ABOUT IT !!
MAYBE IT WOULD MAKE US FEEL LESS LIKE FREAKS.

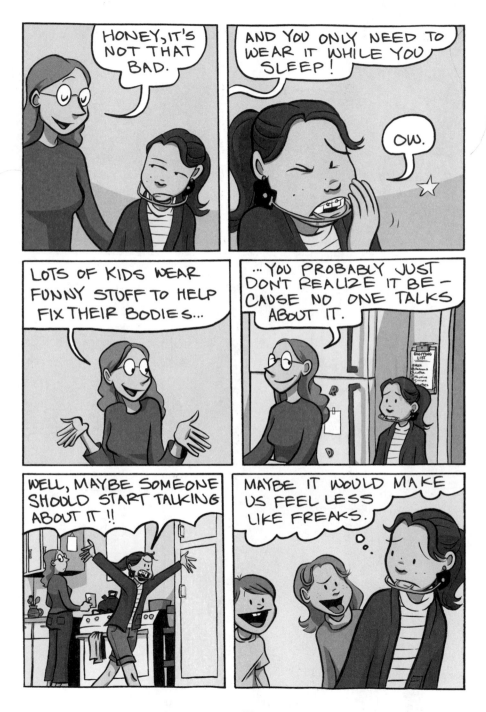

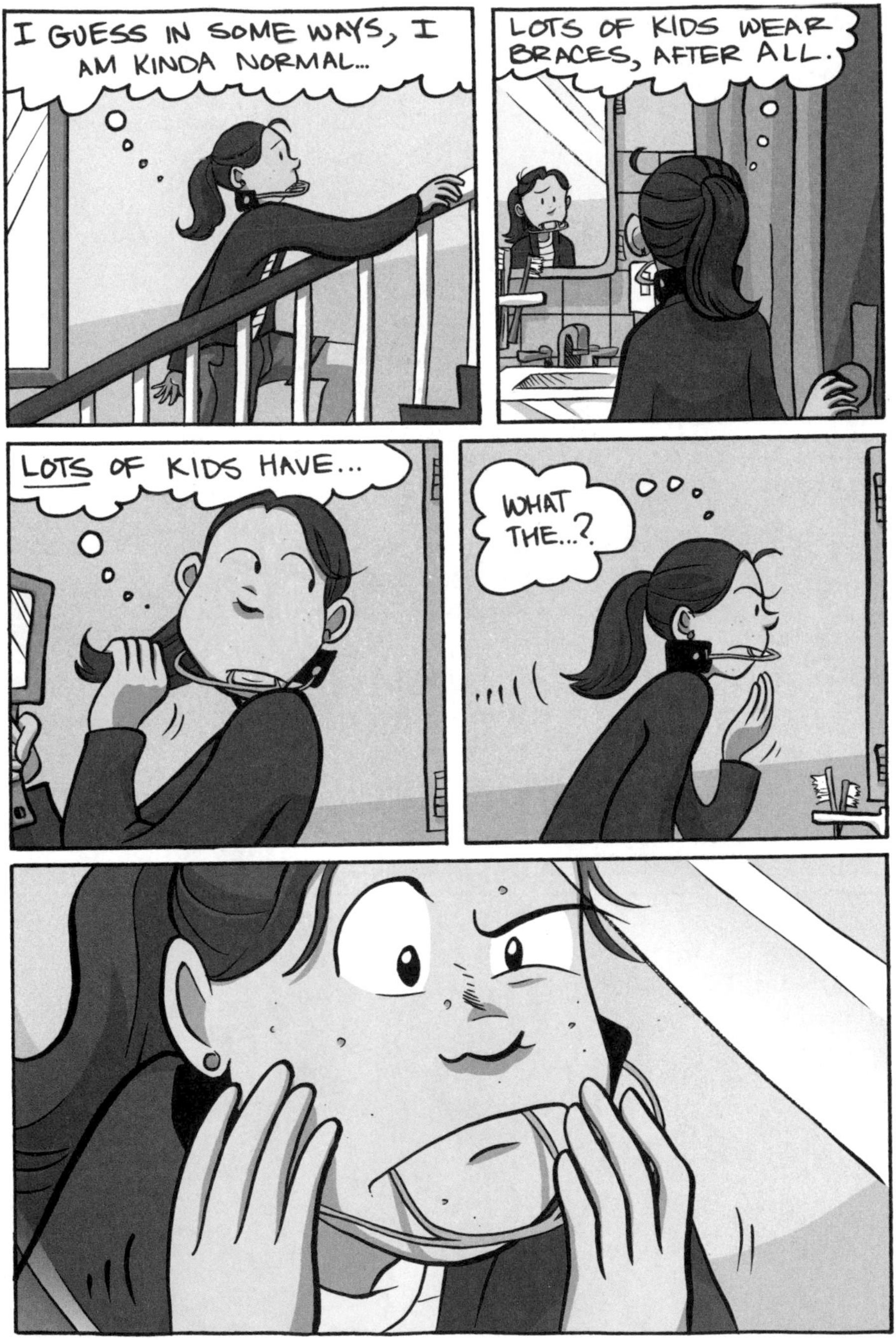
I GUESS IN SOME WAYS, I AM KINDA NORMAL...
LOTS OF KIDS WEAR BRACES, AFTER ALL.
LOTS OF KIDS HAVE...
WHAT THE...?

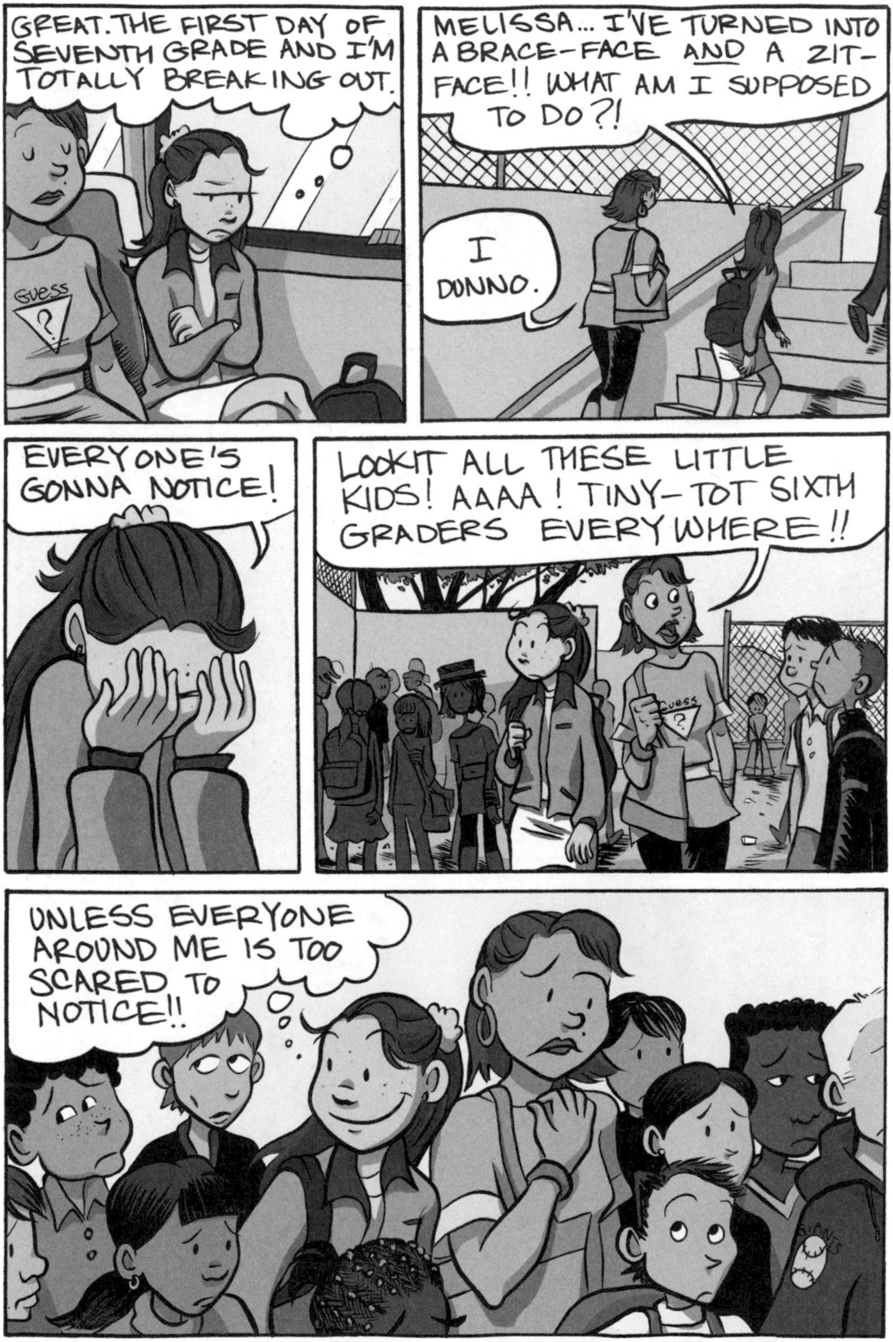
GREAT. THE FIRST DAY OF SEVENTH GRADE AND I'M TOTALLY BREAKING OUT.
MELISSA... I'VE TURNED INTO A BRACE-FACE AND A ZIT-FACE!! WHAT AM I SUPPOSED TO DO?!
I DUNNO.
GUESS
EVERYONE'S GONNA NOTICE!
LOOKIT ALL THESE LITTLE KIDS! AAAA! TINY-TOT SIXTH GRADERS EVERYWHERE!!
UNLESS EVERYONE AROUND ME IS TOO SCARED TO NOTICE!!

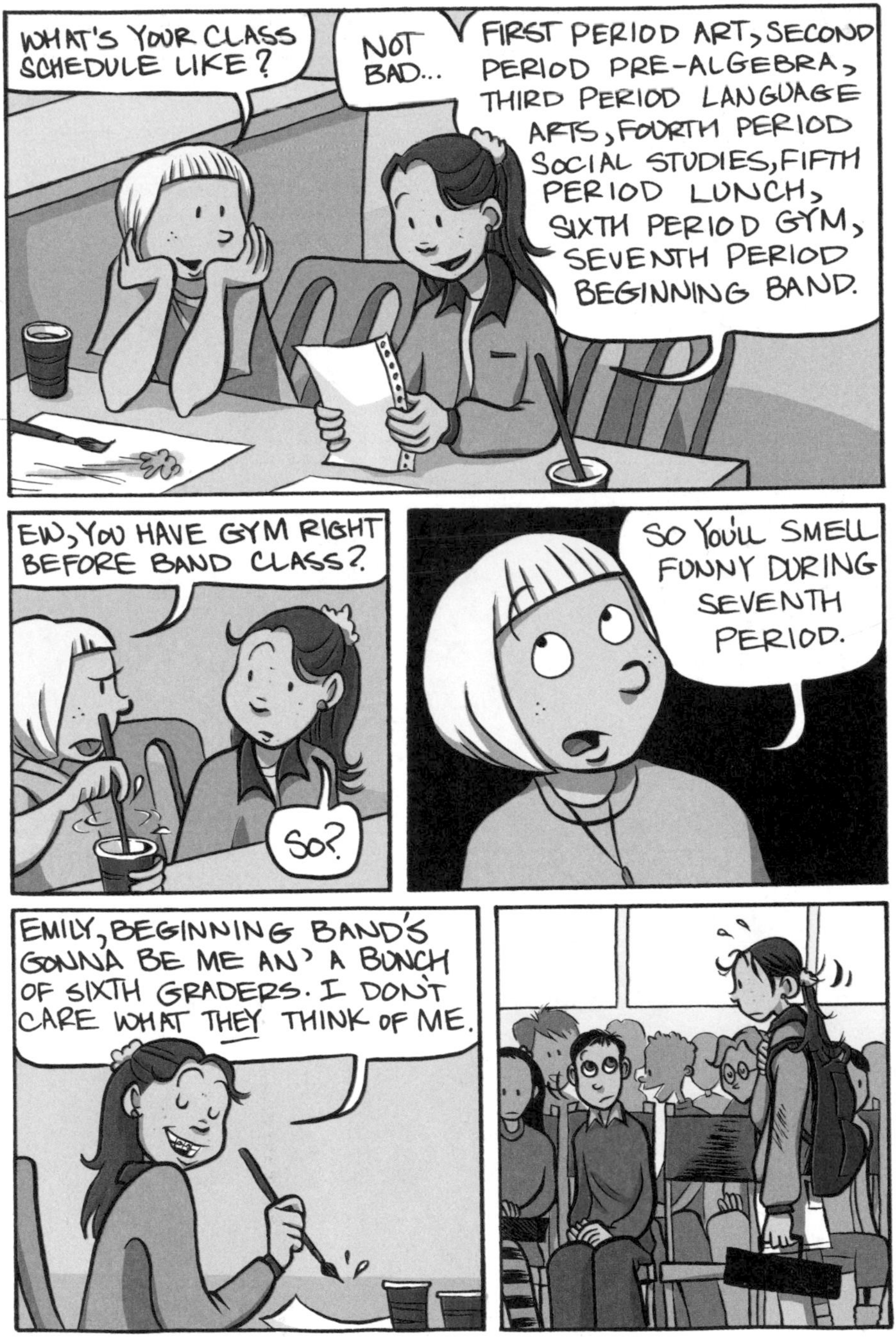
WHAT'S YOUR CLASS SCHEDULE LIKE?
NOT BAD...
FIRST PERIOD ART, SECOND PERIOD PRE-ALGEBRA, THIRD PERIOD LANGUAGE ARTS, FOURTH PERIOD SOCIAL STUDIES, FIFTH PERIOD LUNCH, SIXTH PERIOD GYM, SEVENTH PERIOD BEGINNING BAND.
EW, YOU HAVE GYM RIGHT BEFORE BAND CLASS?
SO?
SO YOU'LL SMELL FUNNY DURING SEVENTH PERIOD.
EMILY, BEGINNING BAND'S GONNA BE ME AN' A BUNCH OF SIXTH GRADERS. I DON'T CARE WHAT THEY THINK OF ME.

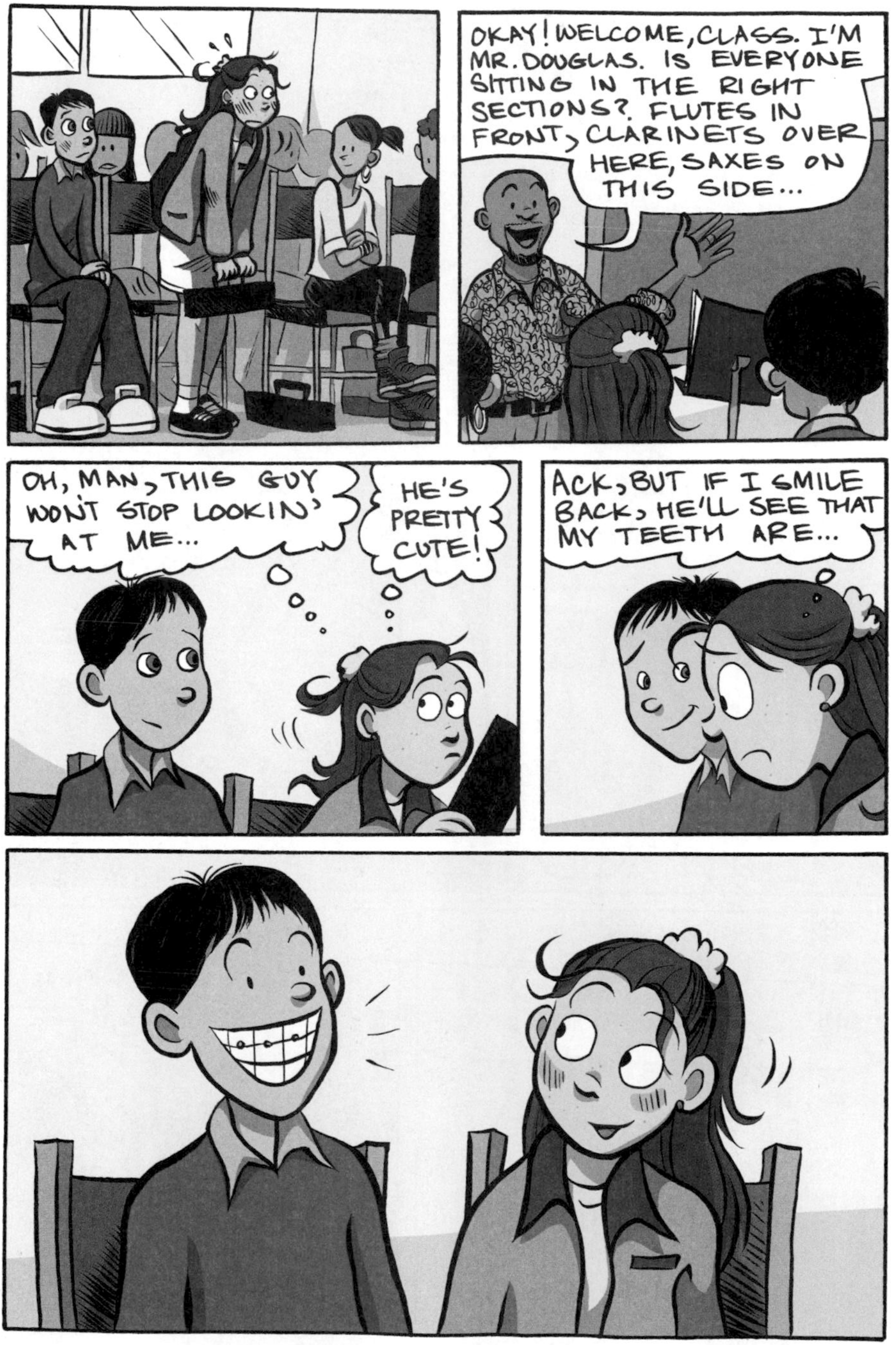
OKAY! WELCOME, CLASS. I'M MR. DOUGLAS. IS EVERYONE SITTING IN THE RIGHT SECTIONS? FLUTES IN FRONT, CLARINETS OVER HERE, SAXES ON THIS SIDE...
OH, MAN, THIS GUY WON'T STOP LOOKIN' AT ME...
HE'S PRETTY CUTE!
ACK, BUT IF I SMILE BACK, HE'LL SEE THAT MY TEETH ARE...

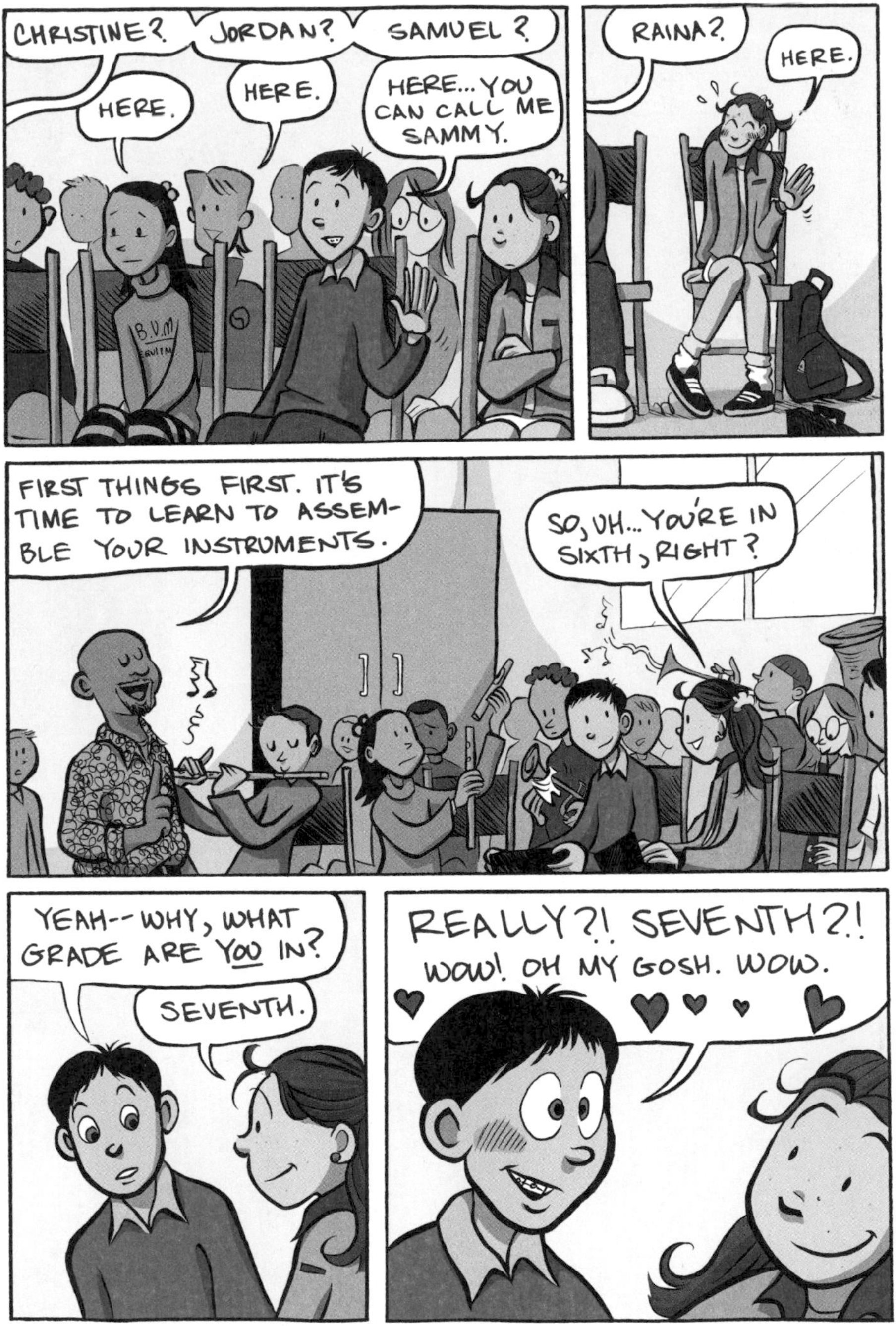
CHRISTINE?
HERE.
JORDAN?
HERE.
SAMUEL?
HERE... YOU CAN CALL ME SAMMY.
RAINA?
HERE.
FIRST THINGS FIRST. IT'S TIME TO LEARN TO ASSEMBLE YOUR INSTRUMENTS.
SO, UH... YOU'RE IN SIXTH, RIGHT?
YEAH-- WHY, WHAT GRADE ARE YOU IN?
SEVENTH.
REALLY?! SEVENTH?!
WOW! OH MY GOSH. WOW.

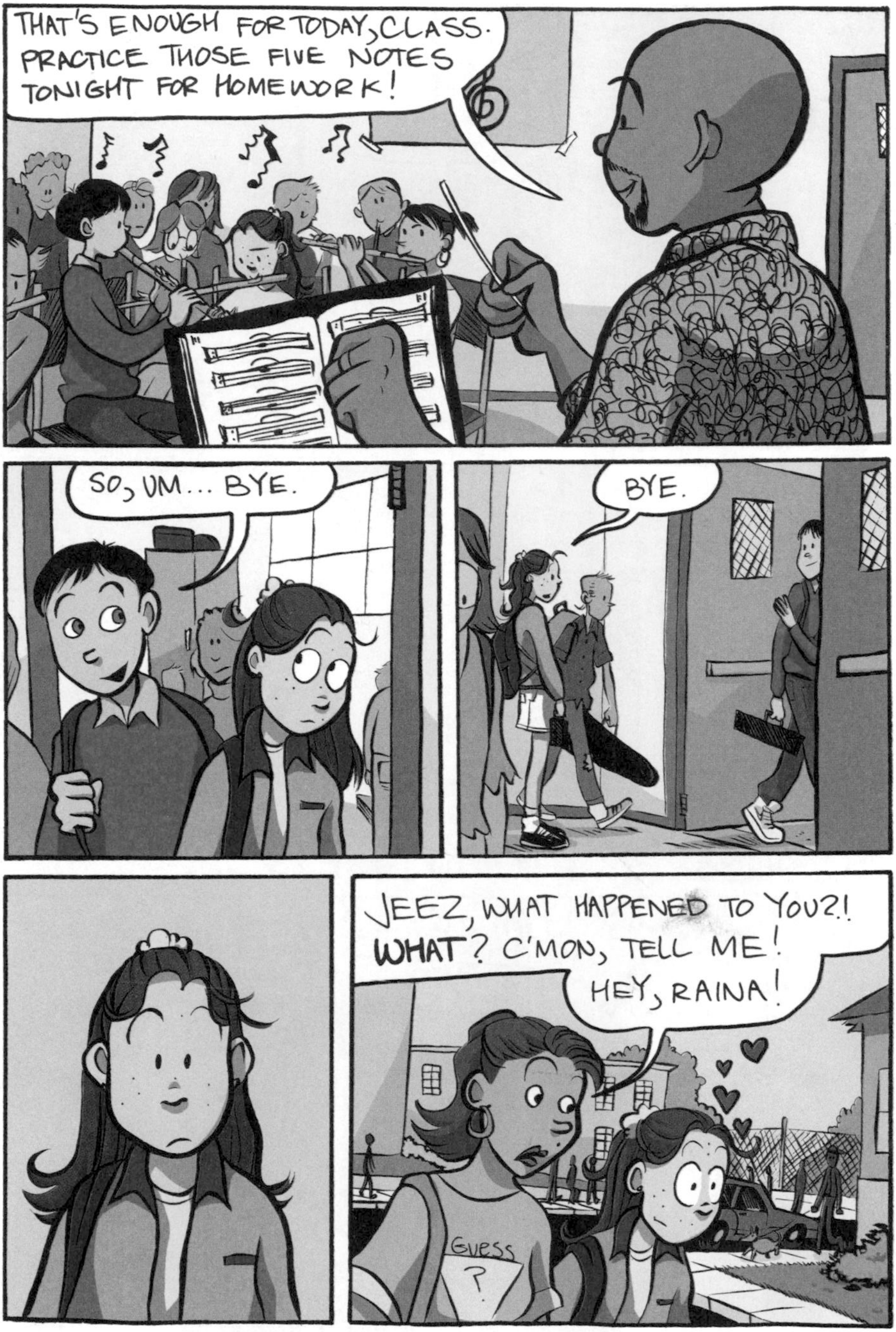
THAT'S ENOUGH FOR TODAY, CLASS. PRACTICE THOSE FIVE NOTES TONIGHT FOR HOMEWORK!
SO, UM... BYE.
BYE.
JEEZ, WHAT HAPPENED TO YOU?!
WHAT? C'MON, TELL ME!
HEY, RAINA!
GUESS
?

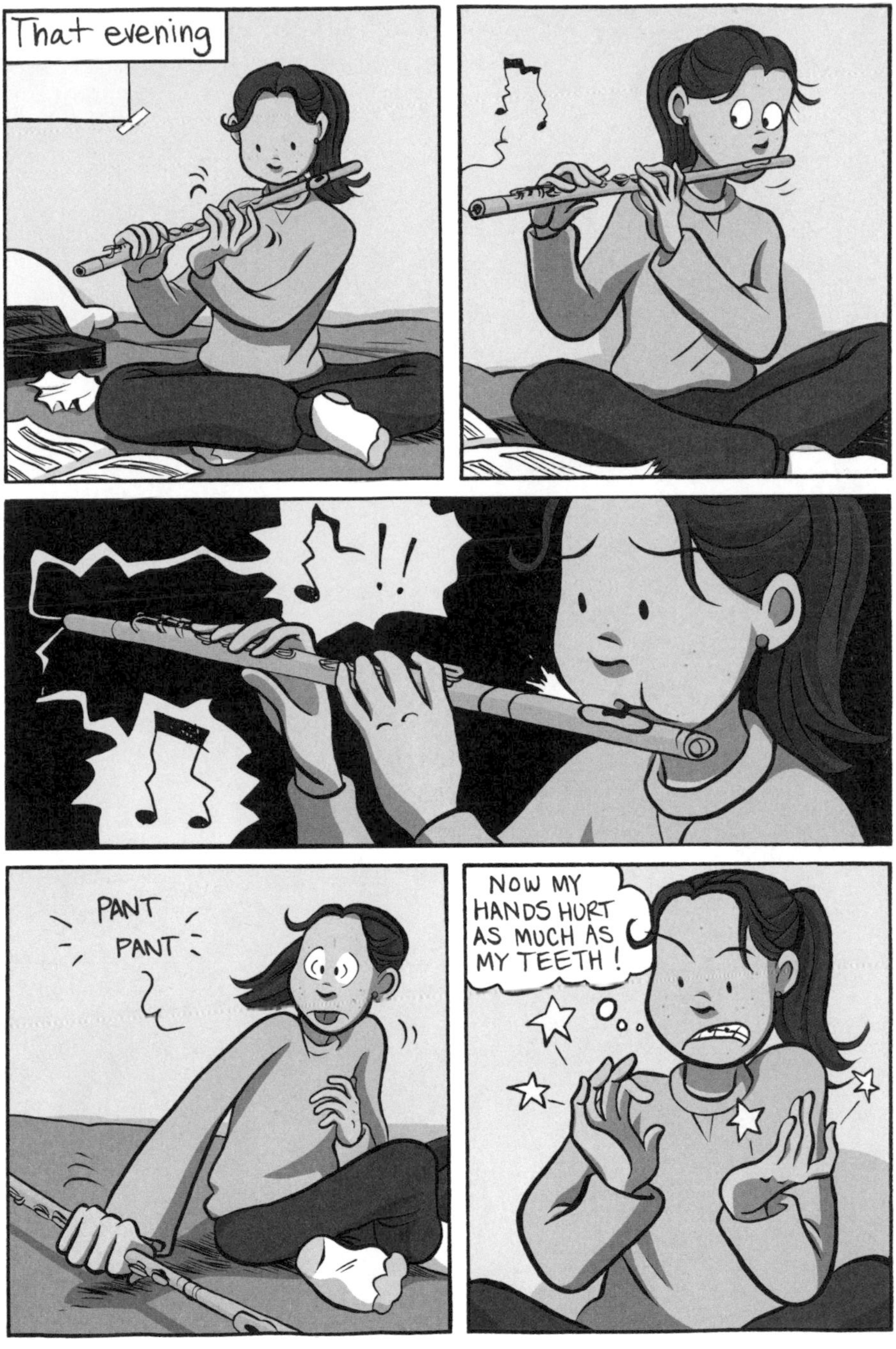
That evening
!!
PANT
PANT
NOW MY HANDS HURT AS MUCH AS MY TEETH!

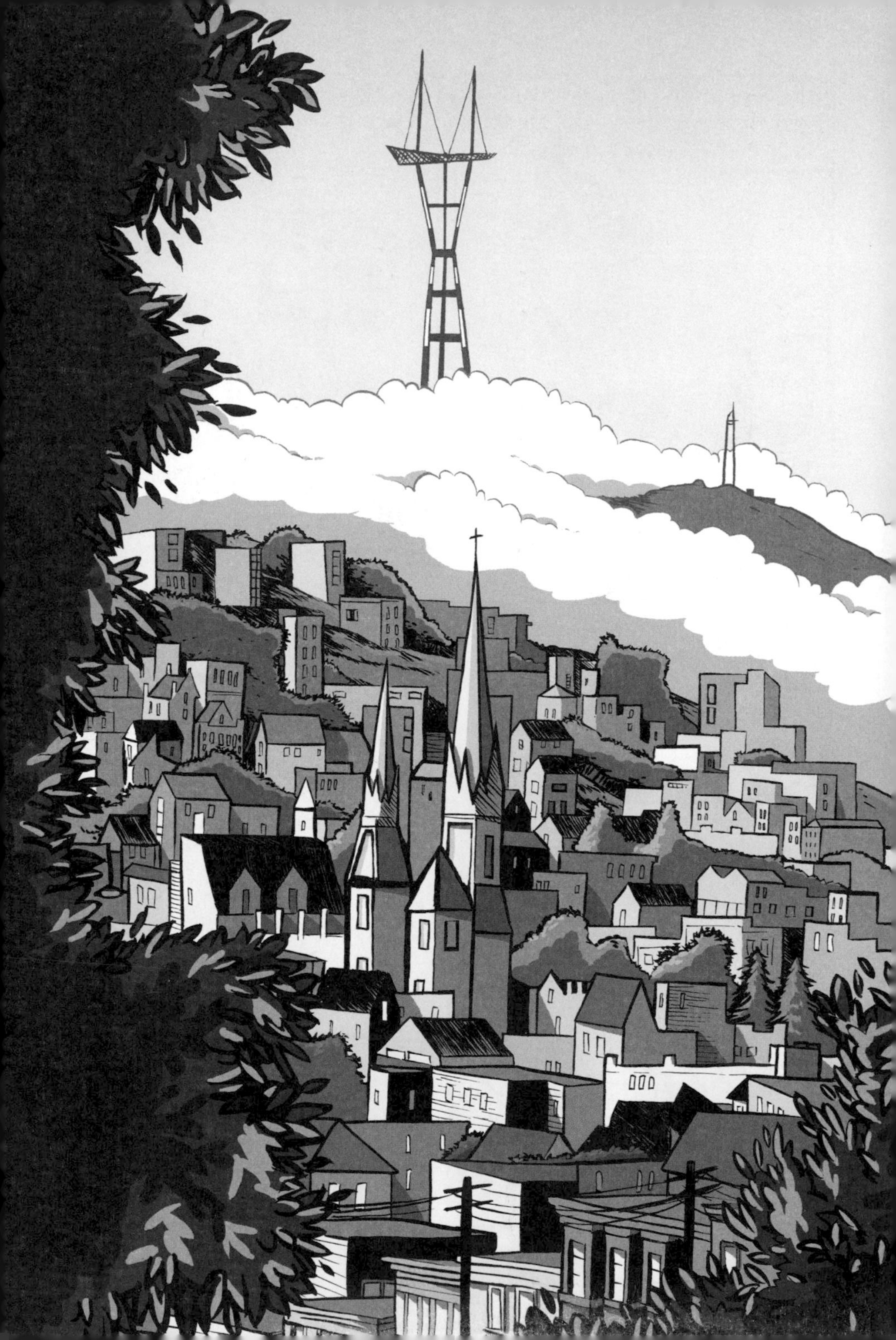

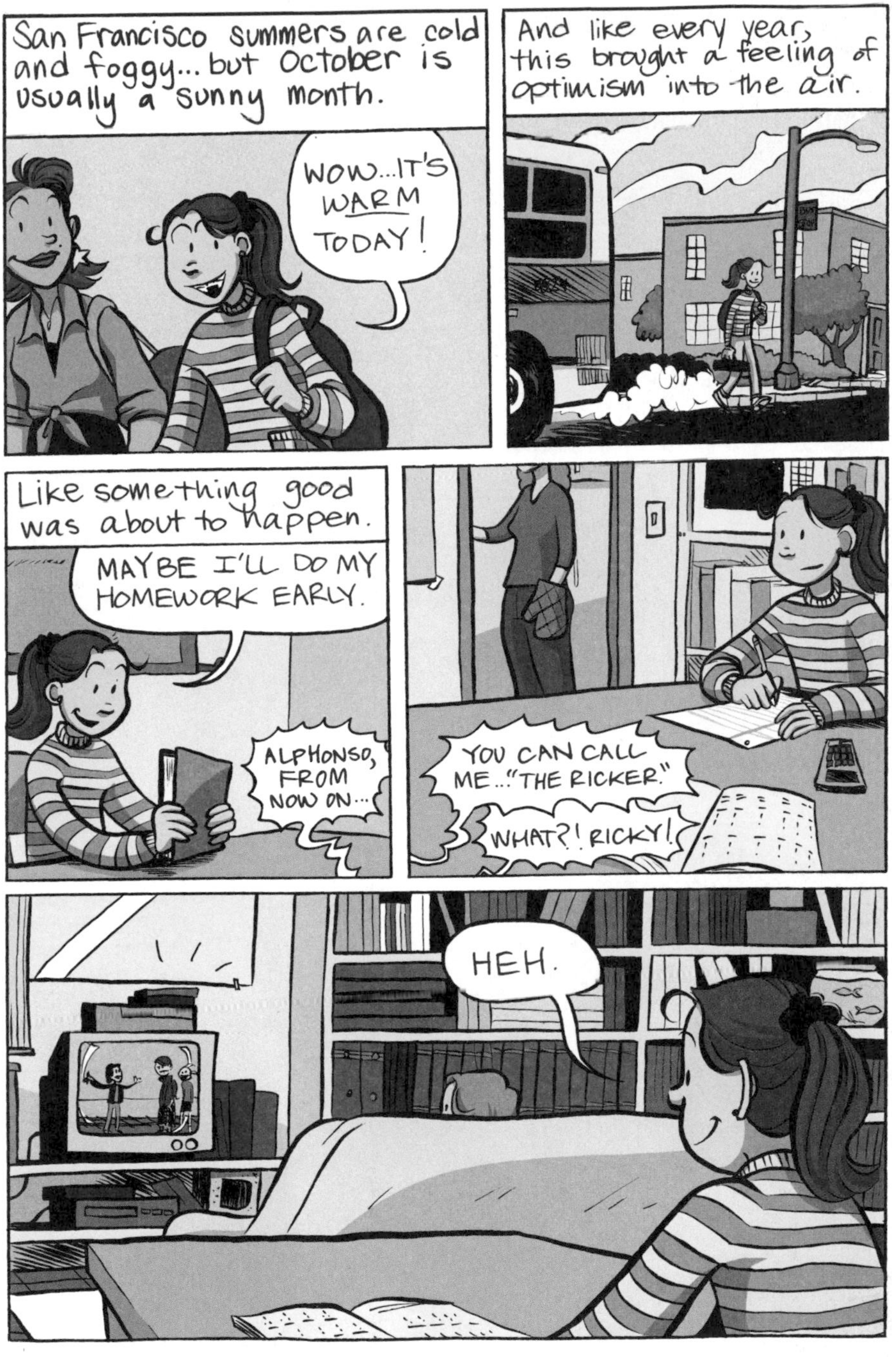
San Francisco summers are cold and foggy... but October is usually a sunny month.
WOW...IT'S WARM TODAY!
And like every year, this brought a feeling of optimism into the air.
Like something good was about to happen.
MAYBE I'LL DO MY HOMEWORK EARLY.
ALPHONSO, FROM NOW ON...
YOU CAN CALL ME..."THE RICKER."
WHAT?! RICKY!
HEH.

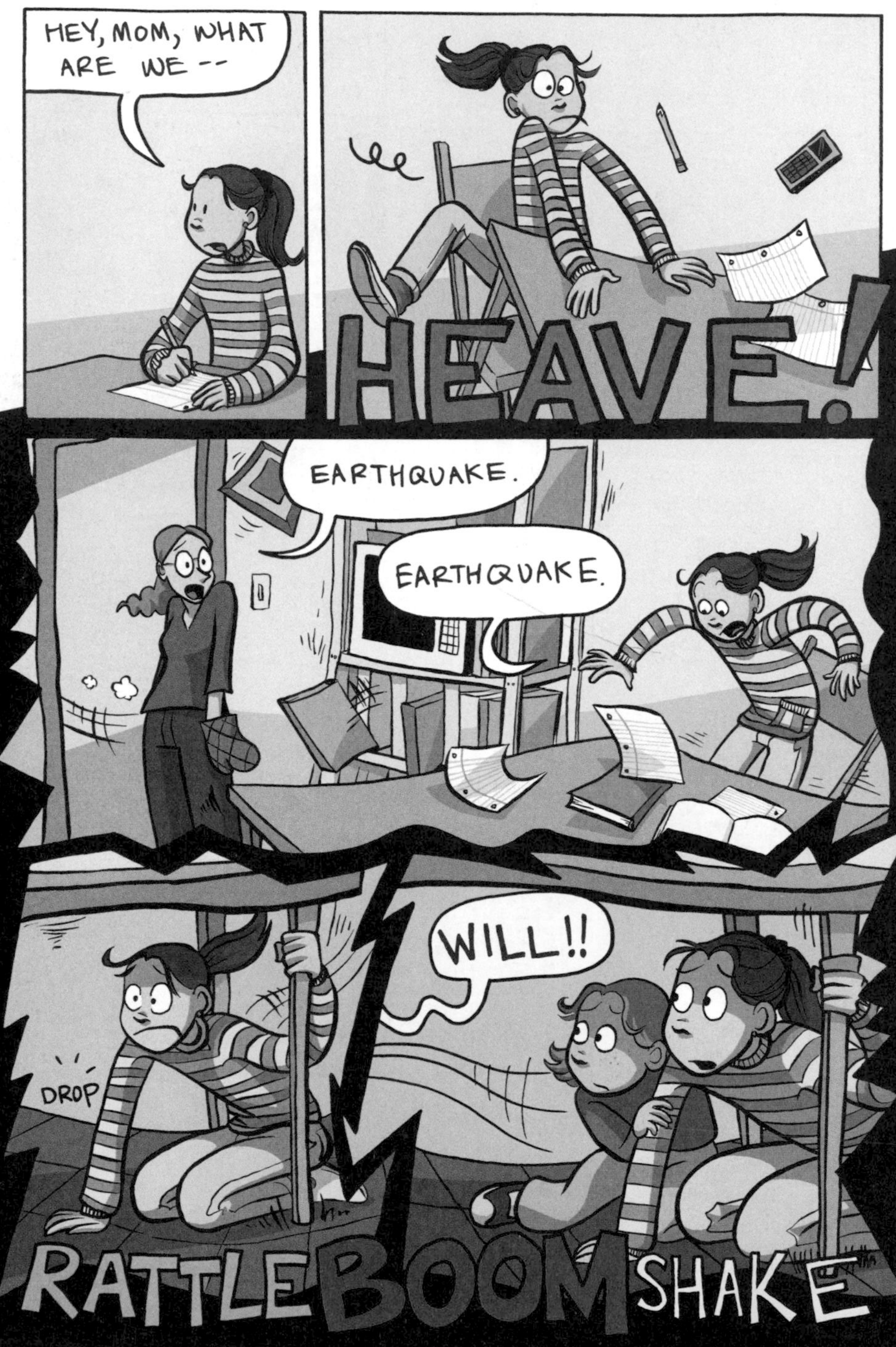
HEY, MOM, WHAT ARE WE --
HEAVE!
EARTHQUAKE.
EARTHQUAKE.
WILL!!
DROP
RATTLE BOOM SHAKE

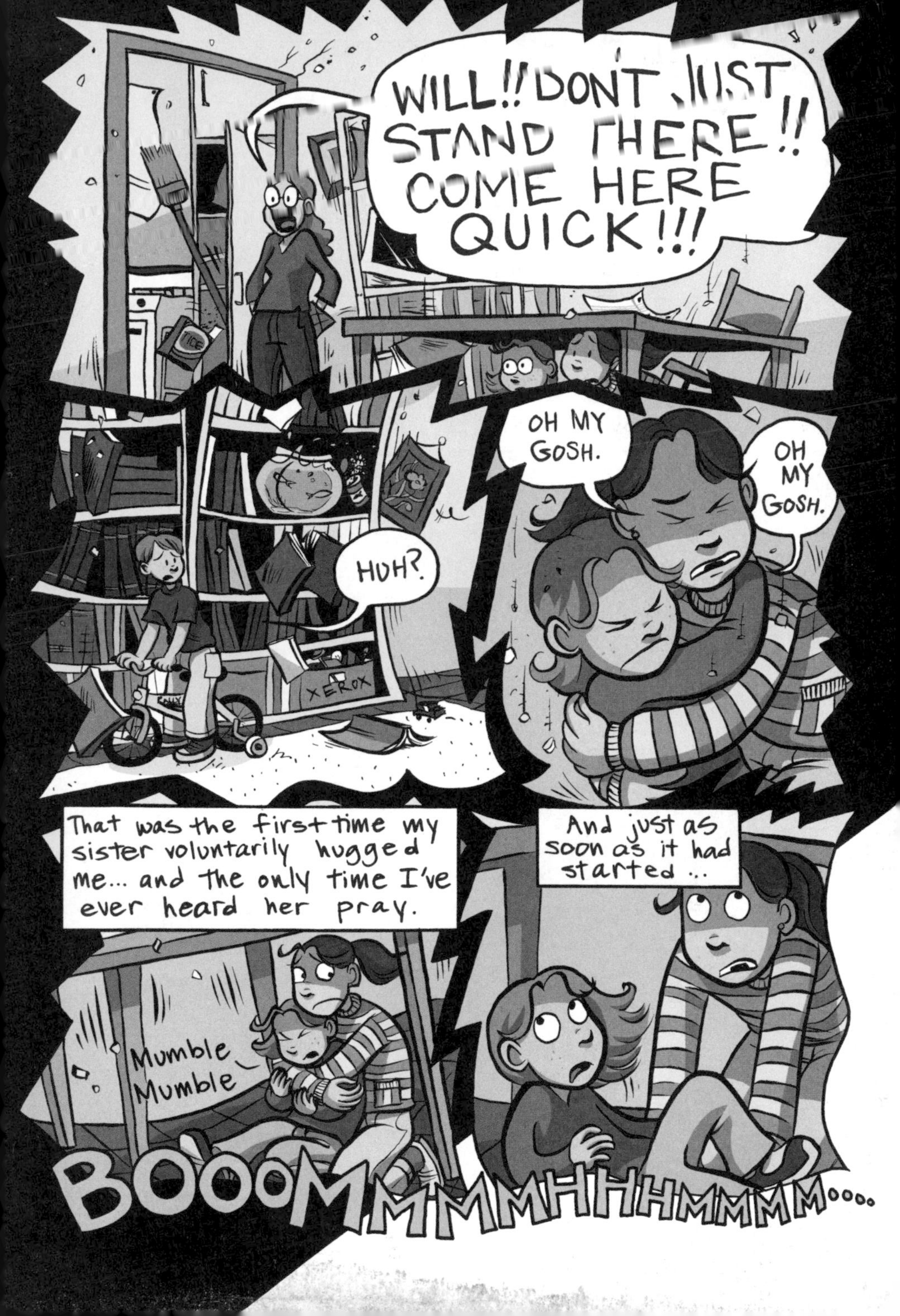
WILL!! DON'T JUST STAND THERE!! COME HERE QUICK!!!
HUH?
OH MY GOSH.
OH MY GOSH.
That was the first time my sister voluntarily hugged me... and the only time I've ever heard her pray.
And just as soon as it had started ...
Mumble Mumble
BOOOMMMMMHHHHMMMM....

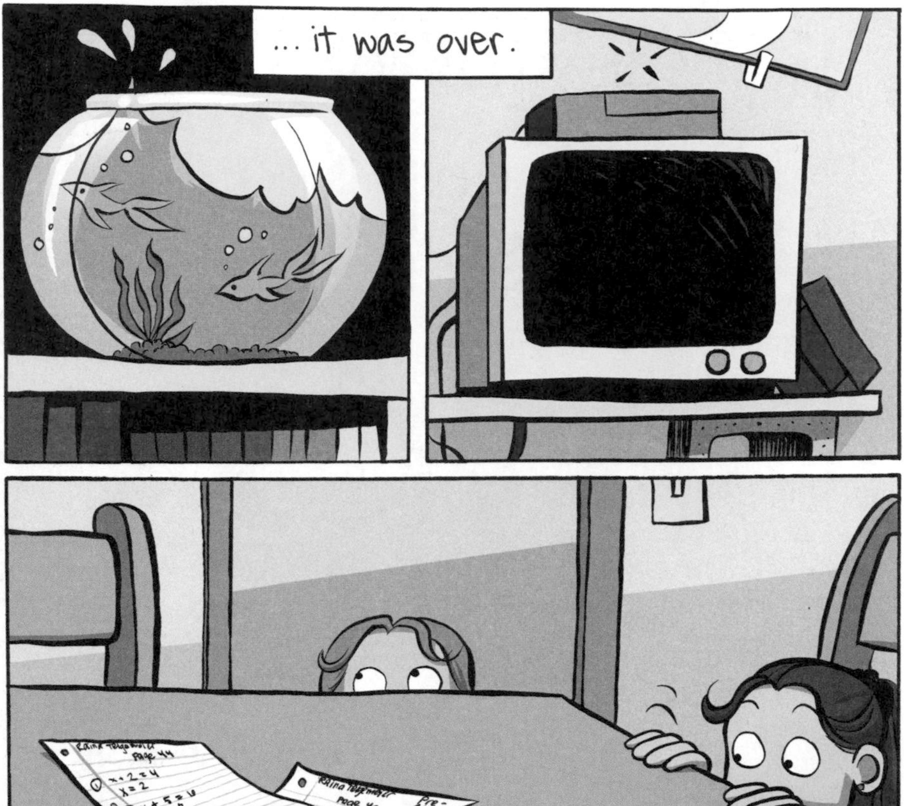
... it was over.
WILL!!!
WHAT?

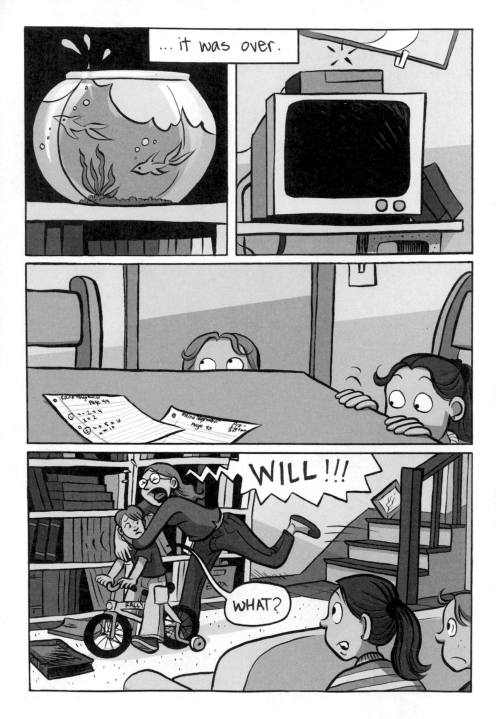

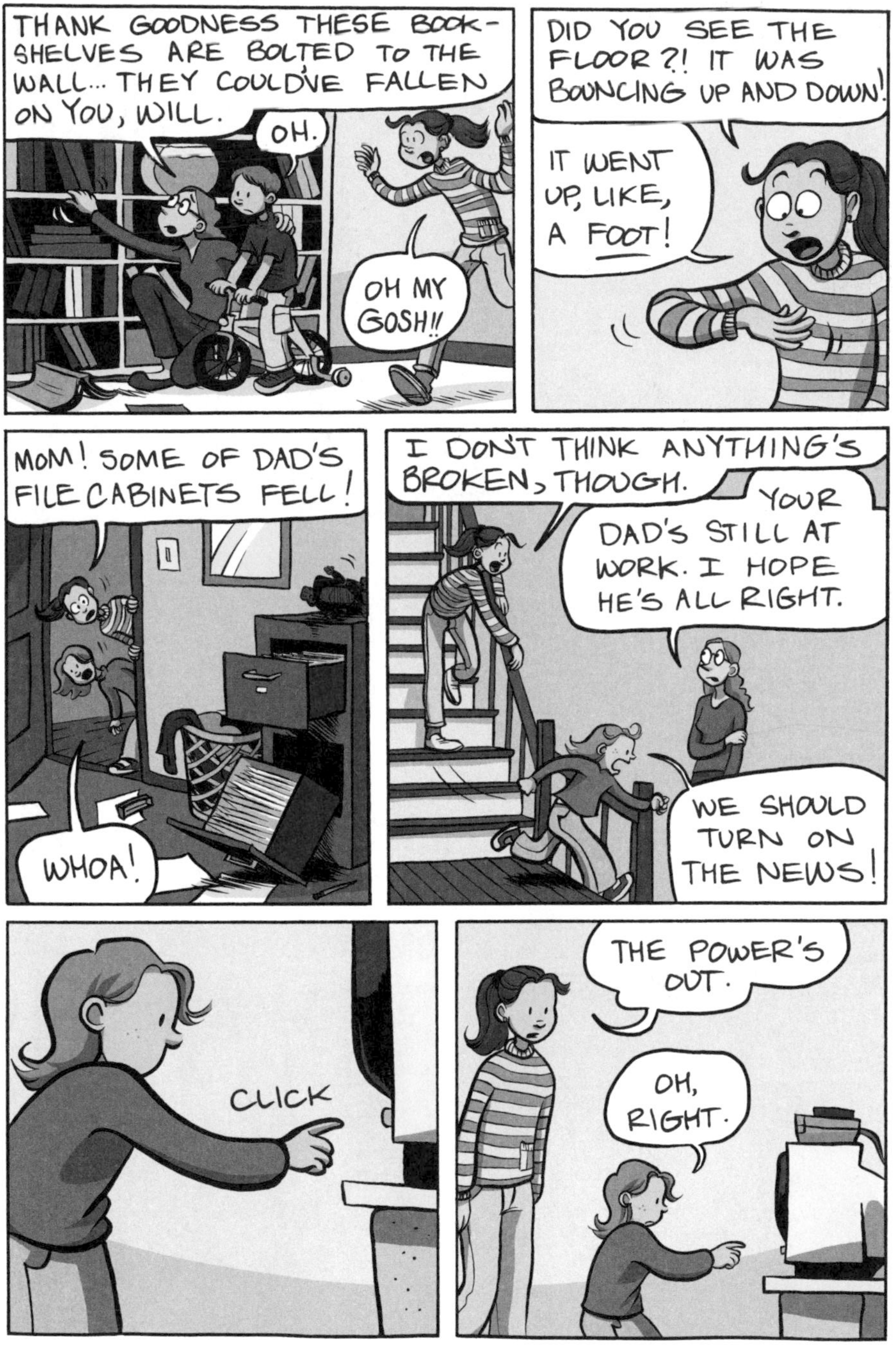
THANK GOODNESS THESE BOOK-SHELVES ARE BOLTED TO THE WALL... THEY COULD'VE FALLEN ON YOU, WILL.
OH.
OH MY GOSH!!
DID YOU SEE THE FLOOR?! IT WAS BOUNCING UP AND DOWN!
IT WENT UP, LIKE, A FOOT!
MOM! SOME OF DAD'S FILE CABINETS FELL!
WHOA!
I DON'T THINK ANYTHING'S BROKEN, THOUGH.
YOUR DAD'S STILL AT WORK. I HOPE HE'S ALL RIGHT.
WE SHOULD TURN ON THE NEWS!
CLICK
THE POWER'S OUT.
OH, RIGHT.

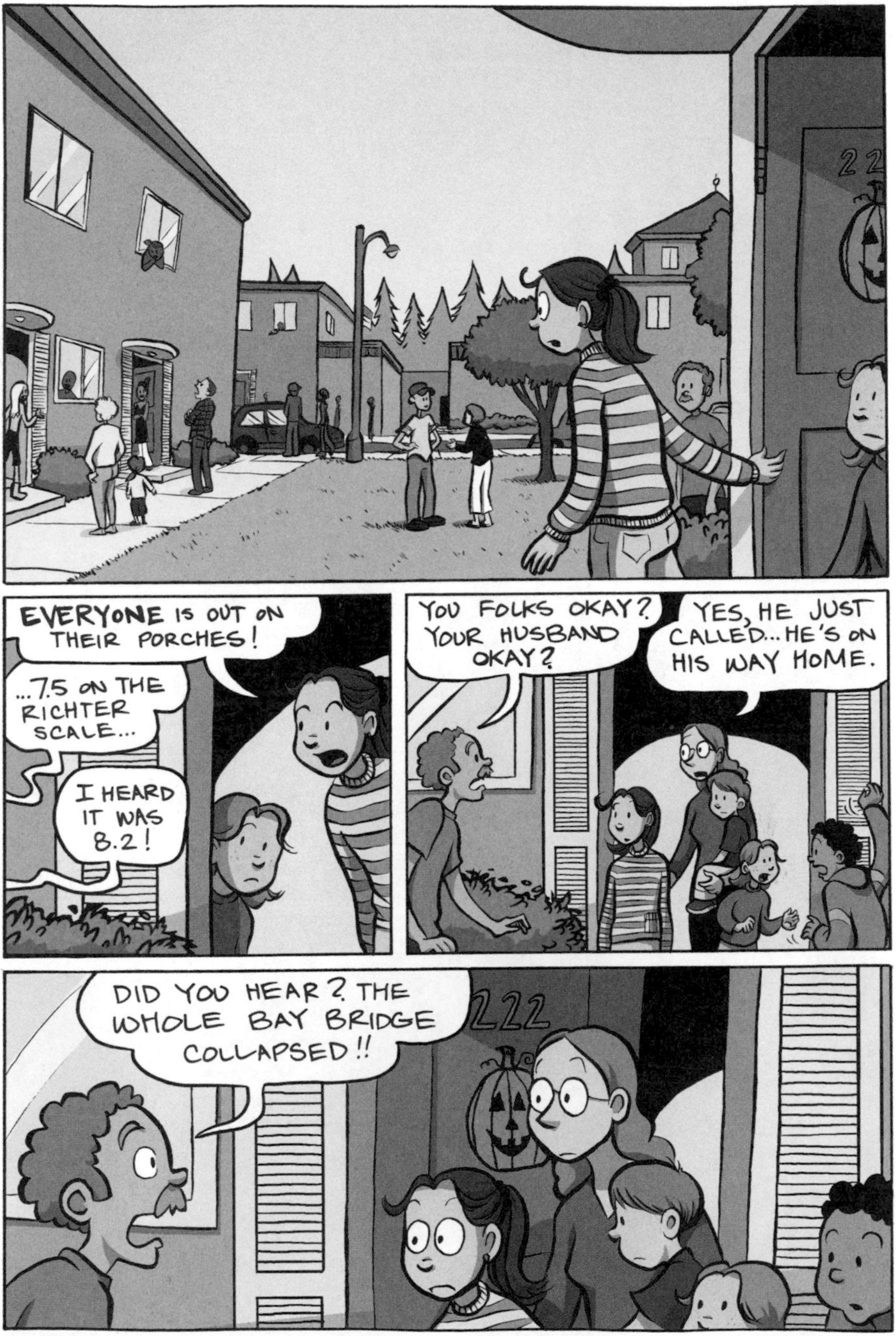
EVERYONE IS OUT ON THEIR PORCHES!
...7.5 ON THE RICHTER SCALE...
I HEARD IT WAS 8.2!
YOU FOLKS OKAY? YOUR HUSBAND OKAY?
YES, HE JUST CALLED... HE'S ON HIS WAY HOME.
DID YOU HEAR? THE WHOLE BAY BRIDGE COLLAPSED!!

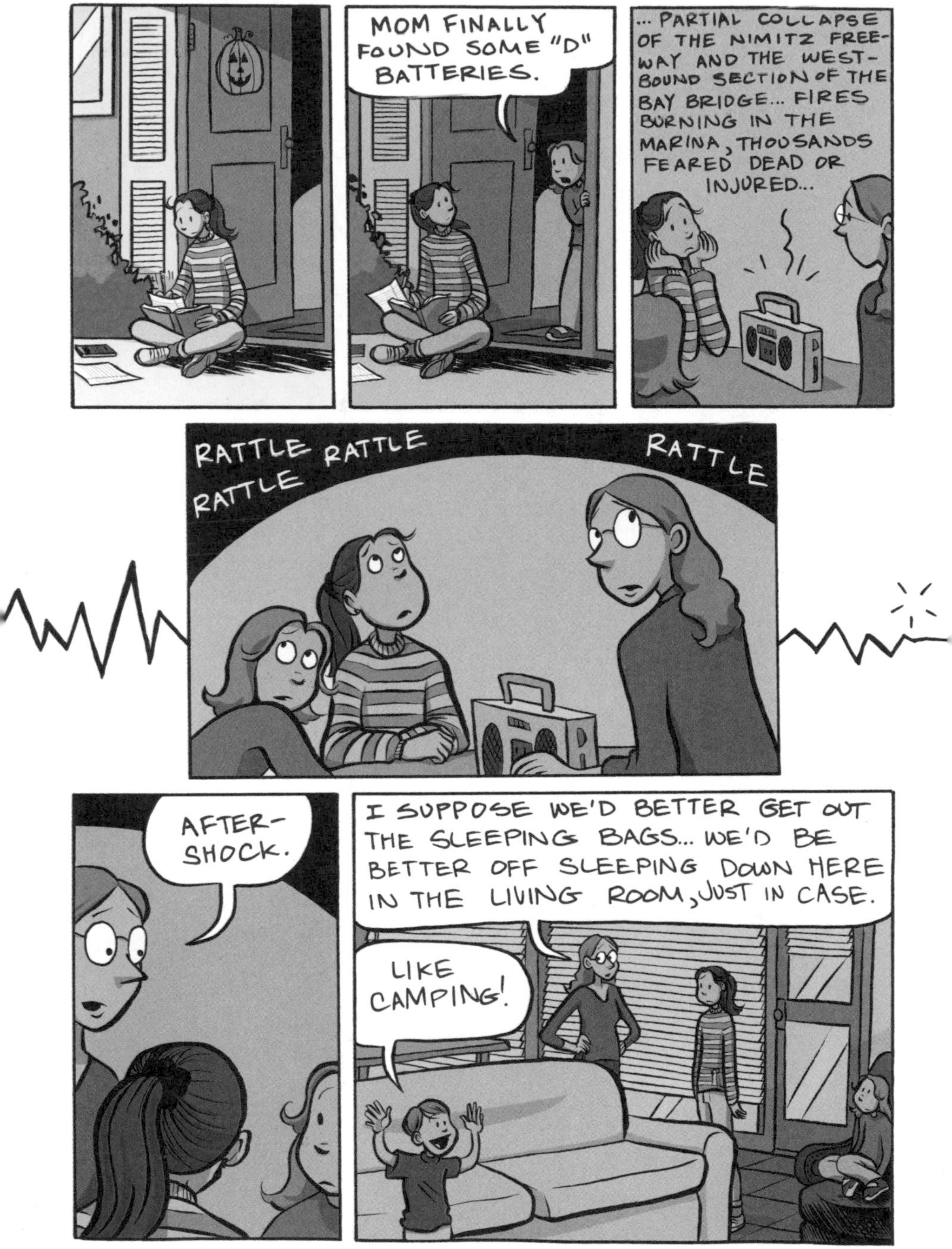
MOM FINALLY FOUND SOME "D" BATTERIES.
... PARTIAL COLLAPSE OF THE NIMITZ FREEWAY AND THE WEST-BOUND SECTION OF THE BAY BRIDGE... FIRES BURNING IN THE MARINA, THOUSANDS FEARED DEAD OR INJURED...
RATTLE RATTLE
RATTLE
RATTLE
AFTER-SHOCK.
I SUPPOSE WE'D BETTER GET OUT THE SLEEPING BAGS... WE'D BE BETTER OFF SLEEPING DOWN HERE IN THE LIVING ROOM, JUST IN CASE.
LIKE CAMPING!

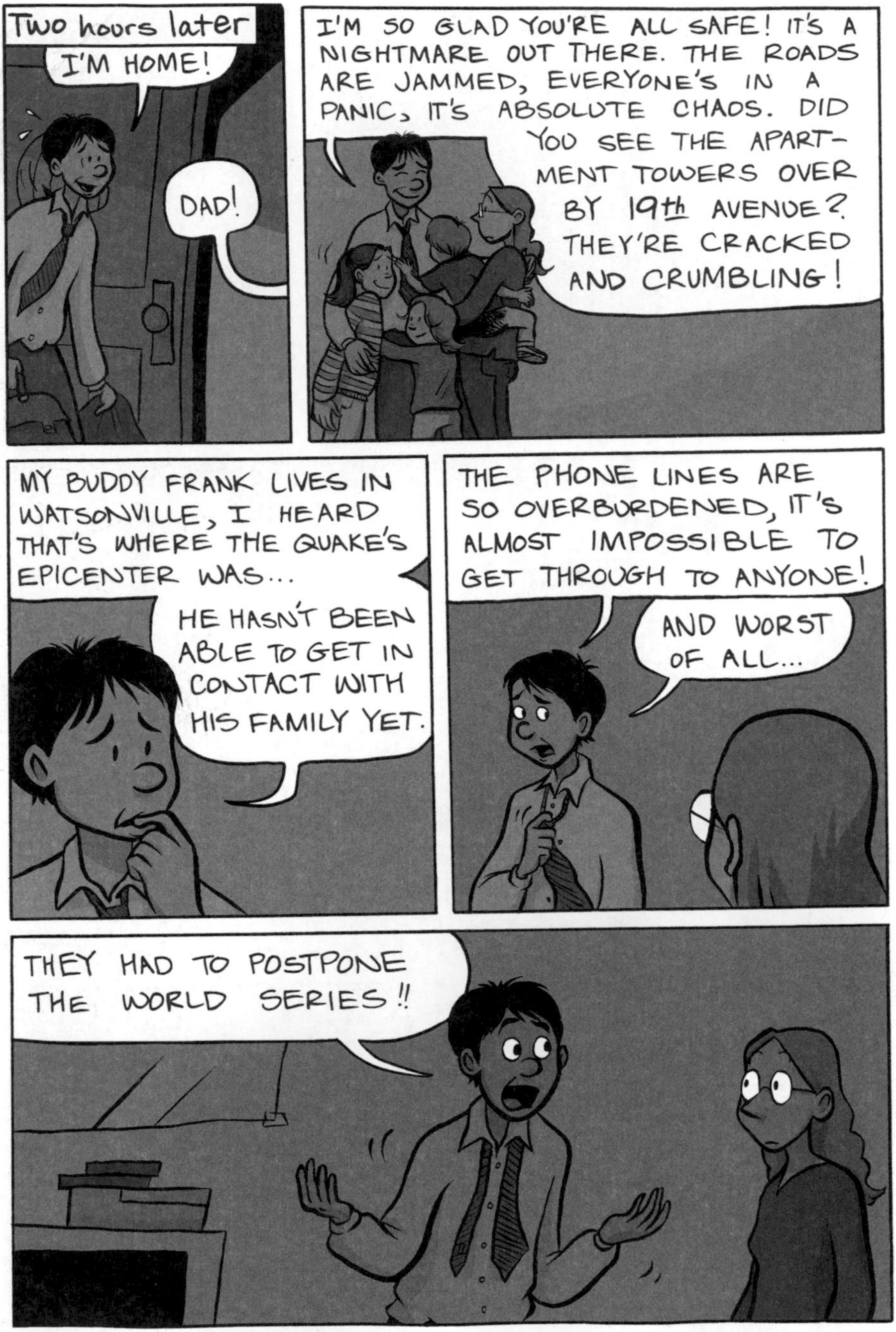

Two hours later
I'M HOME!
DAD!
I'M SO GLAD YOU'RE ALL SAFE! IT'S A NIGHTMARE OUT THERE. THE ROADS ARE JAMMED, EVERYONE'S IN A PANIC, IT'S ABSOLUTE CHAOS. DID YOU SEE THE APARTMENT TOWERS OVER BY 19th AVENUE? THEY'RE CRACKED AND CRUMBLING!
MY BUDDY FRANK LIVES IN WATSONVILLE, I HEARD THAT'S WHERE THE QUAKE'S EPICENTER WAS...
HE HASN'T BEEN ABLE TO GET IN CONTACT WITH HIS FAMILY YET.
THE PHONE LINES ARE SO OVERBURDENED, IT'S ALMOST IMPOSSIBLE TO GET THROUGH TO ANYONE!
AND WORST OF ALL...
THEY HAD TO POSTPONE THE WORLD SERIES!!

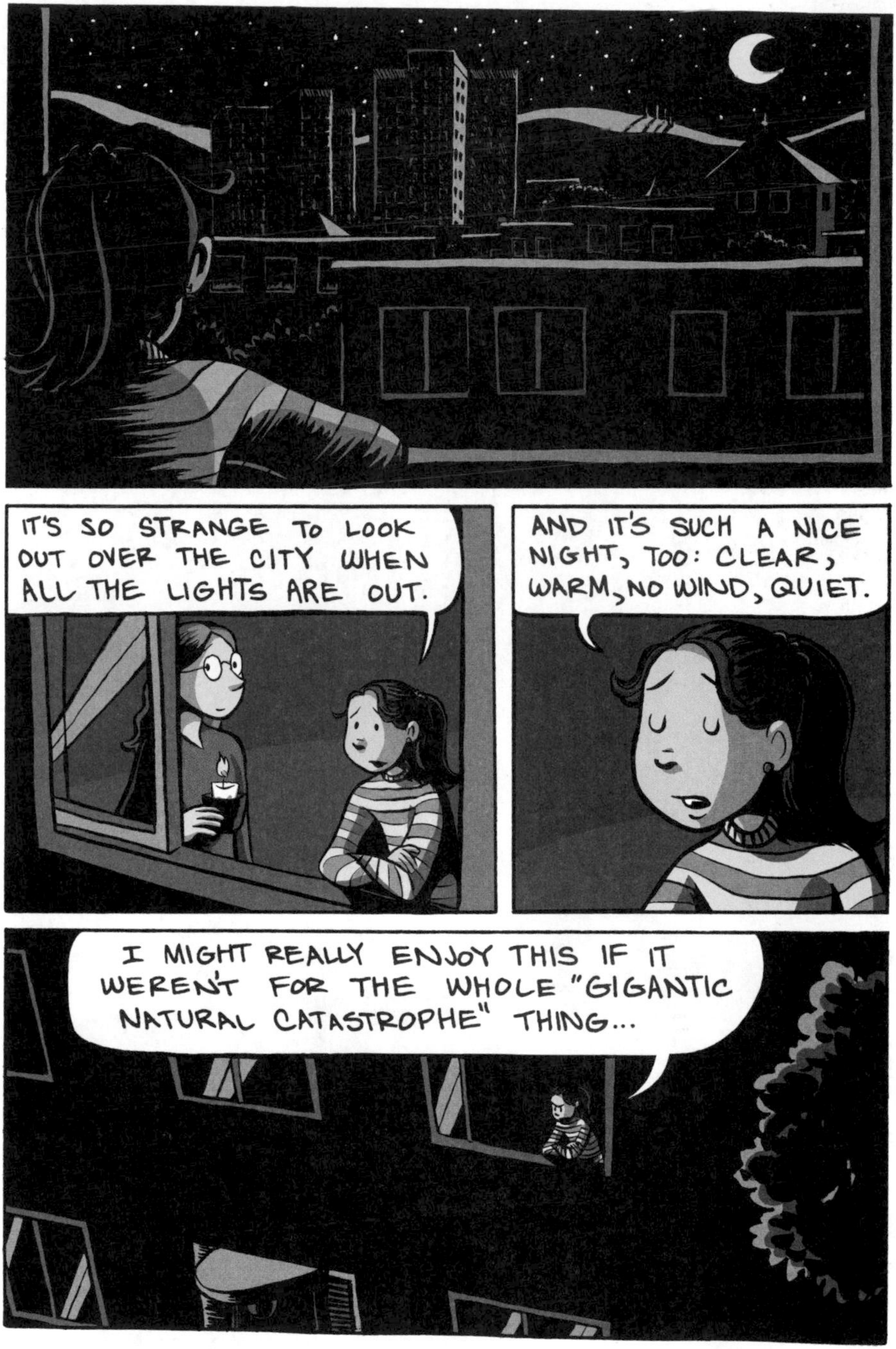
IT'S SO STRANGE TO LOOK OUT OVER THE CITY WHEN ALL THE LIGHTS ARE OUT.
AND IT'S SUCH A NICE NIGHT, TOO: CLEAR, WARM, NO WIND, QUIET.
I MIGHT REALLY ENJOY THIS IF IT WEREN'T FOR THE WHOLE "GIGANTIC NATURAL CATASTROPHE" THING...

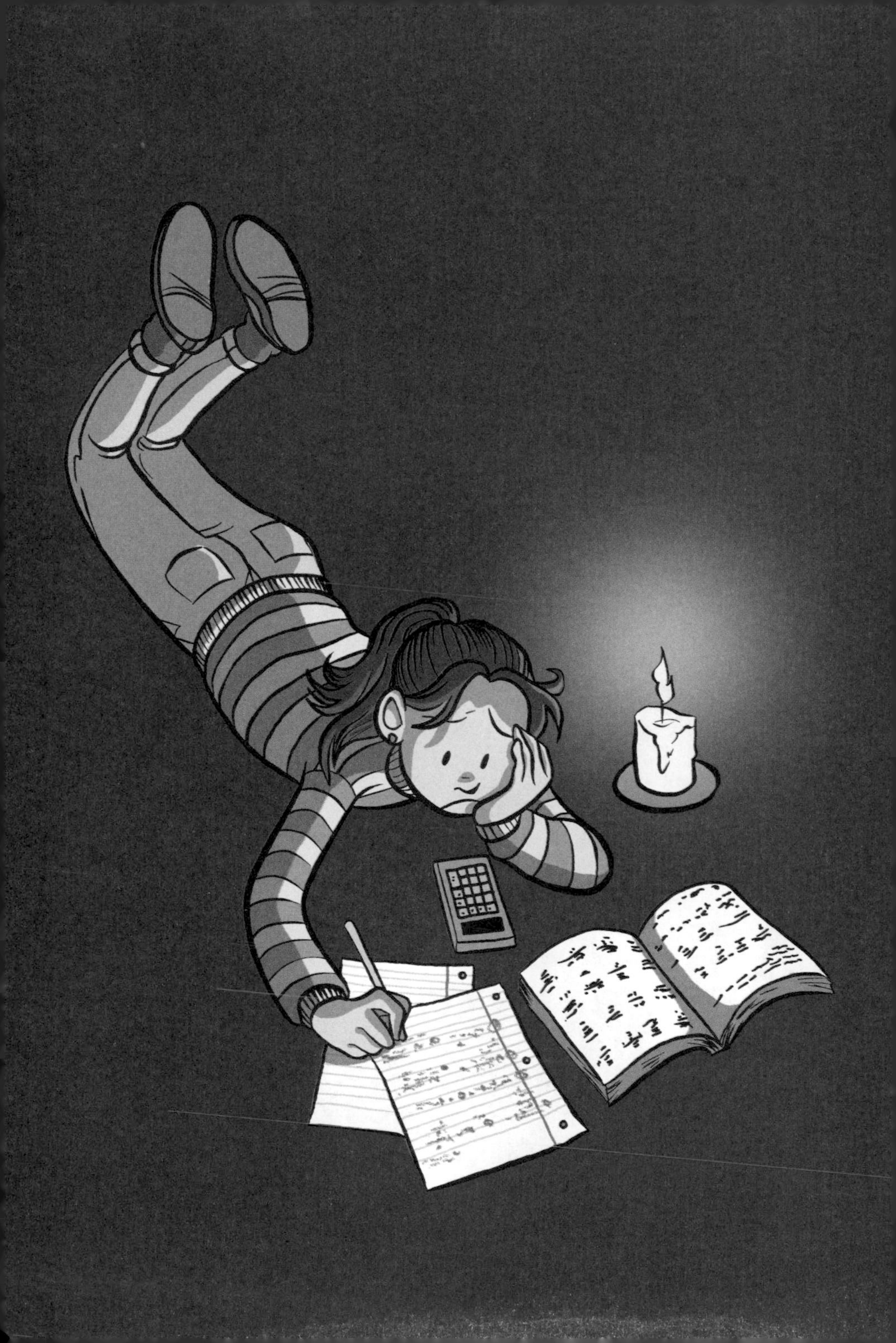

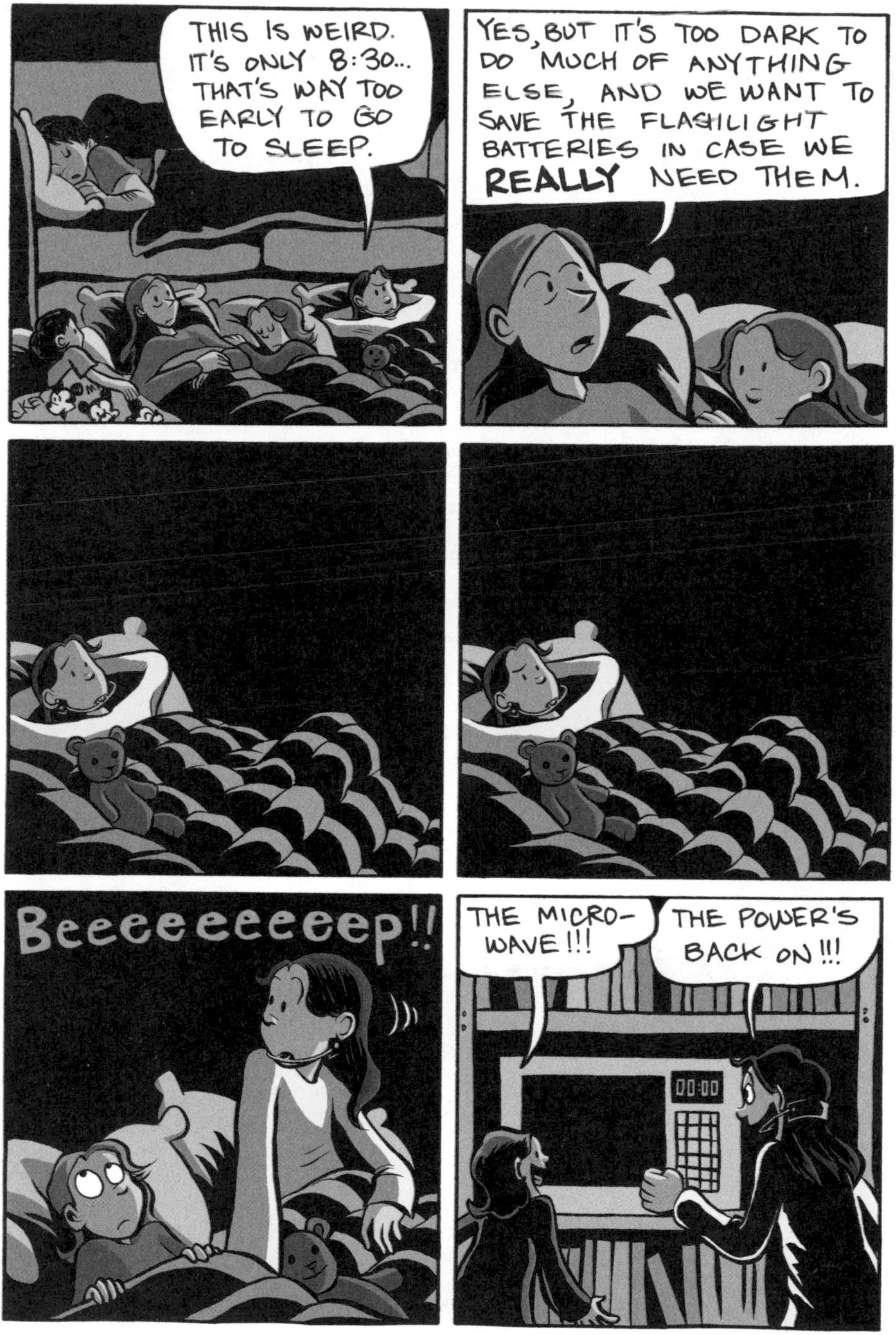

THIS IS WEIRD. IT'S ONLY 8:30... THAT'S WAY TOO EARLY TO GO TO SLEEP.
YES, BUT IT'S TOO DARK TO DO MUCH OF ANYTHING ELSE, AND WE WANT TO SAVE THE FLASHLIGHT BATTERIES IN CASE WE **REALLY** NEED THEM.
Beeeeeeeeep!!
THE MICRO-WAVE!!!
THE POWER'S BACK ON!!!

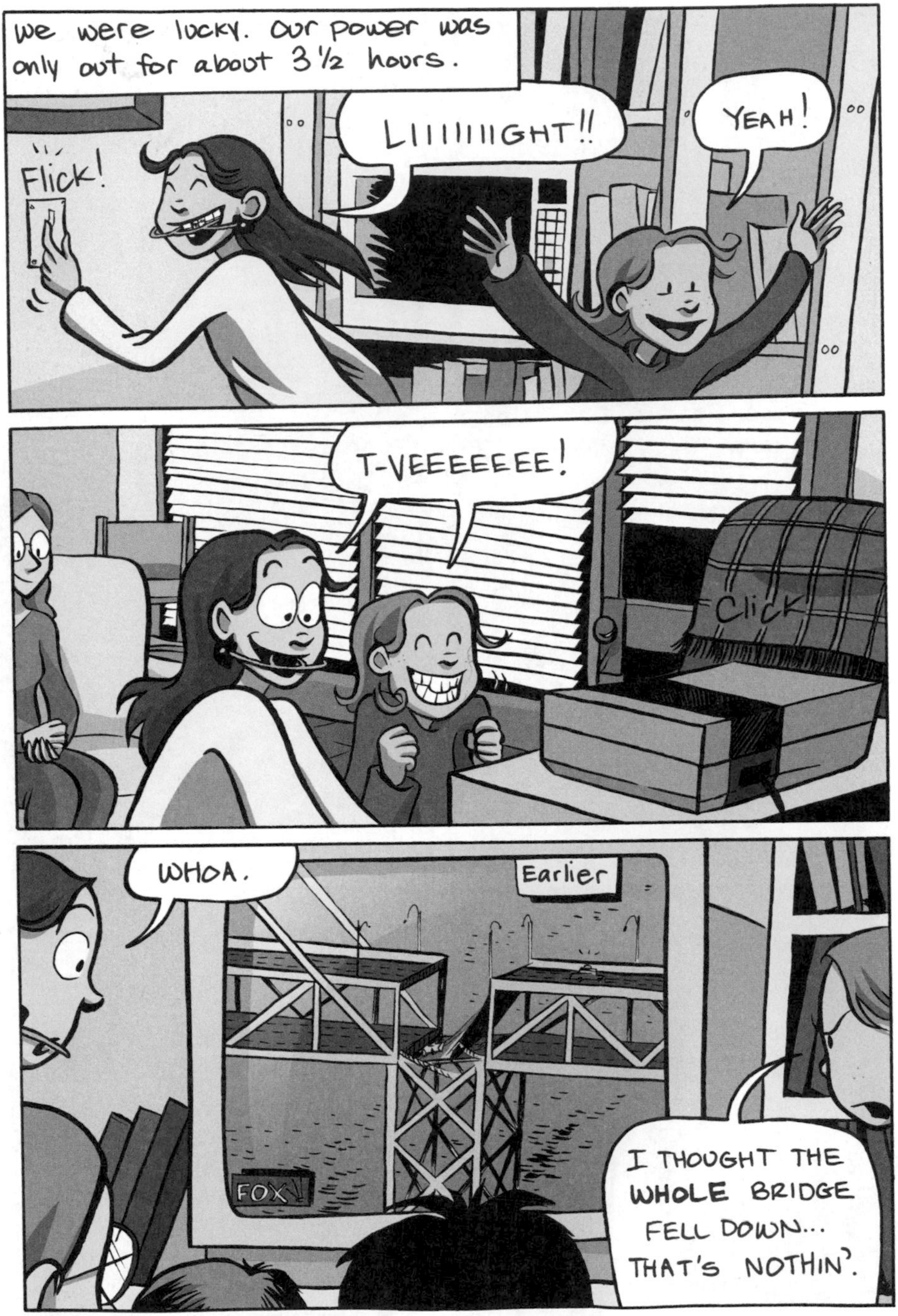
We were lucky. Our power was only out for about 3 ½ hours.
Flick!
LIIIIIIIGHT!!
YEAH!
T-VEEEEEEE!
Click
WHOA.
Earlier
FOX
I THOUGHT THE WHOLE BRIDGE FELL DOWN... THAT'S NOTHIN'.

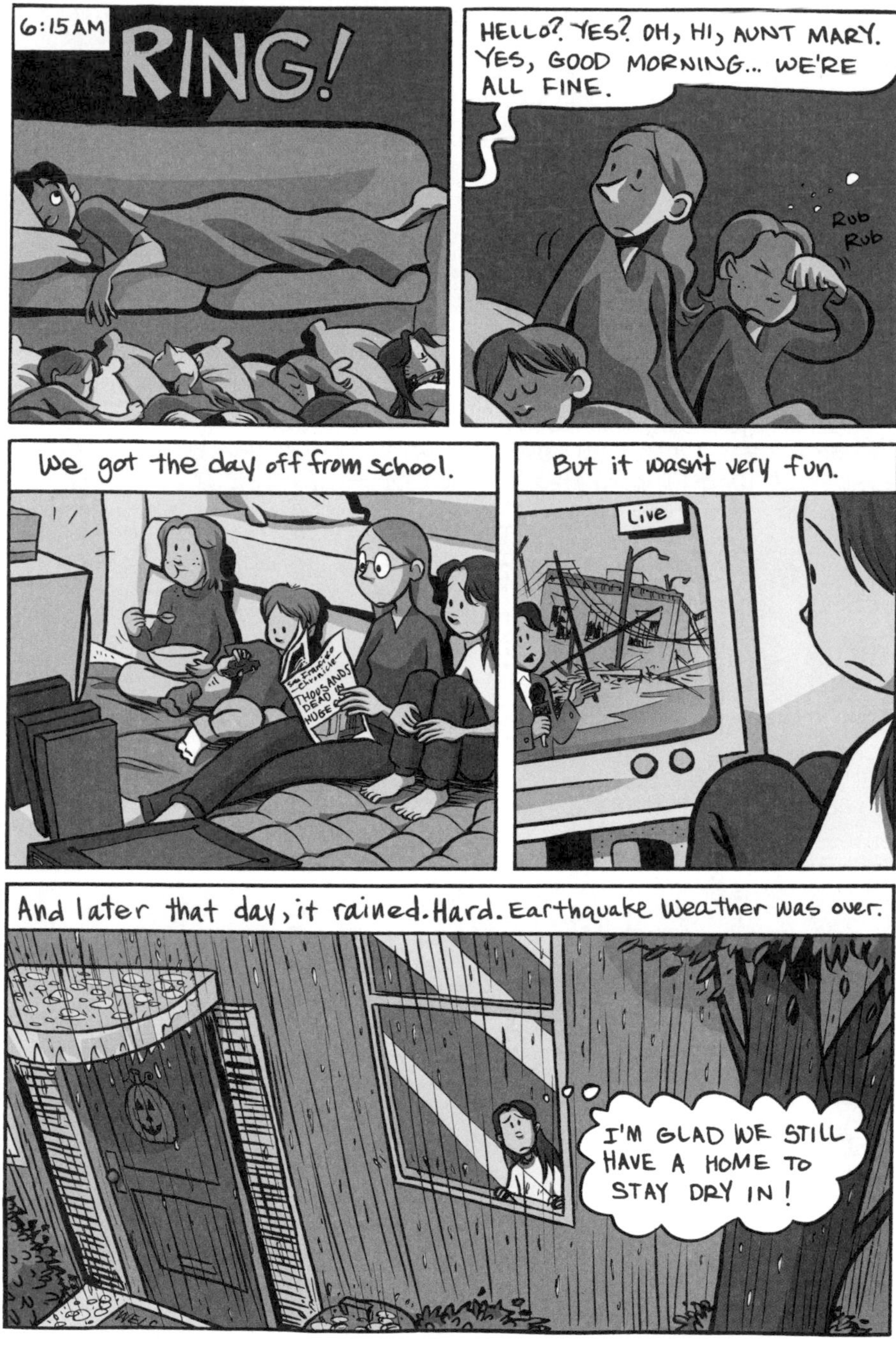
6:15 AM
RING!
HELLO? YES? OH, HI, AUNT MARY. YES, GOOD MORNING... WE'RE ALL FINE.
Rub Rub
We got the day off from school.
But it wasn't very fun.
Live
And later that day, it rained. Hard. Earthquake Weather was over.
I'M GLAD WE STILL HAVE A HOME TO STAY DRY IN!

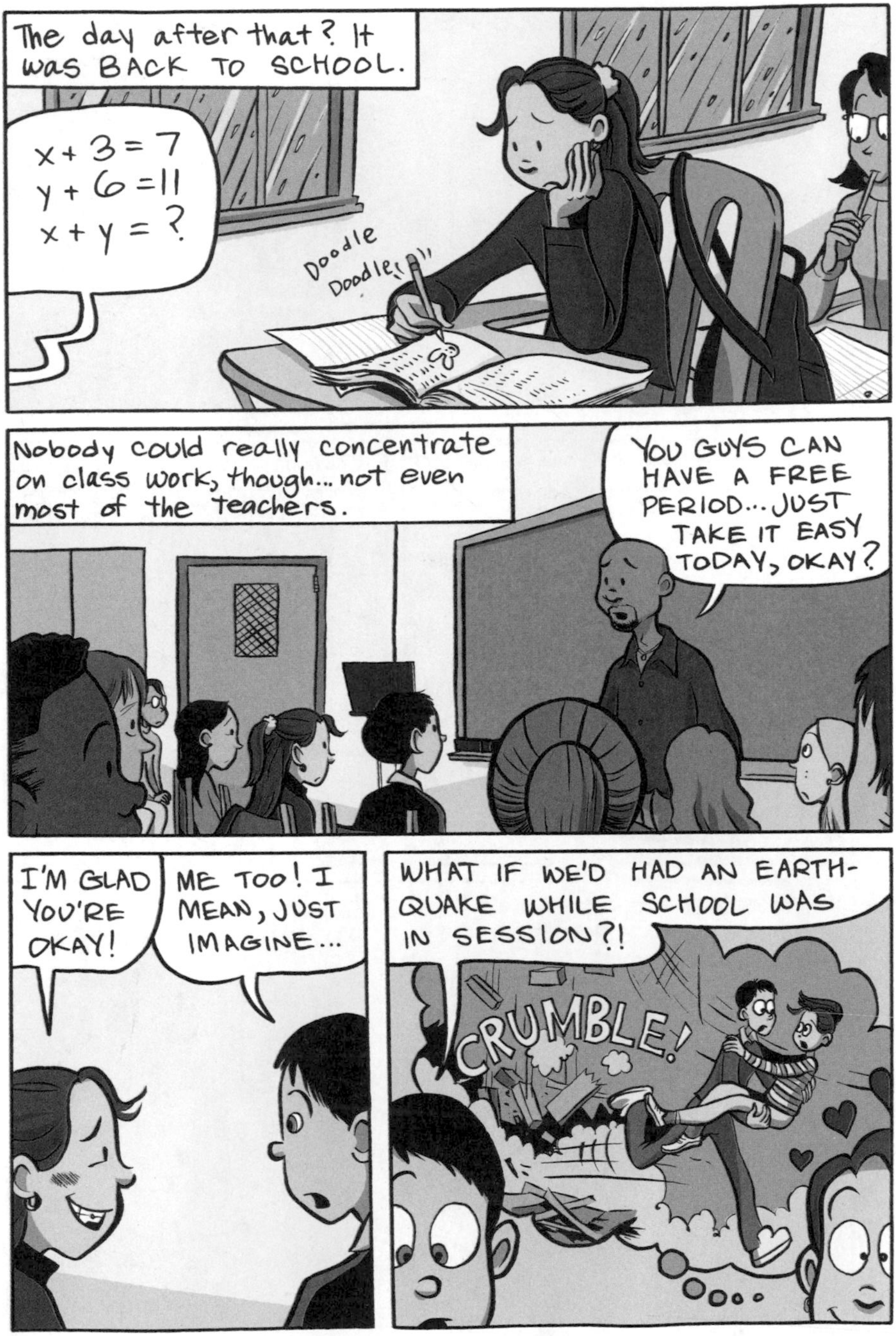
The day after that? It was BACK TO SCHOOL.
x + 3 = 7
y + 6 = 11
x + y = ?
Doodle Doodle
Nobody could really concentrate on class work, though... not even most of the teachers.
YOU GUYS CAN HAVE A FREE PERIOD... JUST TAKE IT EASY TODAY, OKAY?
I'M GLAD YOU'RE OKAY!
ME TOO! I MEAN, JUST IMAGINE...
WHAT IF WE'D HAD AN EARTHQUAKE WHILE SCHOOL WAS IN SESSION?!
CRUMBLE!

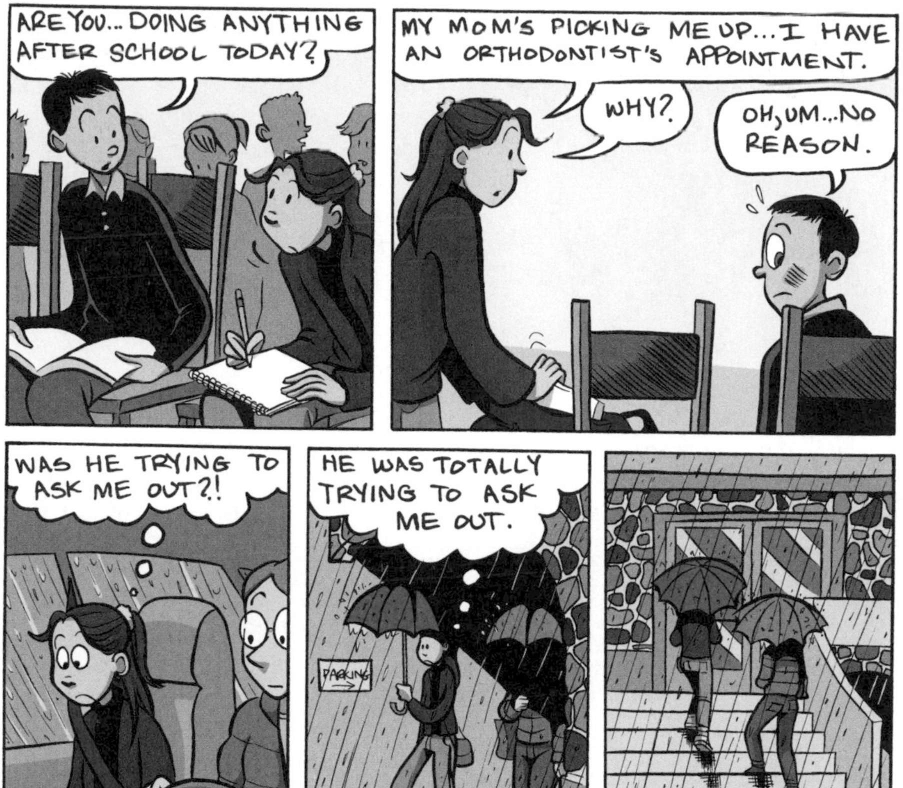
ARE YOU... DOING ANYTHING AFTER SCHOOL TODAY?
MY MOM'S PICKING ME UP... I HAVE AN ORTHODONTIST'S APPOINTMENT.
WHY?
OH, UM... NO REASON.
WAS HE TRYING TO ASK ME OUT?!
HE WAS TOTALLY TRYING TO ASK ME OUT.
PARKING
GOOD THING DR. DRAGONI'S OFFICE DIDN'T FALL DOWN IN THE EARTHQUAKE, HUH?
YEAH, GOOD THING...
Prod
Push

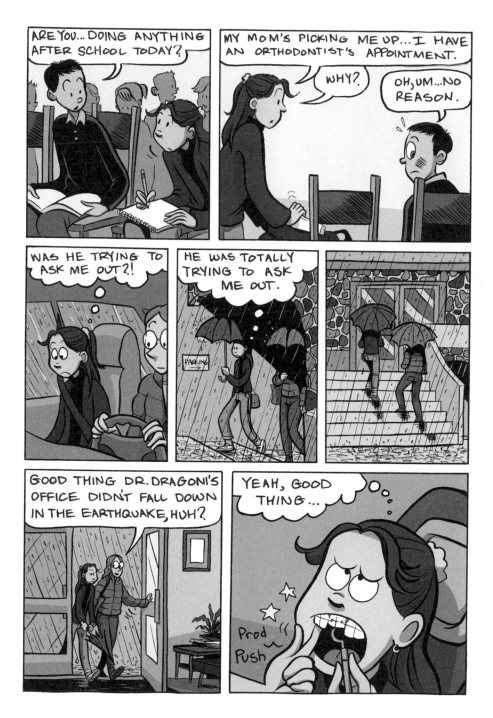

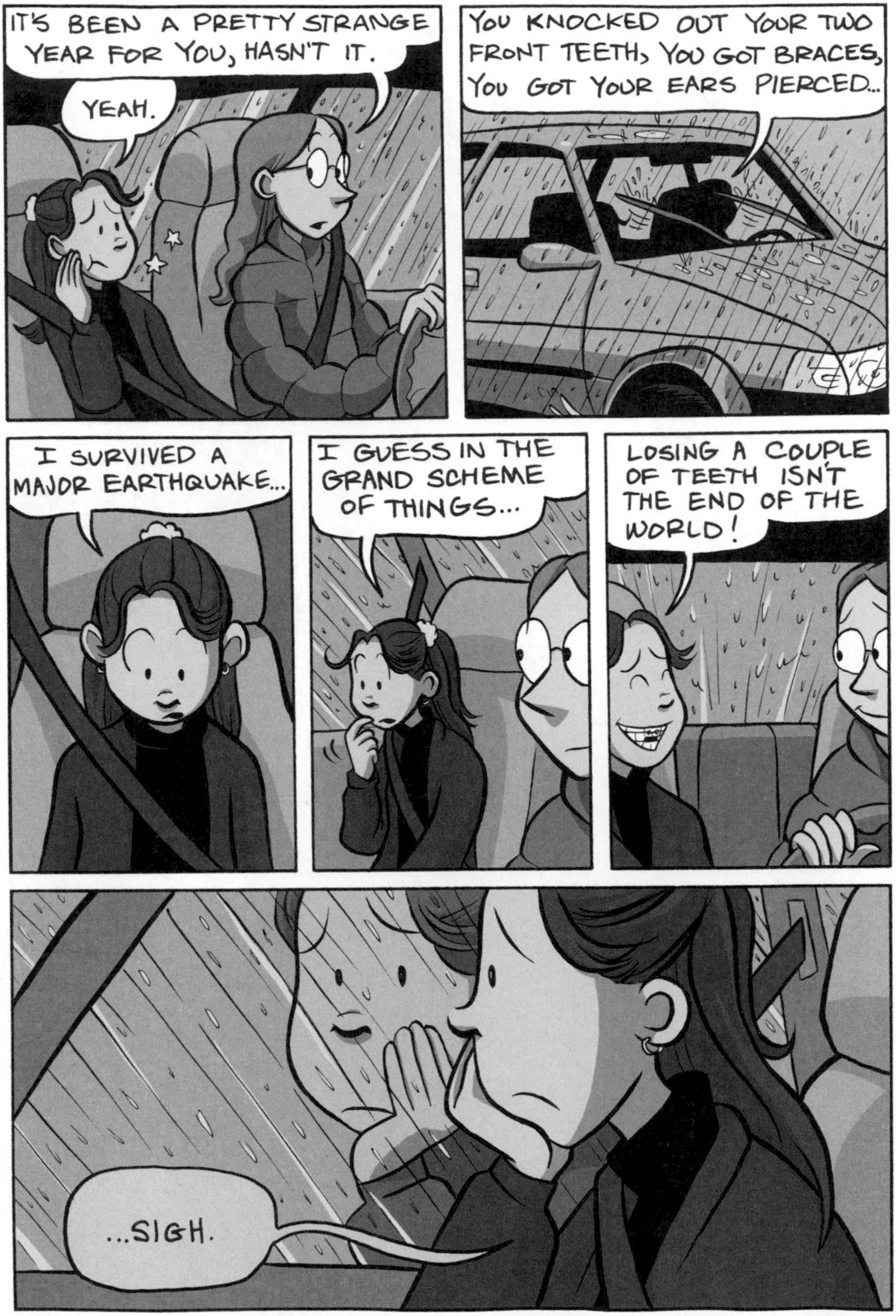
IT'S BEEN A PRETTY STRANGE YEAR FOR YOU, HASN'T IT.
YEAH.
YOU KNOCKED OUT YOUR TWO FRONT TEETH, YOU GOT BRACES, YOU GOT YOUR EARS PIERCED...
I SURVIVED A MAJOR EARTHQUAKE...
I GUESS IN THE GRAND SCHEME OF THINGS...
LOSING A COUPLE OF TEETH ISN'T THE END OF THE WORLD!
...SIGH.

CHAPTER FOUR

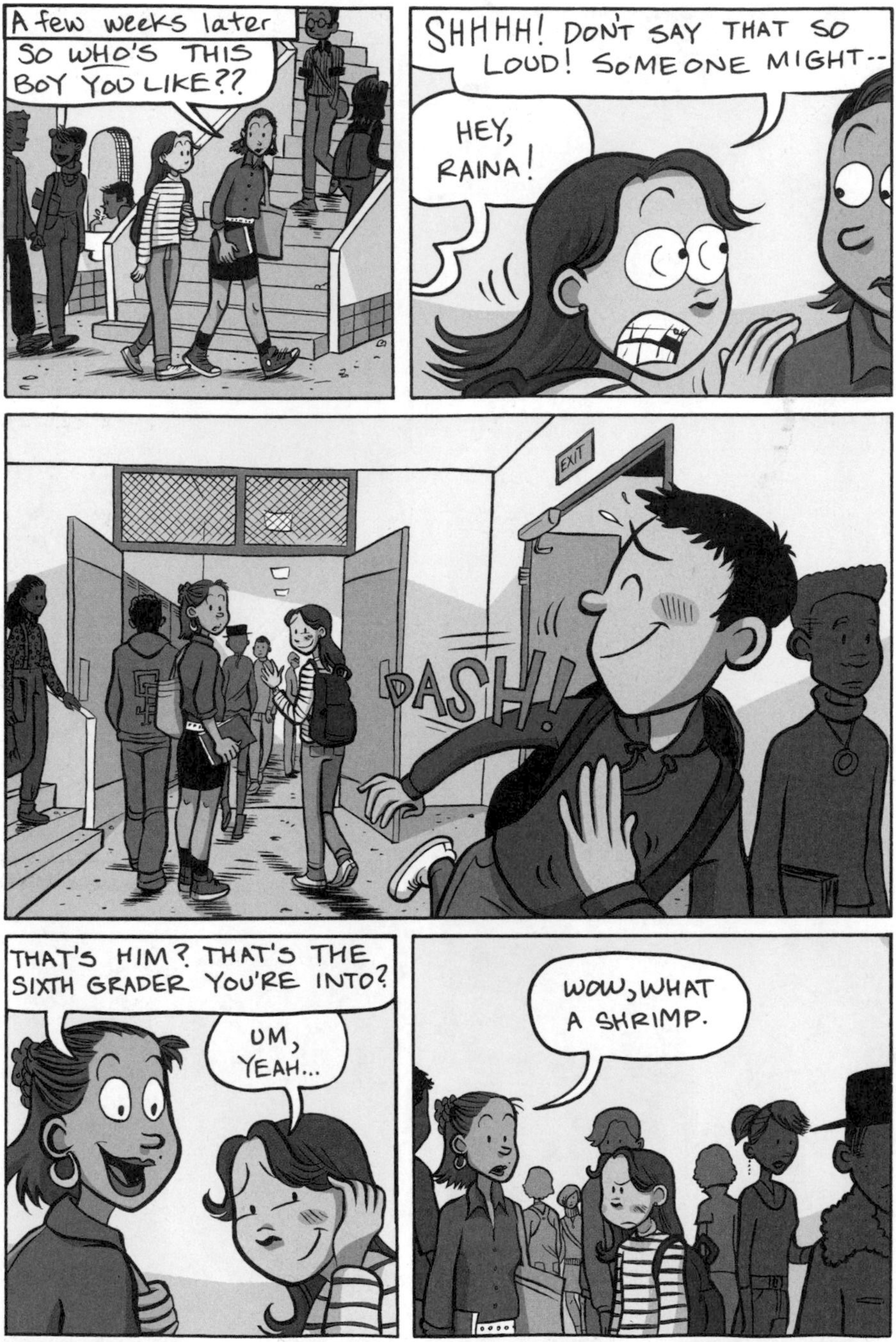
A few weeks later
SO WHO'S THIS BOY YOU LIKE??
SHHHH! DON'T SAY THAT SO LOUD! SOMEONE MIGHT--
HEY, RAINA!
EXIT
DASH!
THAT'S HIM? THAT'S THE SIXTH GRADER YOU'RE INTO?
UM, YEAH...
WOW, WHAT A SHRIMP.

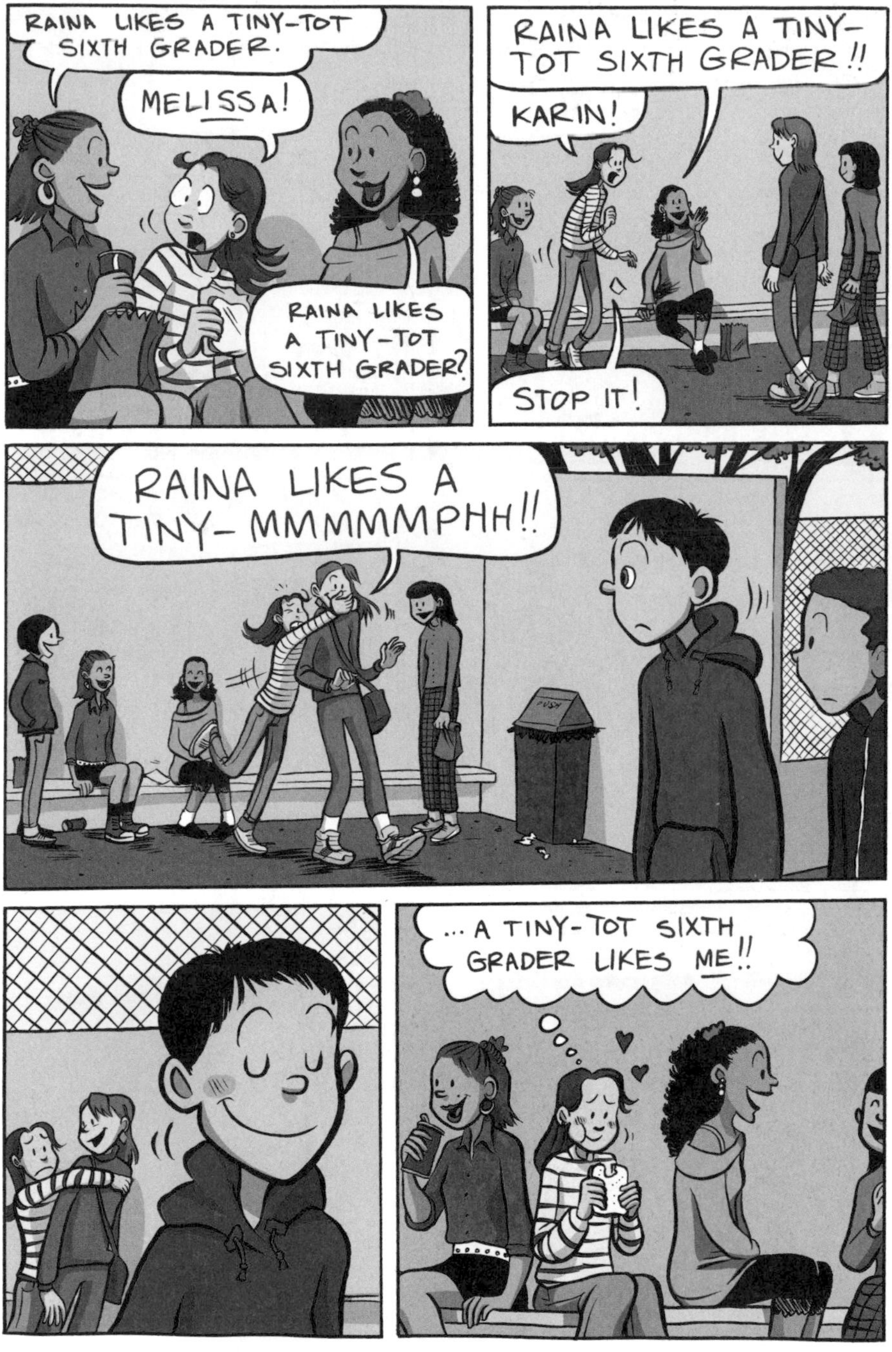
RAINA LIKES A TINY-TOT SIXTH GRADER.
MELISSA!
RAINA LIKES A TINY-TOT SIXTH GRADER?
RAINA LIKES A TINY-TOT SIXTH GRADER!!
KARIN!
STOP IT!
RAINA LIKES A TINY- MMMMMPHH!!
PUSH
... A TINY-TOT SIXTH GRADER LIKES ME!!

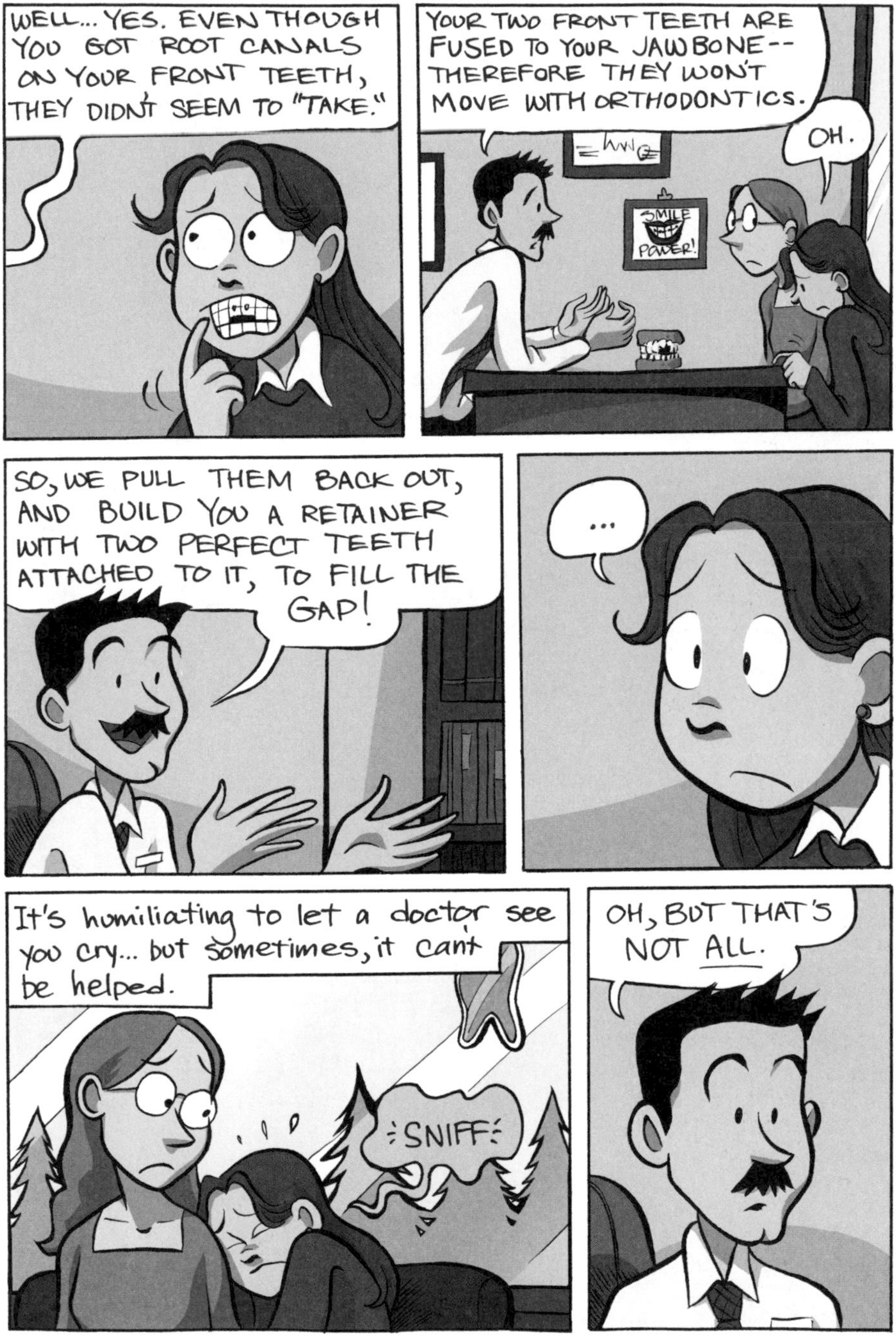
WELL... YES. EVEN THOUGH YOU GOT ROOT CANALS ON YOUR FRONT TEETH, THEY DIDN'T SEEM TO "TAKE."
YOUR TWO FRONT TEETH ARE FUSED TO YOUR JAWBONE-- THEREFORE THEY WON'T MOVE WITH ORTHODONTICS.
OH.
SMILE POWER!
SO, WE PULL THEM BACK OUT, AND BUILD YOU A RETAINER WITH TWO PERFECT TEETH ATTACHED TO IT, TO FILL THE GAP!
...
It's humiliating to let a doctor see you cry... but sometimes, it can't be helped.
SNIFF
OH, BUT THAT'S NOT ALL.

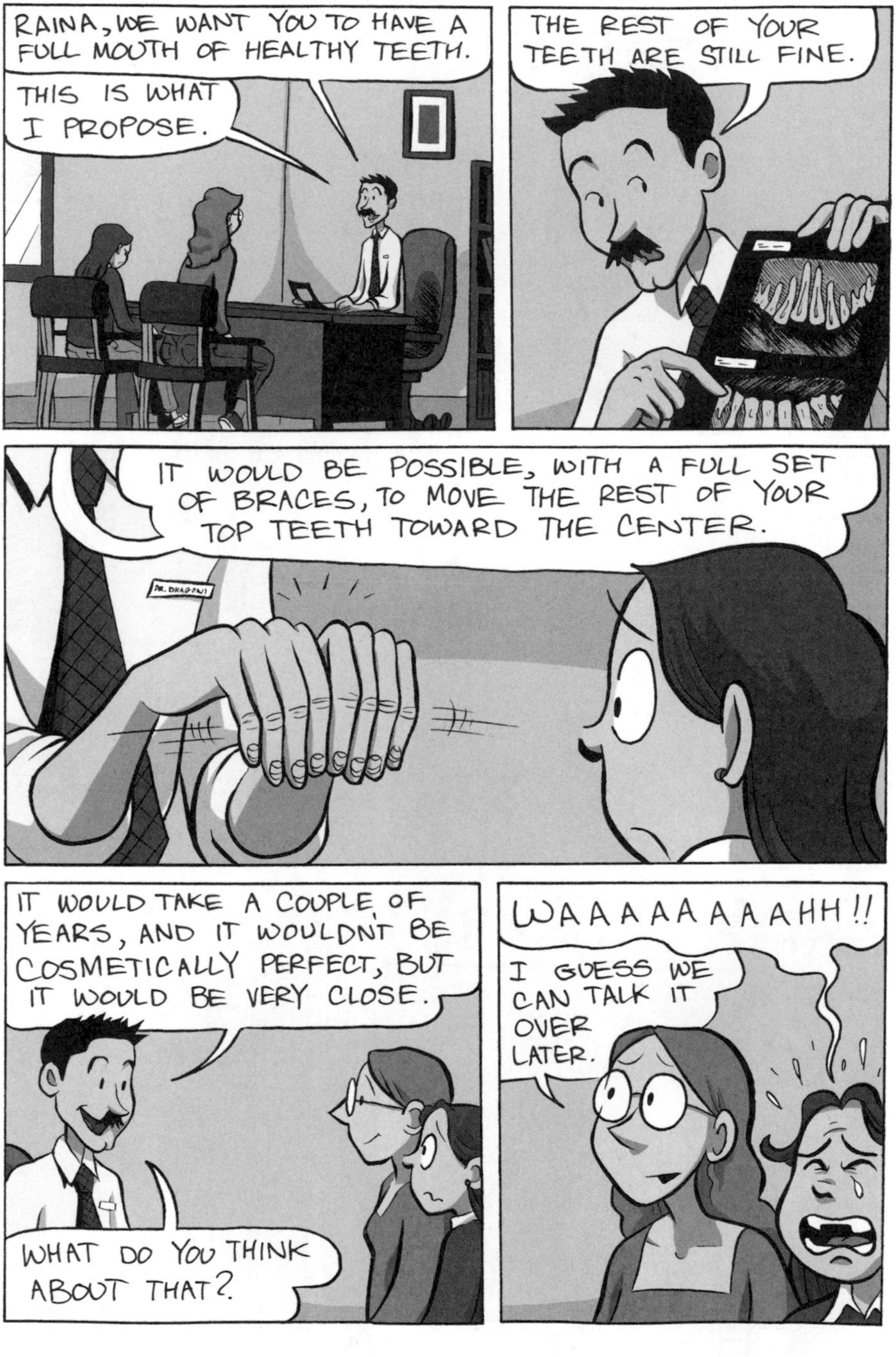
RAINA, WE WANT YOU TO HAVE A FULL MOUTH OF HEALTHY TEETH.
THIS IS WHAT I PROPOSE.
THE REST OF YOUR TEETH ARE STILL FINE.
IT WOULD BE POSSIBLE, WITH A FULL SET OF BRACES, TO MOVE THE REST OF YOUR TOP TEETH TOWARD THE CENTER.
DR. DRAGONI
IT WOULD TAKE A COUPLE OF YEARS, AND IT WOULDN'T BE COSMETICALLY PERFECT, BUT IT WOULD BE VERY CLOSE.
WHAT DO YOU THINK ABOUT THAT?
WAAAAAAAAAHH!!
I GUESS WE CAN TALK IT OVER LATER.

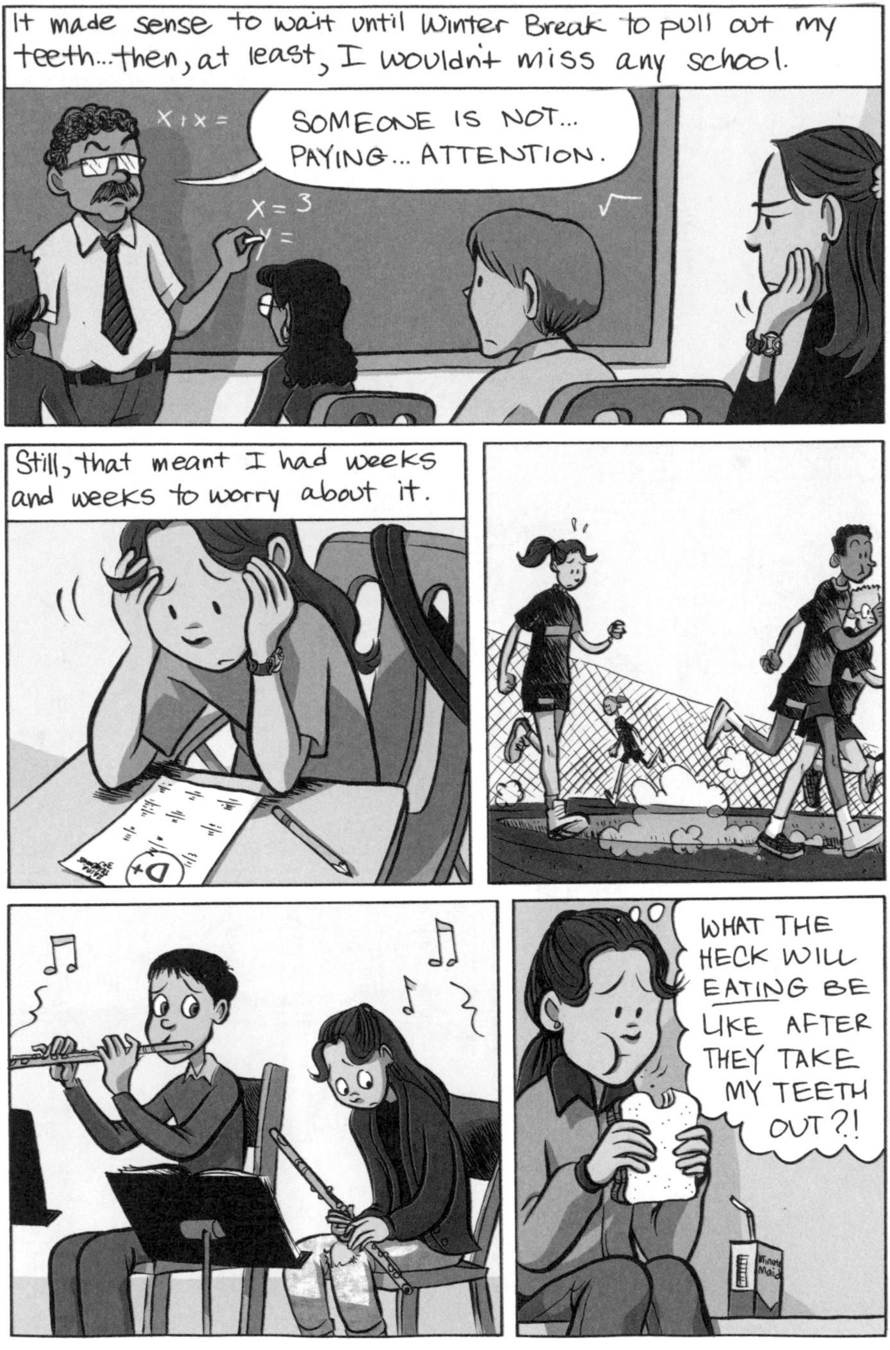
It made sense to wait until Winter Break to pull out my teeth...then, at least, I wouldn't miss any school.
SOMEONE IS NOT... PAYING... ATTENTION.
x = 3
Still, that meant I had weeks and weeks to worry about it.
D+
WHAT THE HECK WILL EATING BE LIKE AFTER THEY TAKE MY TEETH OUT?!

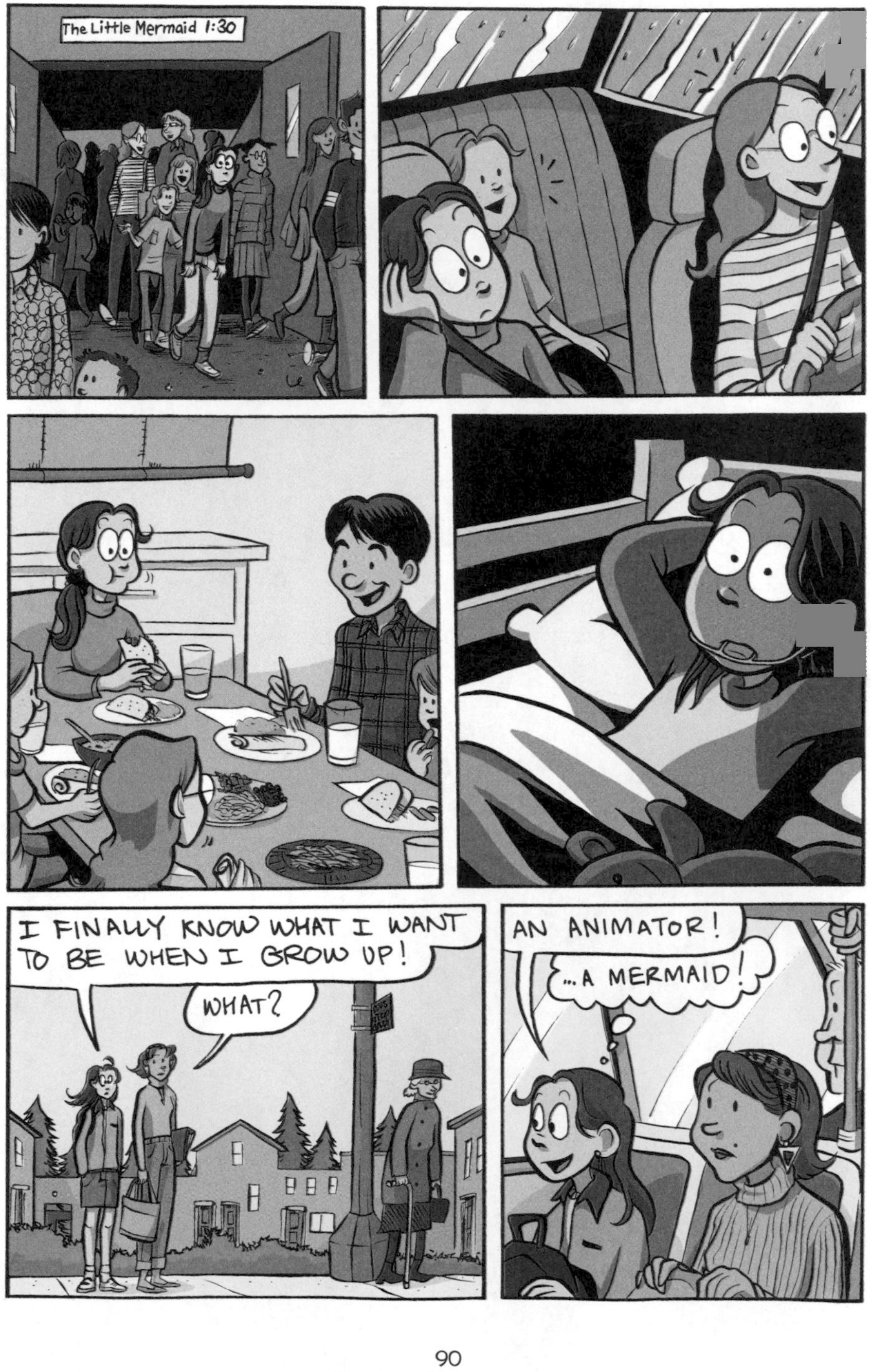
The Little Mermaid 1:30
I FINALLY KNOW WHAT I WANT TO BE WHEN I GROW UP!
WHAT?
AN ANIMATOR!
...A MERMAID!

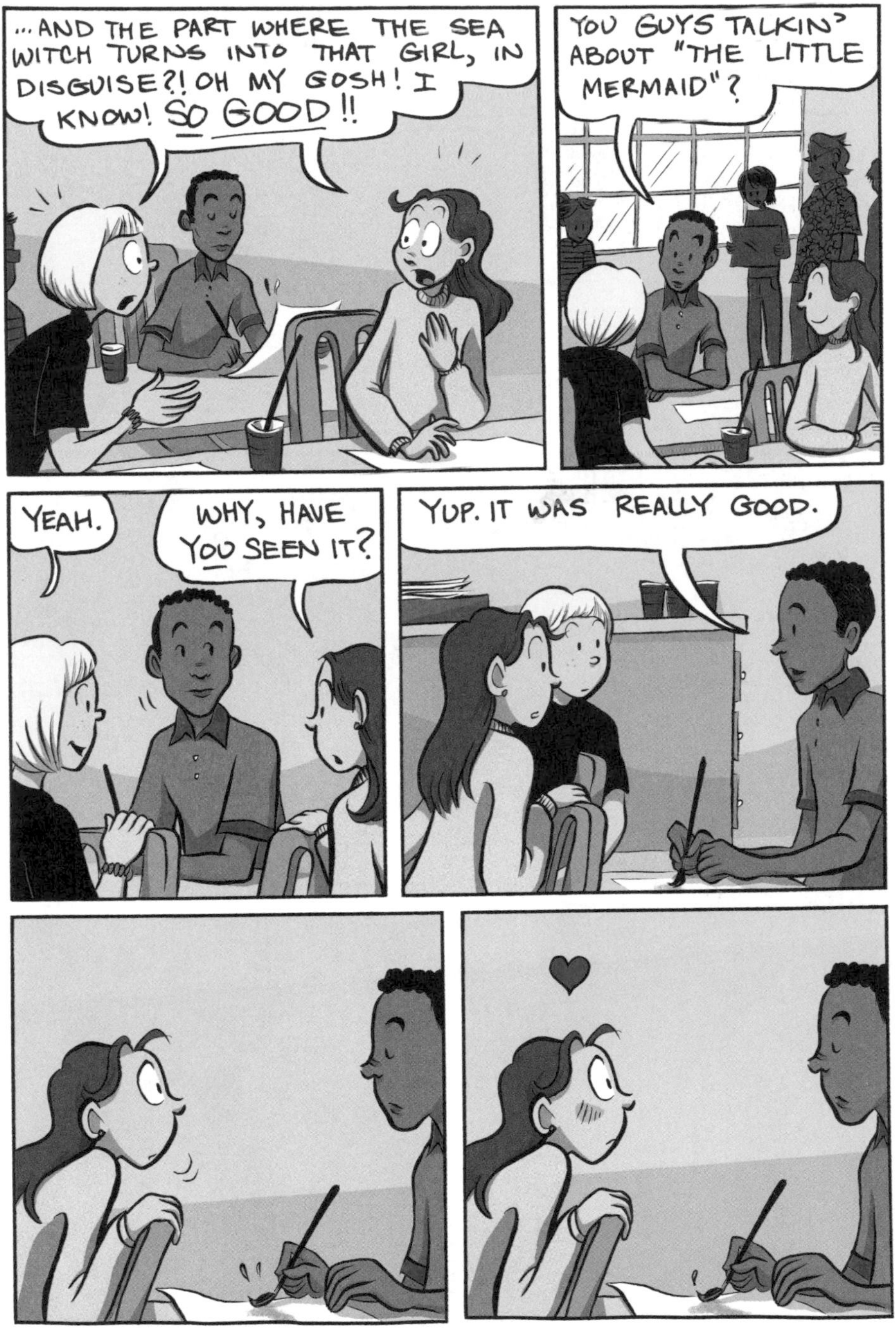
...AND THE PART WHERE THE SEA WITCH TURNS INTO THAT GIRL, IN DISGUISE?! OH MY GOSH! I KNOW! SO GOOD!!
YOU GUYS TALKIN' ABOUT "THE LITTLE MERMAID"?
YEAH.
WHY, HAVE YOU SEEN IT?
YUP. IT WAS REALLY GOOD.

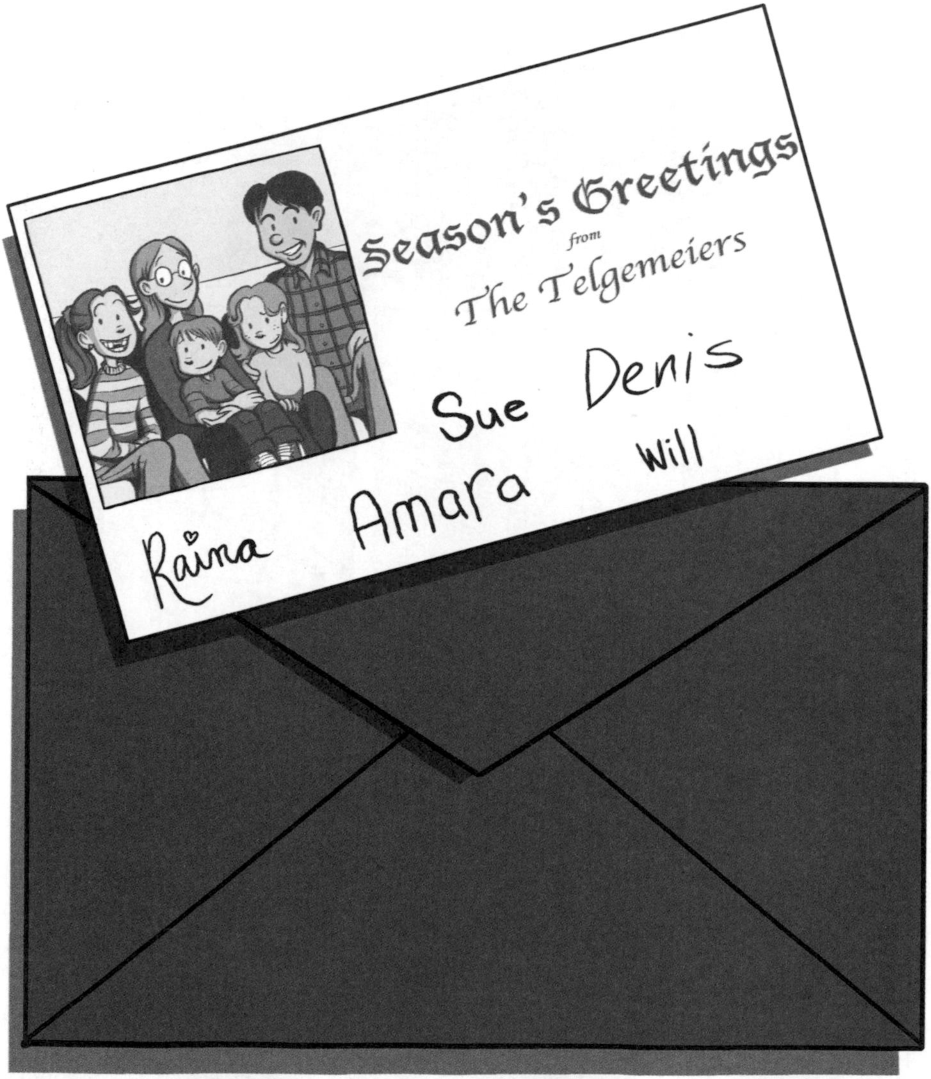
Season's Greetings
from
The Telgemeiers
Sue
Denis
Will
Raina
Amara

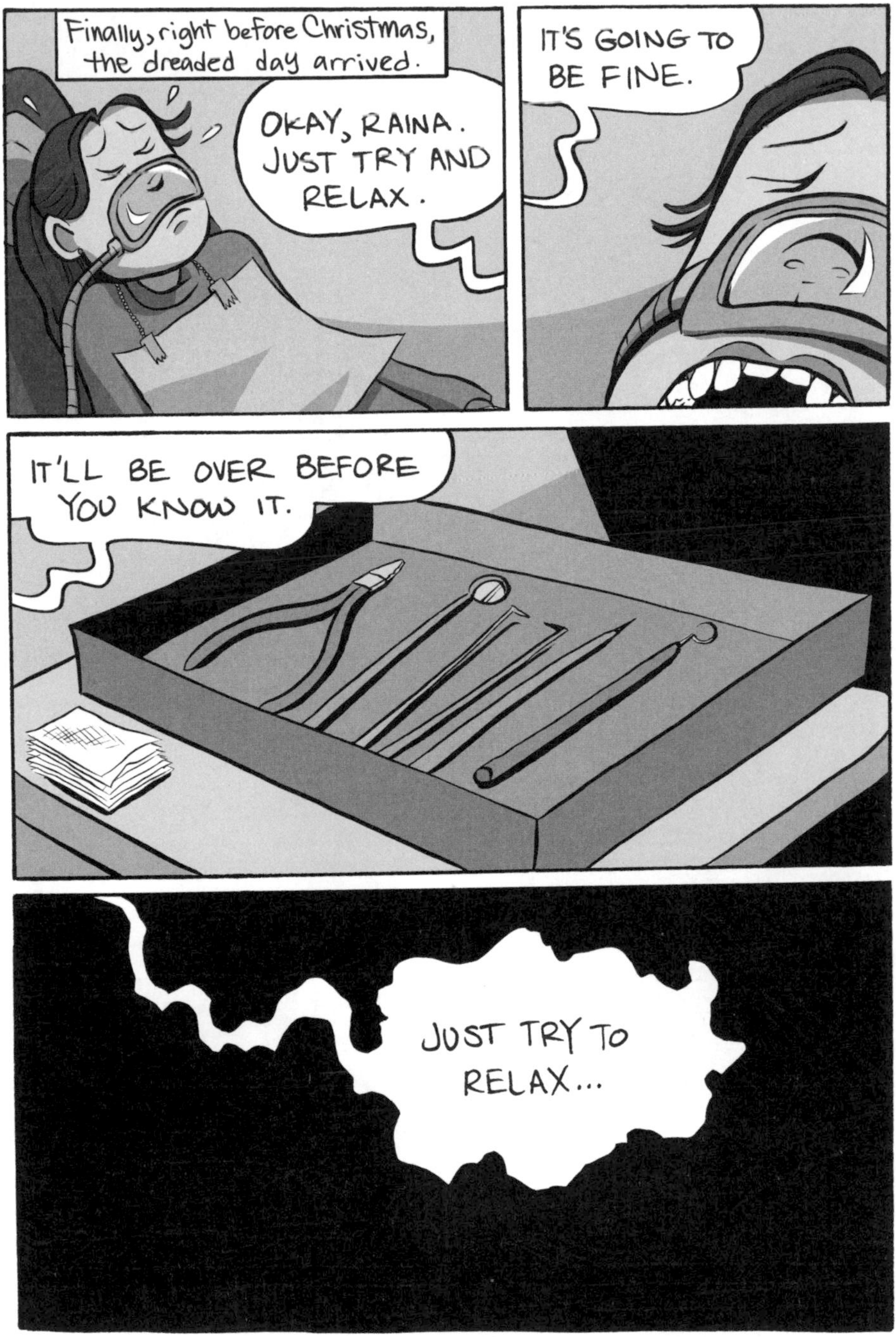
Finally, right before Christmas, the dreaded day arrived.
OKAY, RAINA. JUST TRY AND RELAX.
IT'S GOING TO BE FINE.
IT'LL BE OVER BEFORE YOU KNOW IT.
JUST TRY TO RELAX...

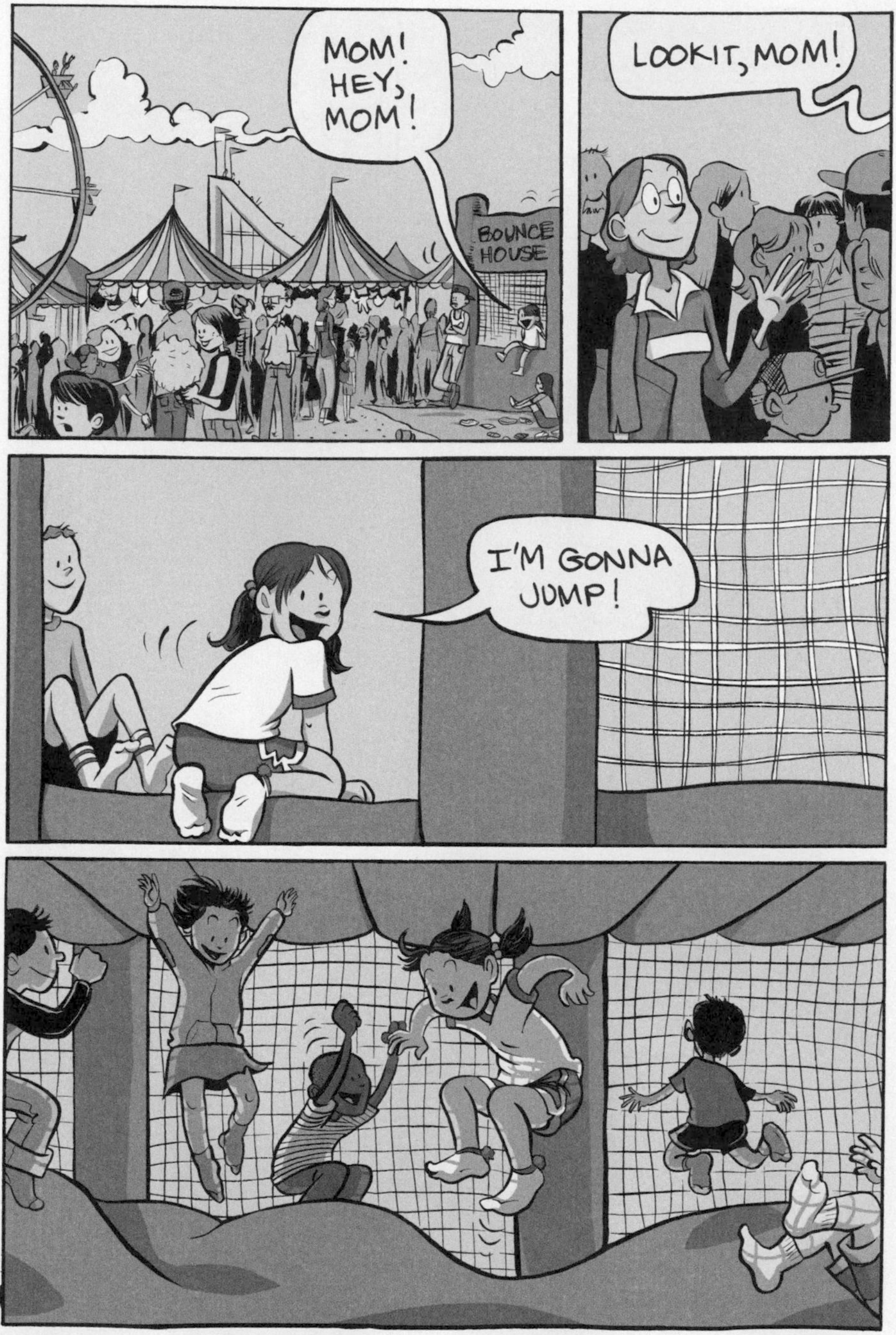
MOM! HEY, MOM!
BOUNCE HOUSE
LOOKIT, MOM!
I'M GONNA JUMP!

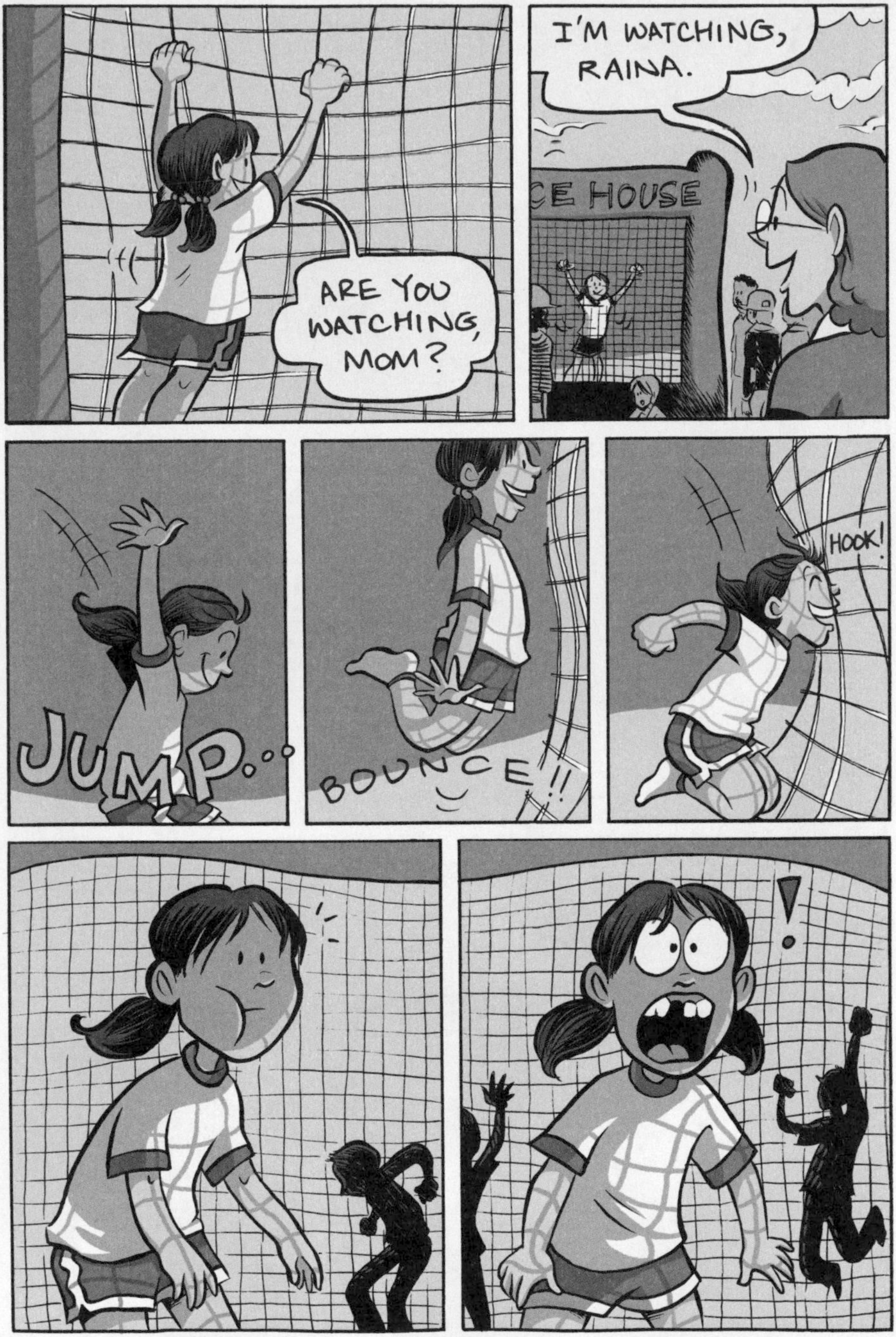
ARE YOU WATCHING, MOM?
I'M WATCHING, RAINA.
CE HOUSE
JUMP...
BOUNCE!!
HOOK!
!

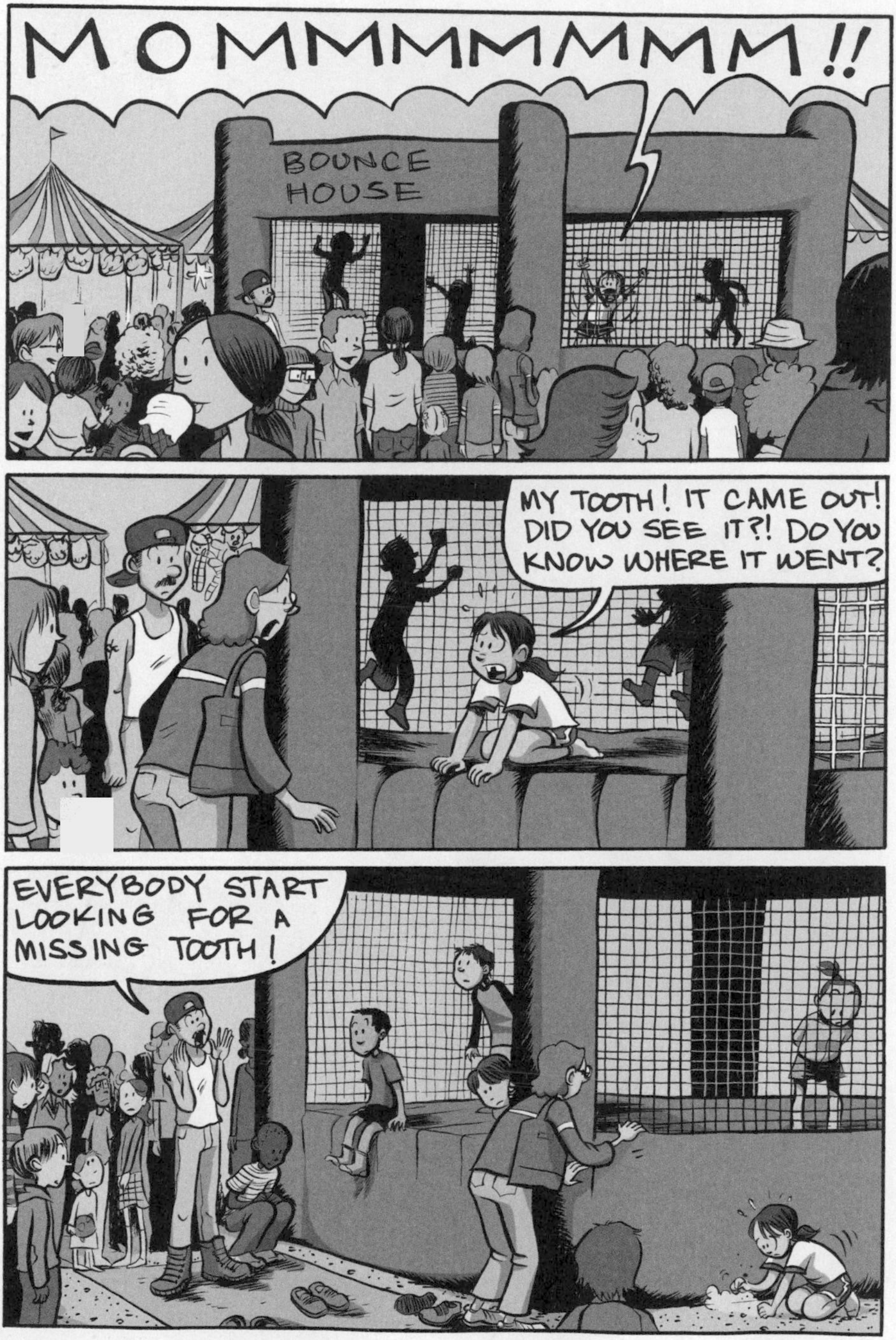
MOMMMMMMM!!
BOUNCE HOUSE
MY TOOTH! IT CAME OUT! DID YOU SEE IT?! DO YOU KNOW WHERE IT WENT?
EVERYBODY START LOOKING FOR A MISSING TOOTH!

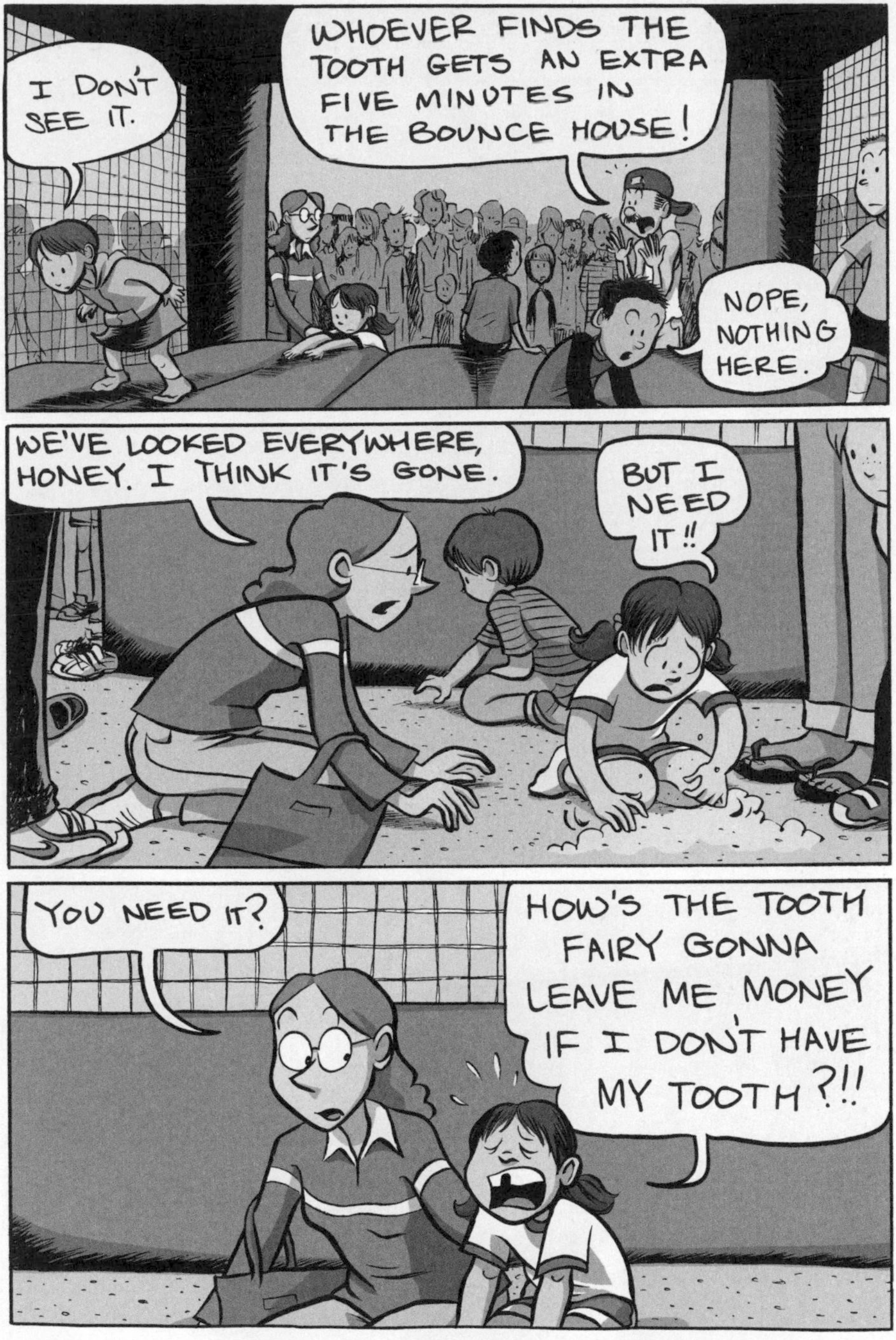
I DON'T SEE IT.
WHOEVER FINDS THE TOOTH GETS AN EXTRA FIVE MINUTES IN THE BOUNCE HOUSE!
NOPE, NOTHING HERE.
WE'VE LOOKED EVERYWHERE, HONEY. I THINK IT'S GONE.
BUT I NEED IT!!
YOU NEED IT?
HOW'S THE TOOTH FAIRY GONNA LEAVE ME MONEY IF I DON'T HAVE MY TOOTH?!!

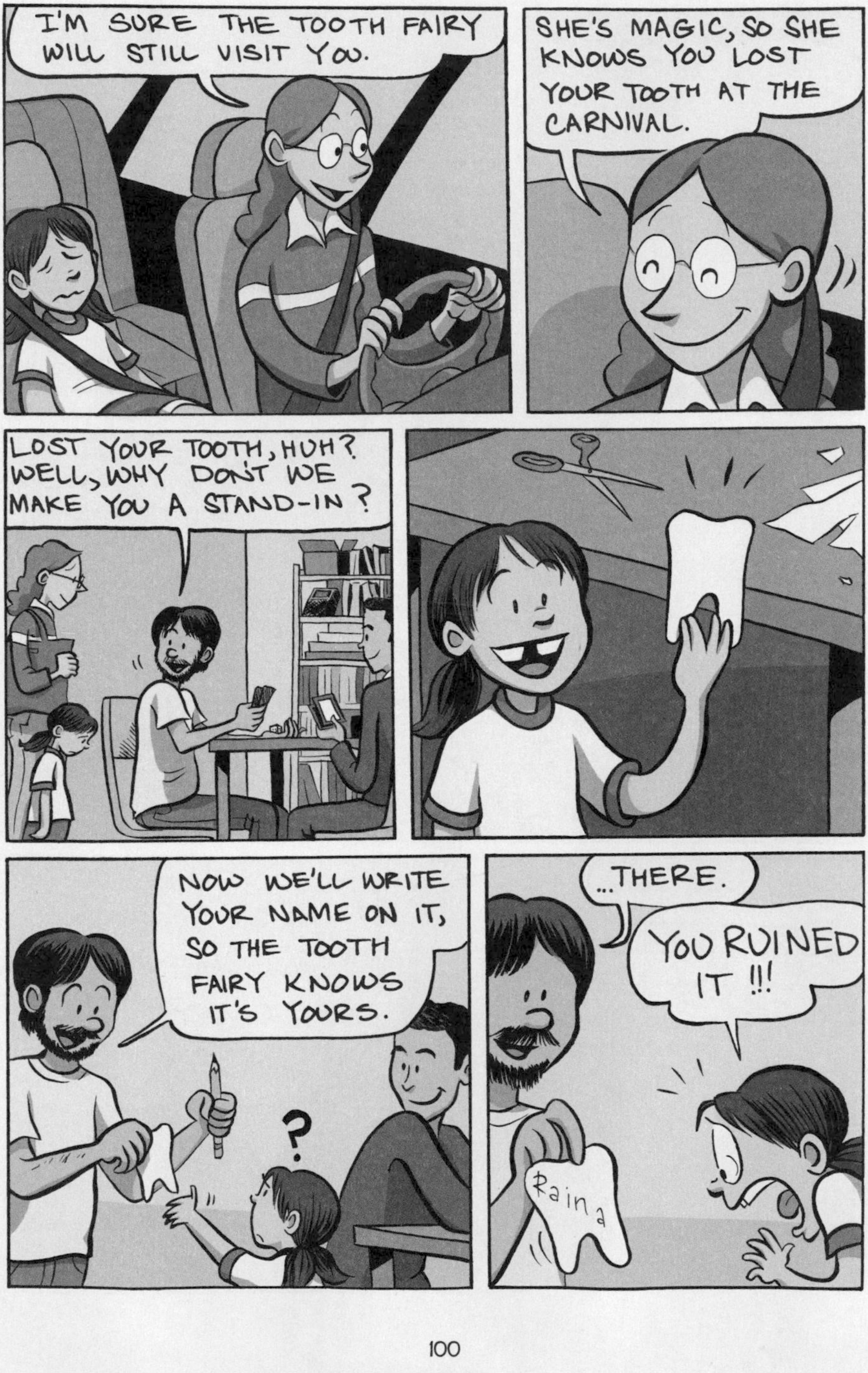
I'M SURE THE TOOTH FAIRY WILL STILL VISIT YOU.
SHE'S MAGIC, SO SHE KNOWS YOU LOST YOUR TOOTH AT THE CARNIVAL.
LOST YOUR TOOTH, HUH? WELL, WHY DON'T WE MAKE YOU A STAND-IN?
NOW WE'LL WRITE YOUR NAME ON IT, SO THE TOOTH FAIRY KNOWS IT'S YOURS.
?
...THERE.
YOU RUINED IT !!!
Raina

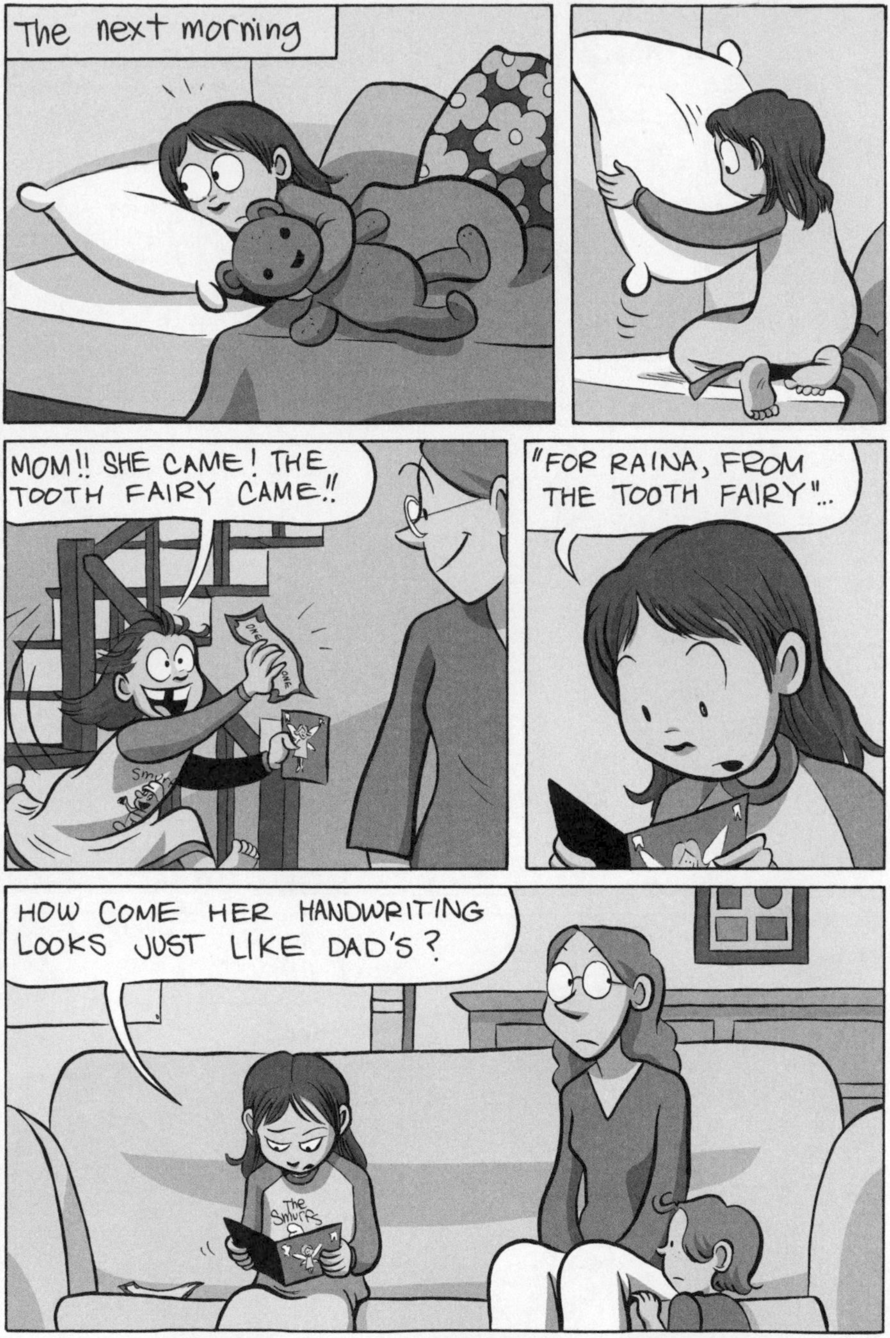
The next morning
MOM!! SHE CAME! THE TOOTH FAIRY CAME!!
ONE
"FOR RAINA, FROM THE TOOTH FAIRY"...
HOW COME HER HANDWRITING LOOKS JUST LIKE DAD'S?
The Smurfs

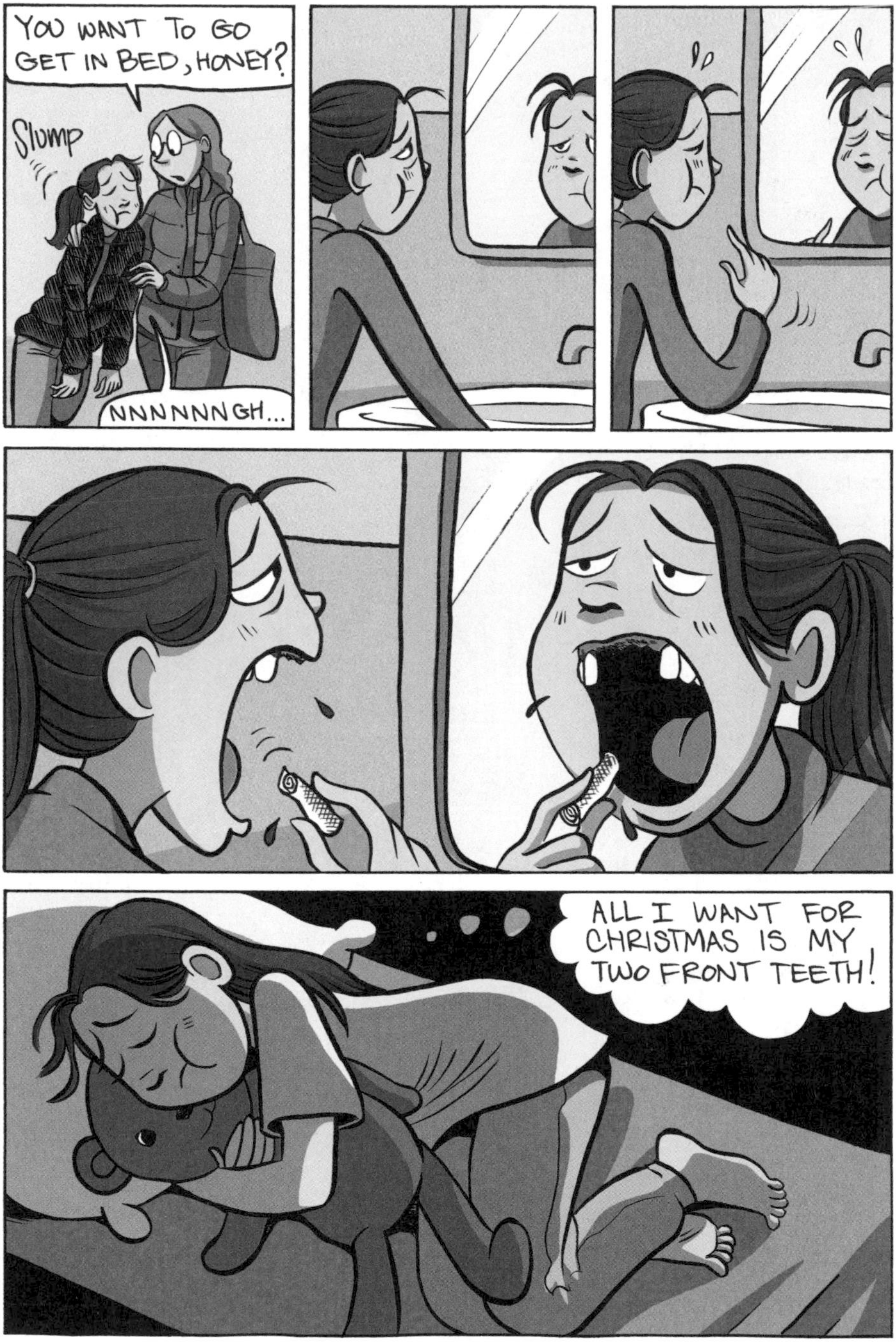
YOU WANT TO GO GET IN BED, HONEY?
Slump
NNNNNNGH...
ALL I WANT FOR CHRISTMAS IS MY TWO FRONT TEETH!

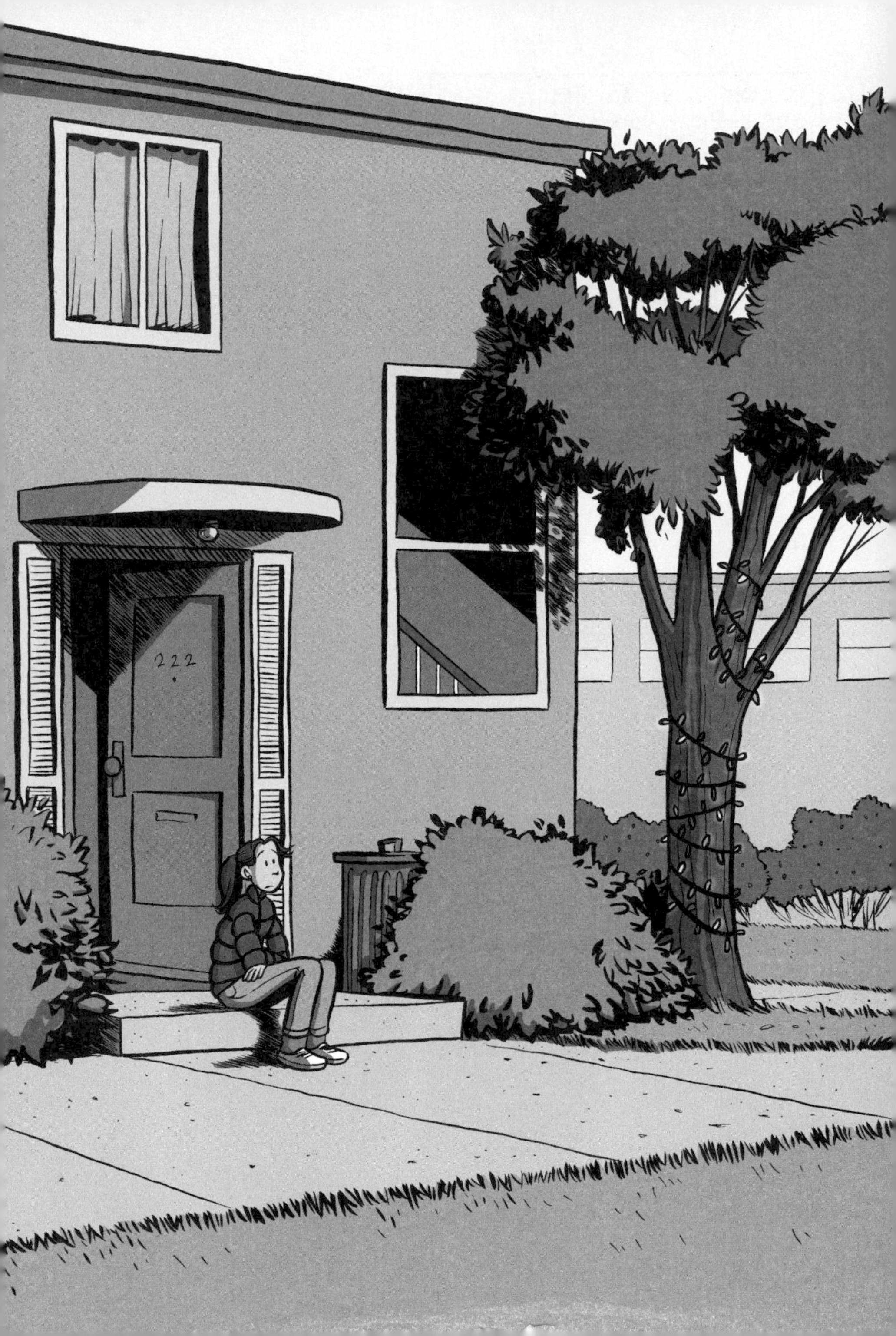
222

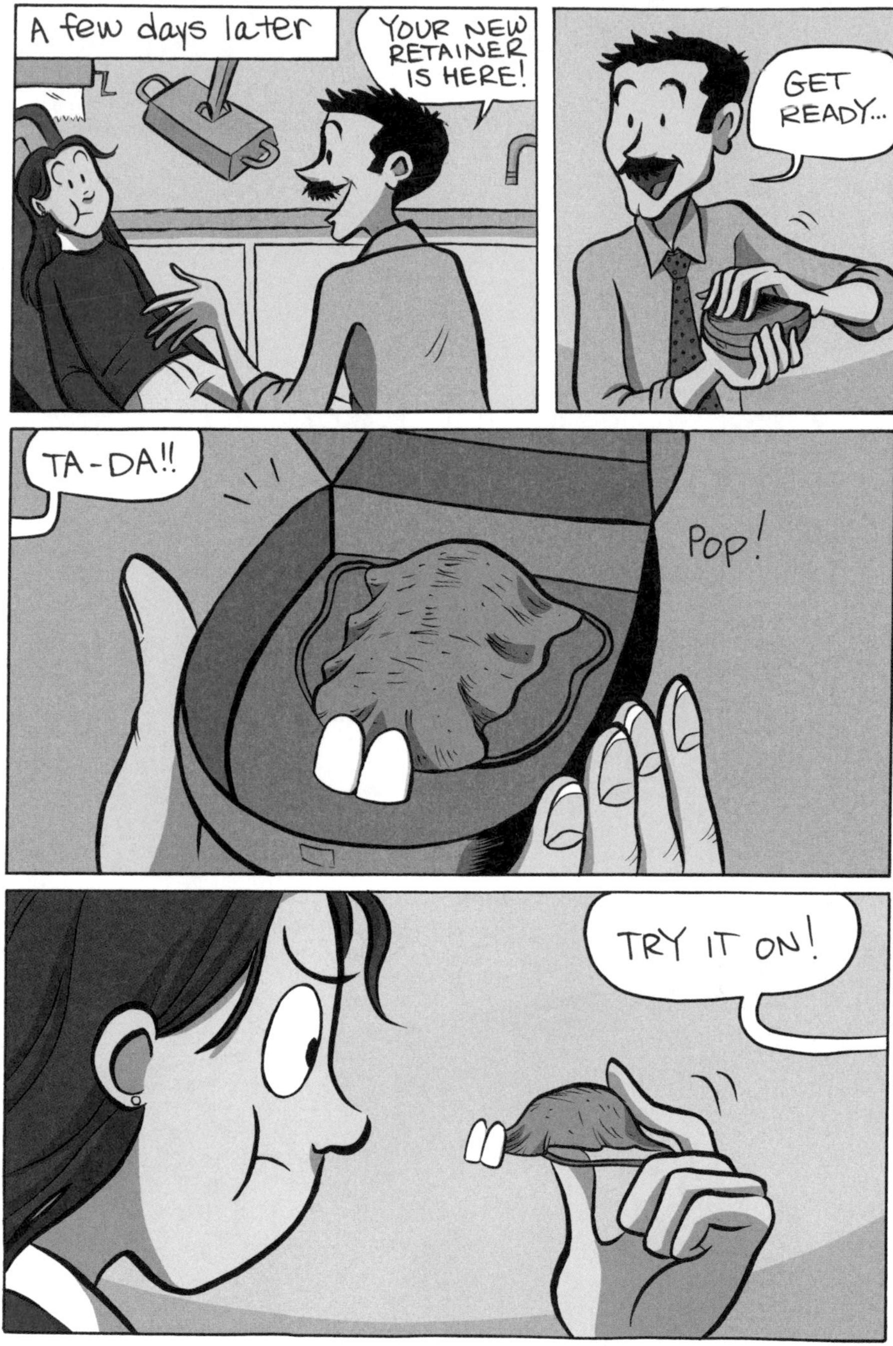

A few days later
YOUR NEW RETAINER IS HERE!
GET READY...
TA-DA!!
POP!
TRY IT ON!

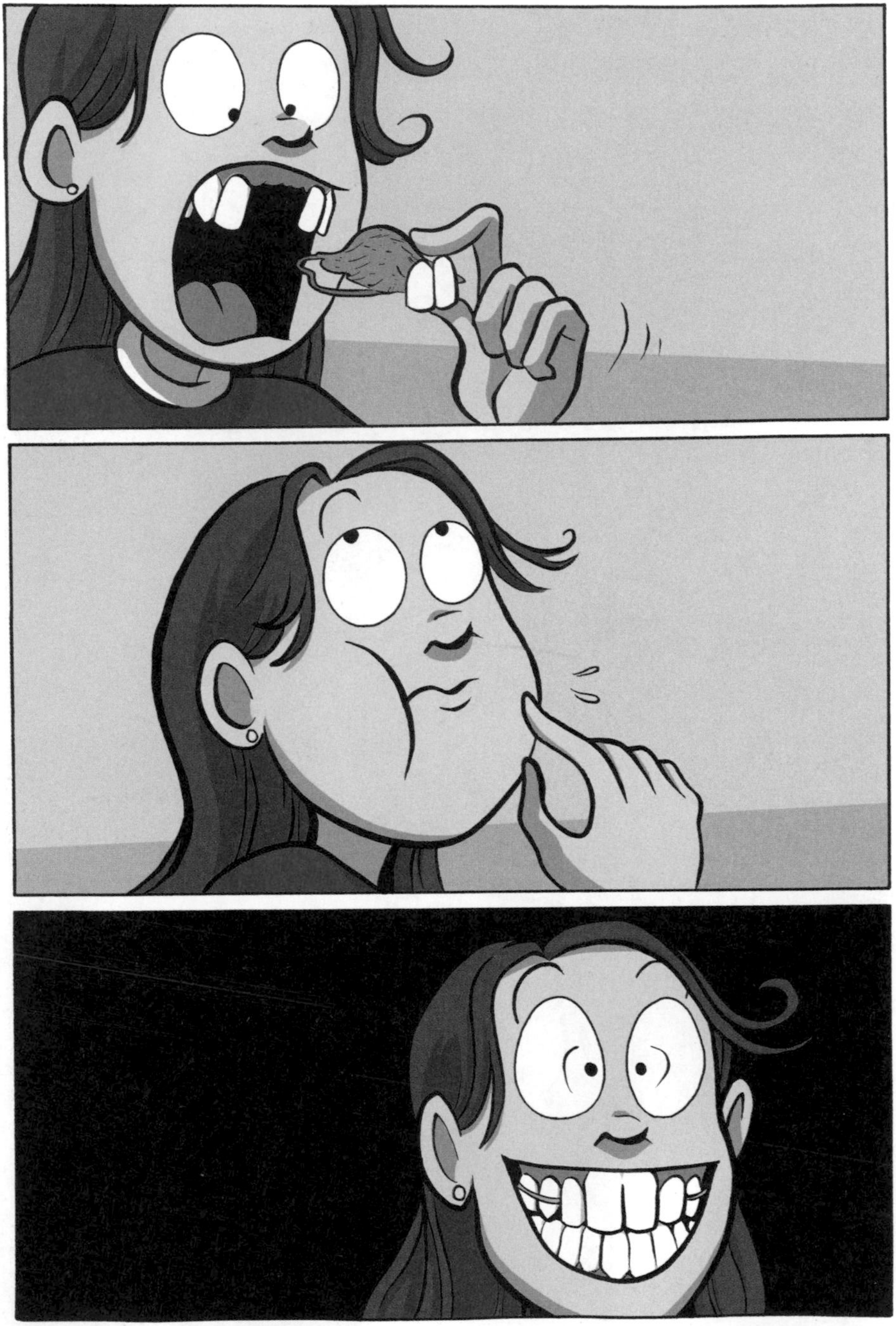

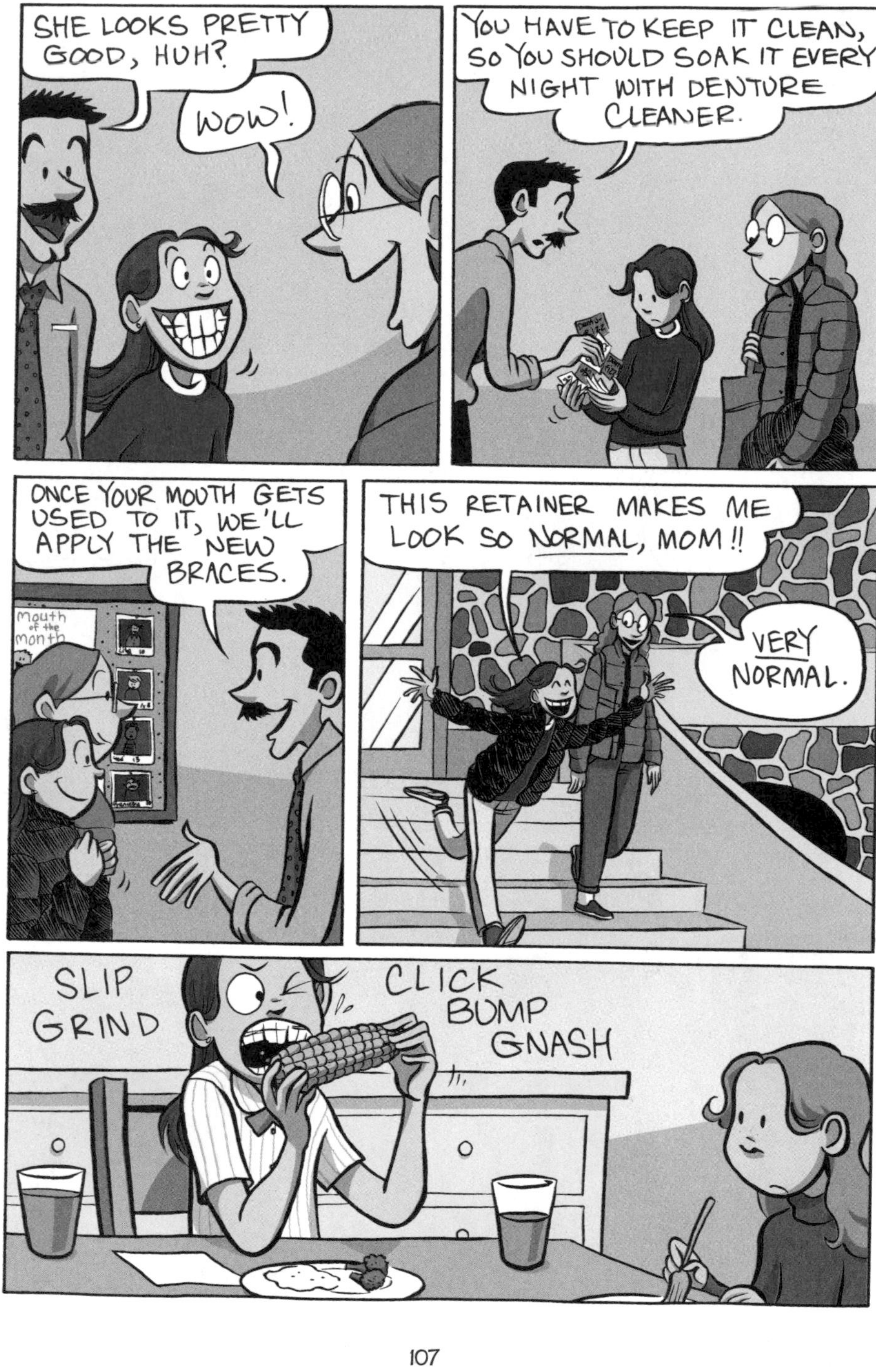
SHE LOOKS PRETTY GOOD, HUH?
WOW!
YOU HAVE TO KEEP IT CLEAN, SO YOU SHOULD SOAK IT EVERY NIGHT WITH DENTURE CLEANER.
ONCE YOUR MOUTH GETS USED TO IT, WE'LL APPLY THE NEW BRACES.
Mouth of the Month
THIS RETAINER MAKES ME LOOK SO NORMAL, MOM!!
VERY NORMAL.
SLIP
GRIND
CLICK
BUMP
GNASH

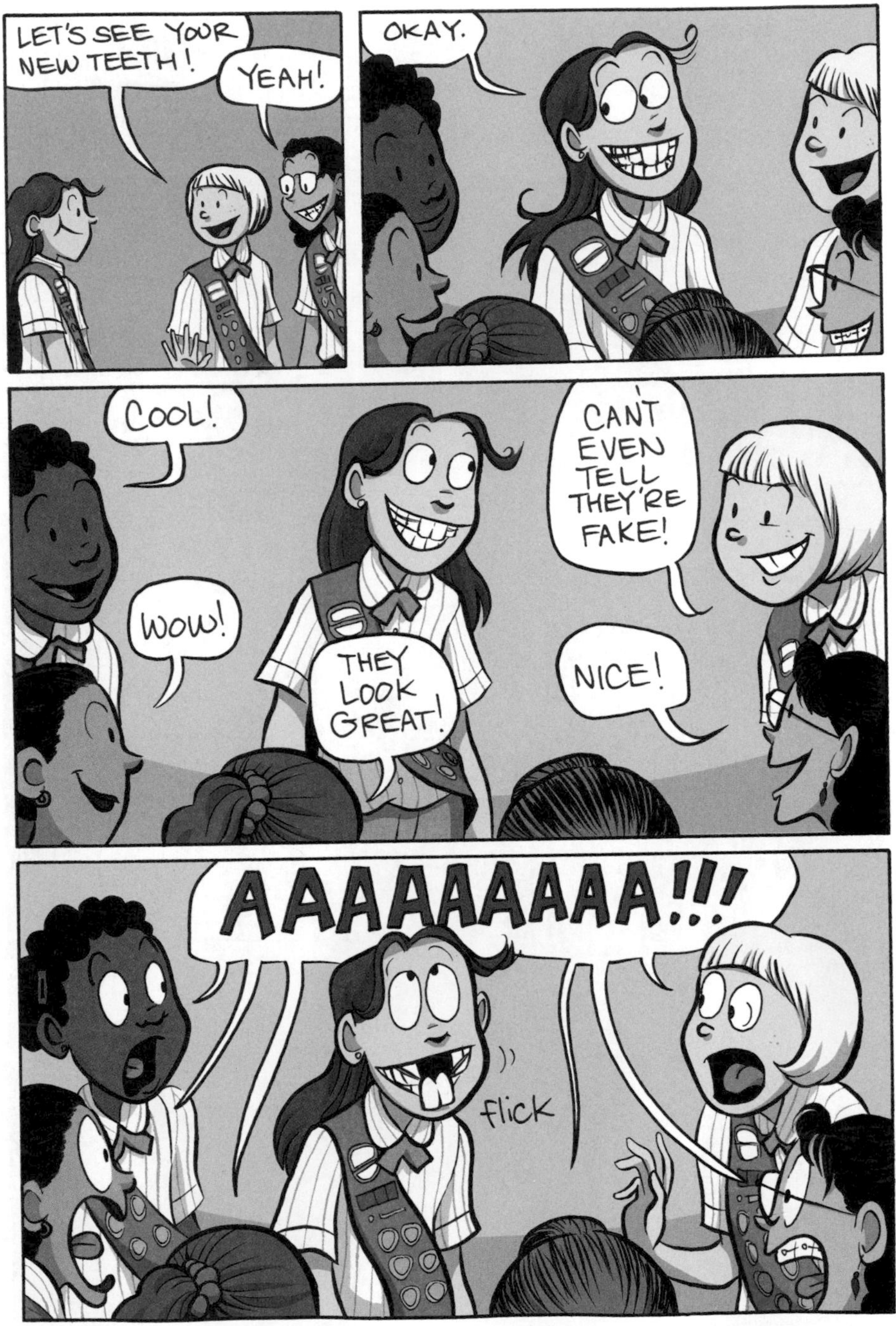
LET'S SEE YOUR NEW TEETH!
YEAH!
OKAY.
COOL!
CAN'T EVEN TELL THEY'RE FAKE!
WOW!
THEY LOOK GREAT!
NICE!
AAAAAAAAA!!!
flick

* FROM NEW KIDS ON THE BLOCK!

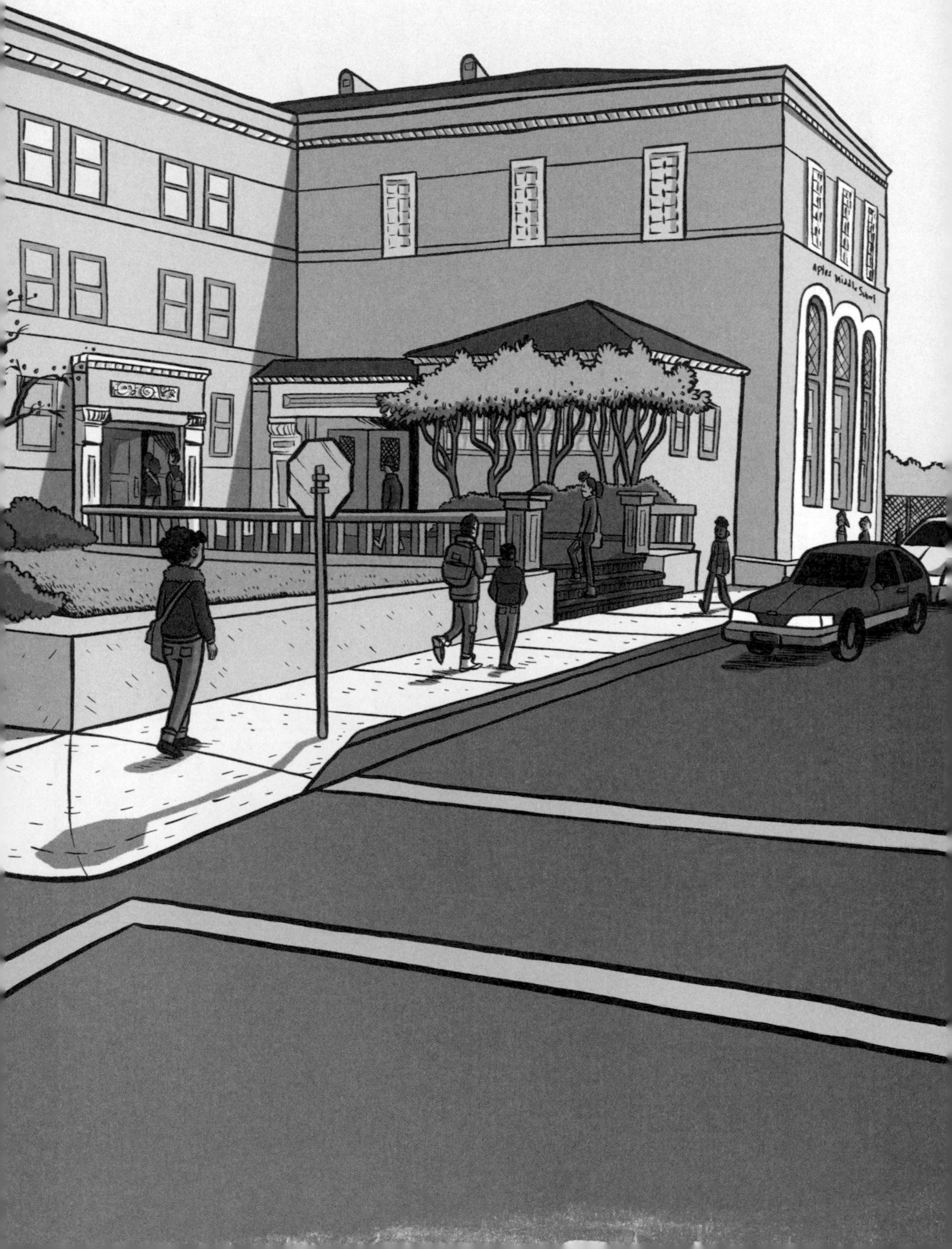

CHAPTER FIVE

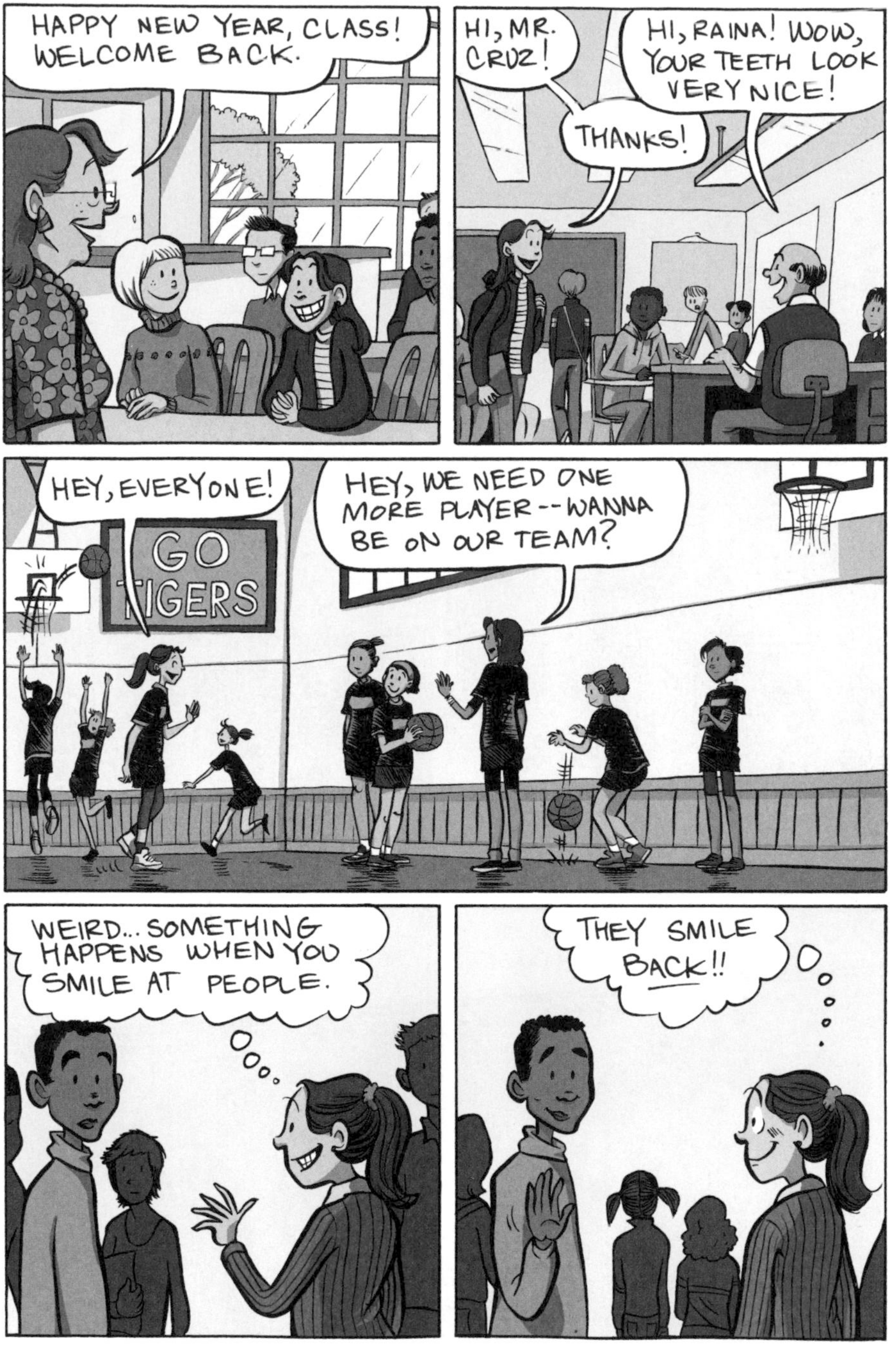
HAPPY NEW YEAR, CLASS! WELCOME BACK.
HI, MR. CRUZ!
HI, RAINA! WOW, YOUR TEETH LOOK VERY NICE!
THANKS!
HEY, EVERYONE!
GO TIGERS
HEY, WE NEED ONE MORE PLAYER--WANNA BE ON OUR TEAM?
WEIRD... SOMETHING HAPPENS WHEN YOU SMILE AT PEOPLE.
THEY SMILE BACK!!

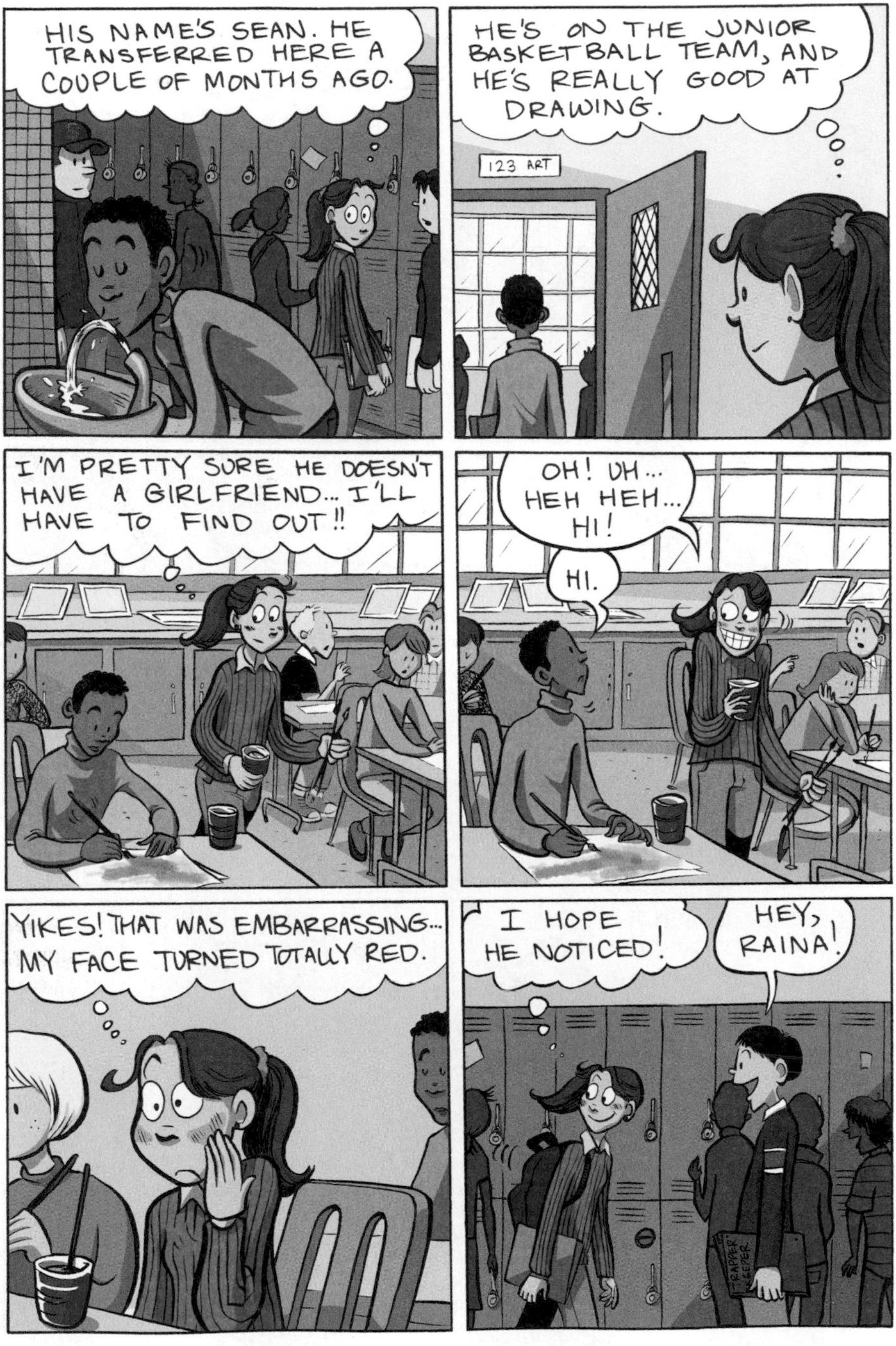
HIS NAME'S SEAN. HE TRANSFERRED HERE A COUPLE OF MONTHS AGO.
HE'S ON THE JUNIOR BASKETBALL TEAM, AND HE'S REALLY GOOD AT DRAWING.
123 ART
I'M PRETTY SURE HE DOESN'T HAVE A GIRLFRIEND... I'LL HAVE TO FIND OUT!!
OH! UH... HEH HEH... HI!
HI.
YIKES! THAT WAS EMBARRASSING... MY FACE TURNED TOTALLY RED.
I HOPE HE NOTICED!
HEY, RAINA!
TRAPPER KEEPER

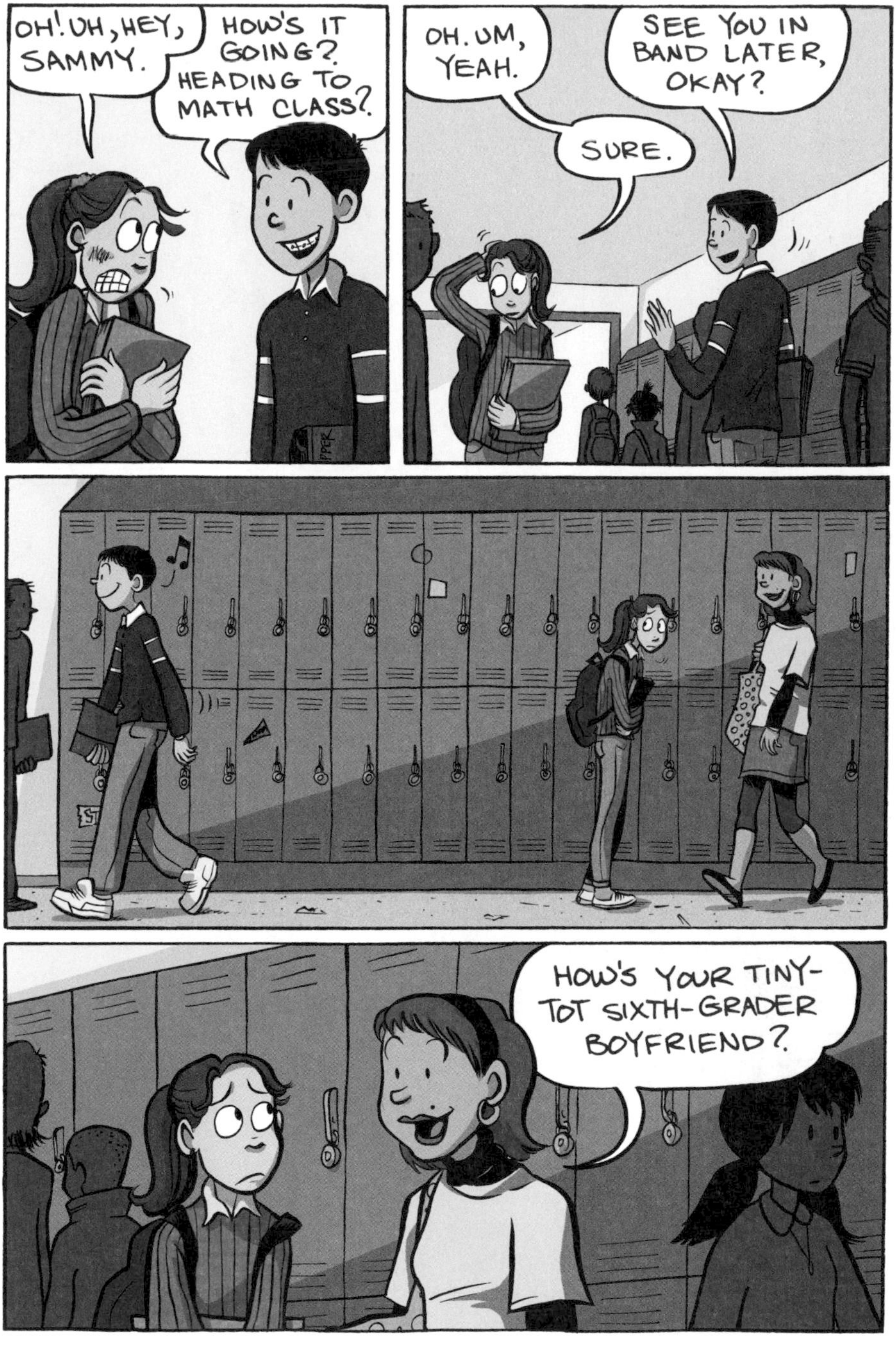
OH! UH, HEY, SAMMY.
HOW'S IT GOING? HEADING TO MATH CLASS?
OH. UM, YEAH.
SEE YOU IN BAND LATER, OKAY?
SURE.
HOW'S YOUR TINY-TOT SIXTH-GRADER BOYFRIEND?

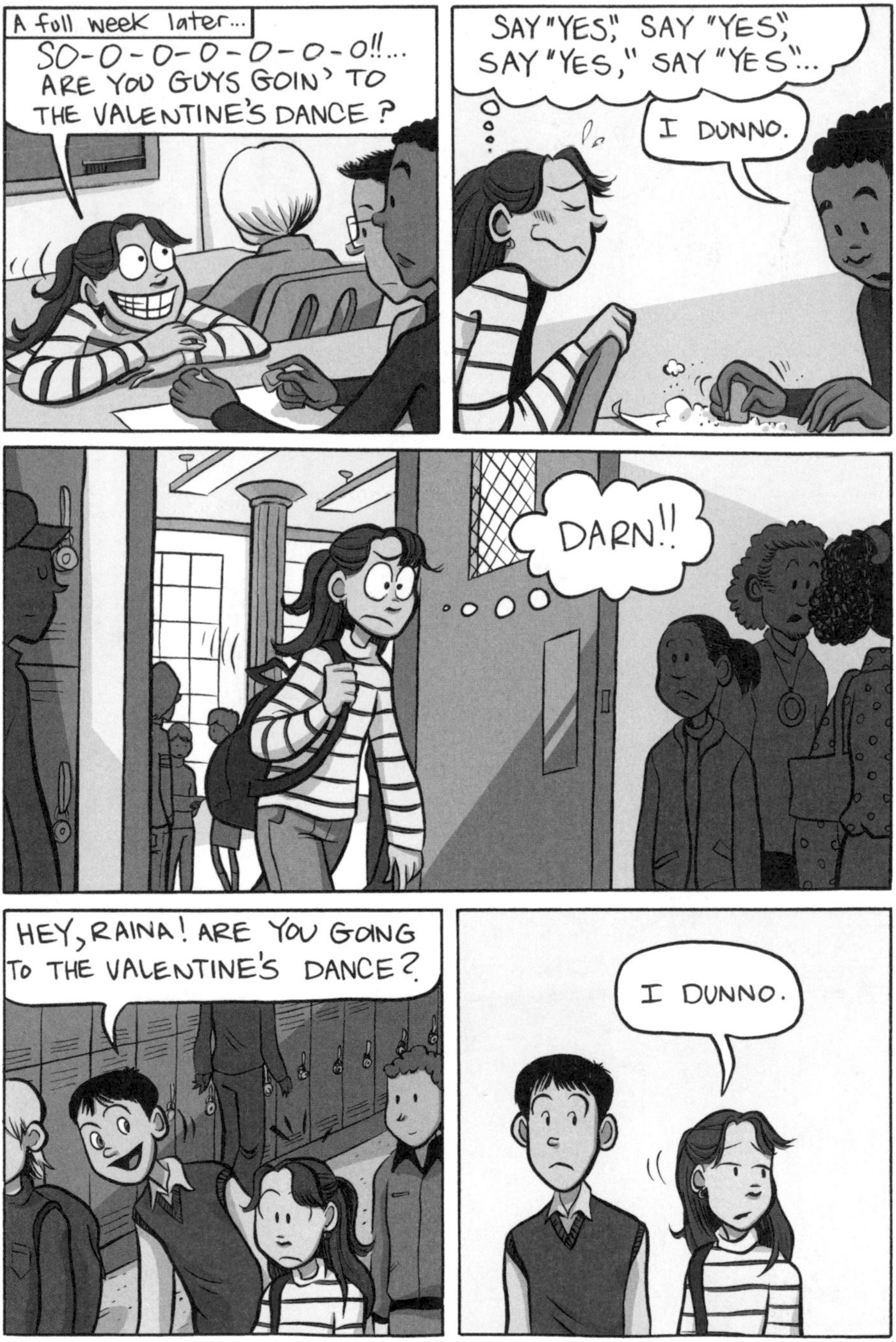

A full week later...
SO-O-O-O-O-O-O!!... ARE YOU GUYS GOIN' TO THE VALENTINE'S DANCE?
SAY "YES," SAY "YES," SAY "YES," SAY "YES"...
I DUNNO.
DARN!!
HEY, RAINA! ARE YOU GOING TO THE VALENTINE'S DANCE?
I DUNNO.

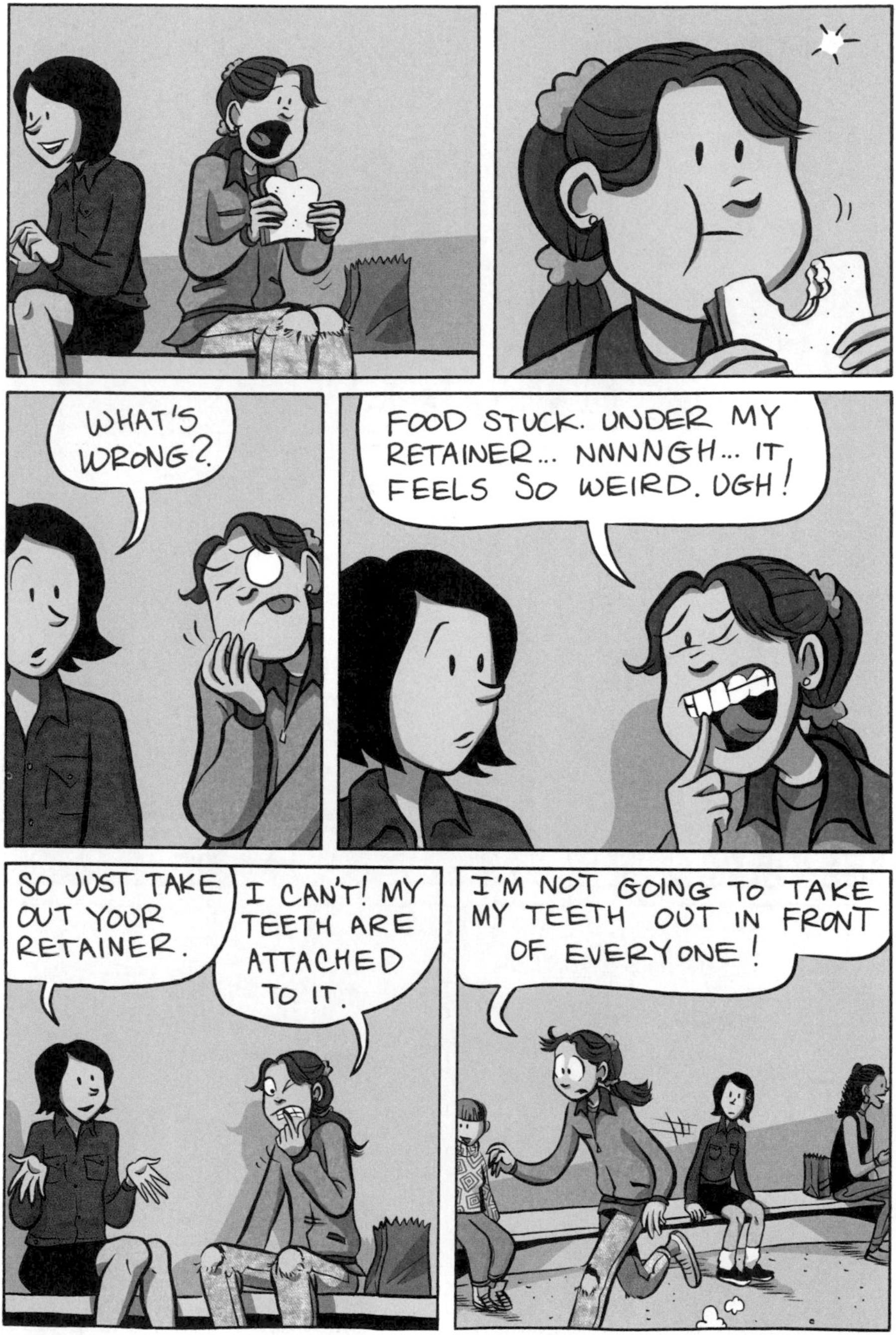
WHAT'S WRONG?
FOOD STUCK. UNDER MY RETAINER... NNNNGH... IT FEELS SO WEIRD. UGH!
SO JUST TAKE OUT YOUR RETAINER.
I CAN'T! MY TEETH ARE ATTACHED TO IT.
I'M NOT GOING TO TAKE MY TEETH OUT IN FRONT OF EVERYONE!

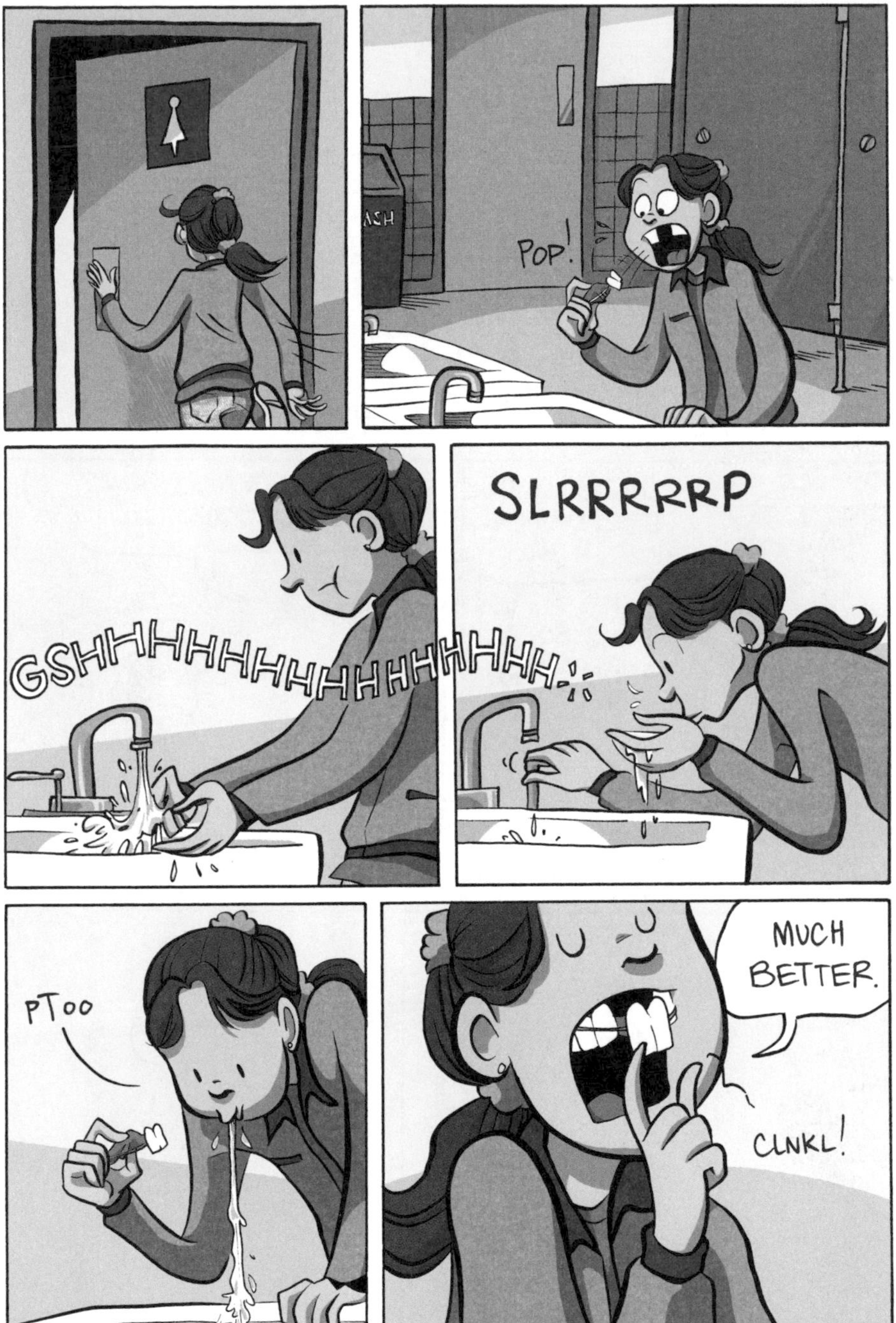
POP!
SLRRRRRP
GSHHHHHHHHHHHHHHH
PTOO
MUCH BETTER.
CLNKL!

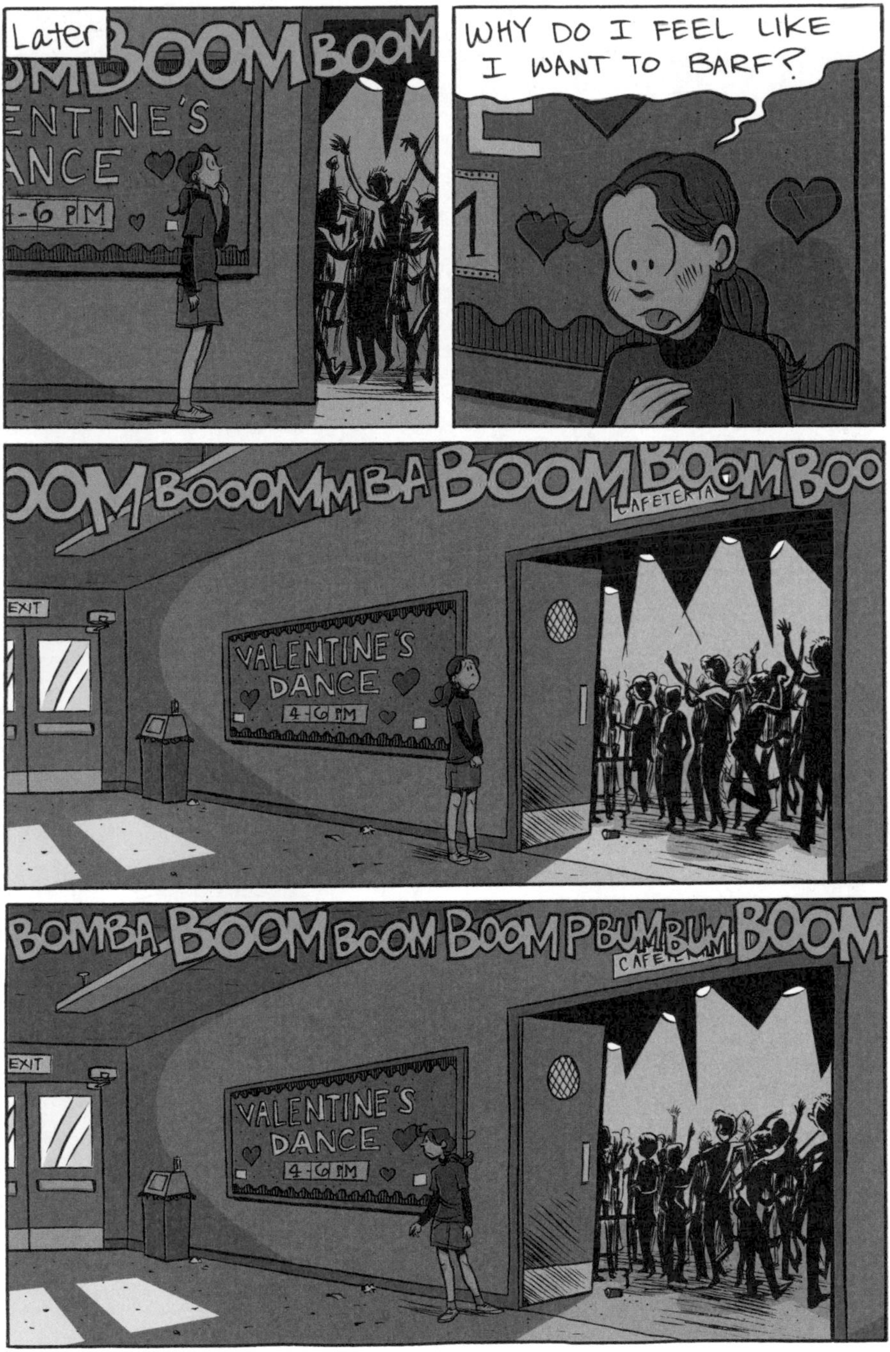
Later
BOOM BOOM
WHY DO I FEEL LIKE I WANT TO BARF?
BOOOMM BA BOOM BOOM
CAFETERIA
EXIT
VALENTINE'S DANCE
4-6 PM
BOMBA BOOM BOOM BOOM P BUM BUM BOOM
EXIT
VALENTINE'S DANCE
4-6 PM

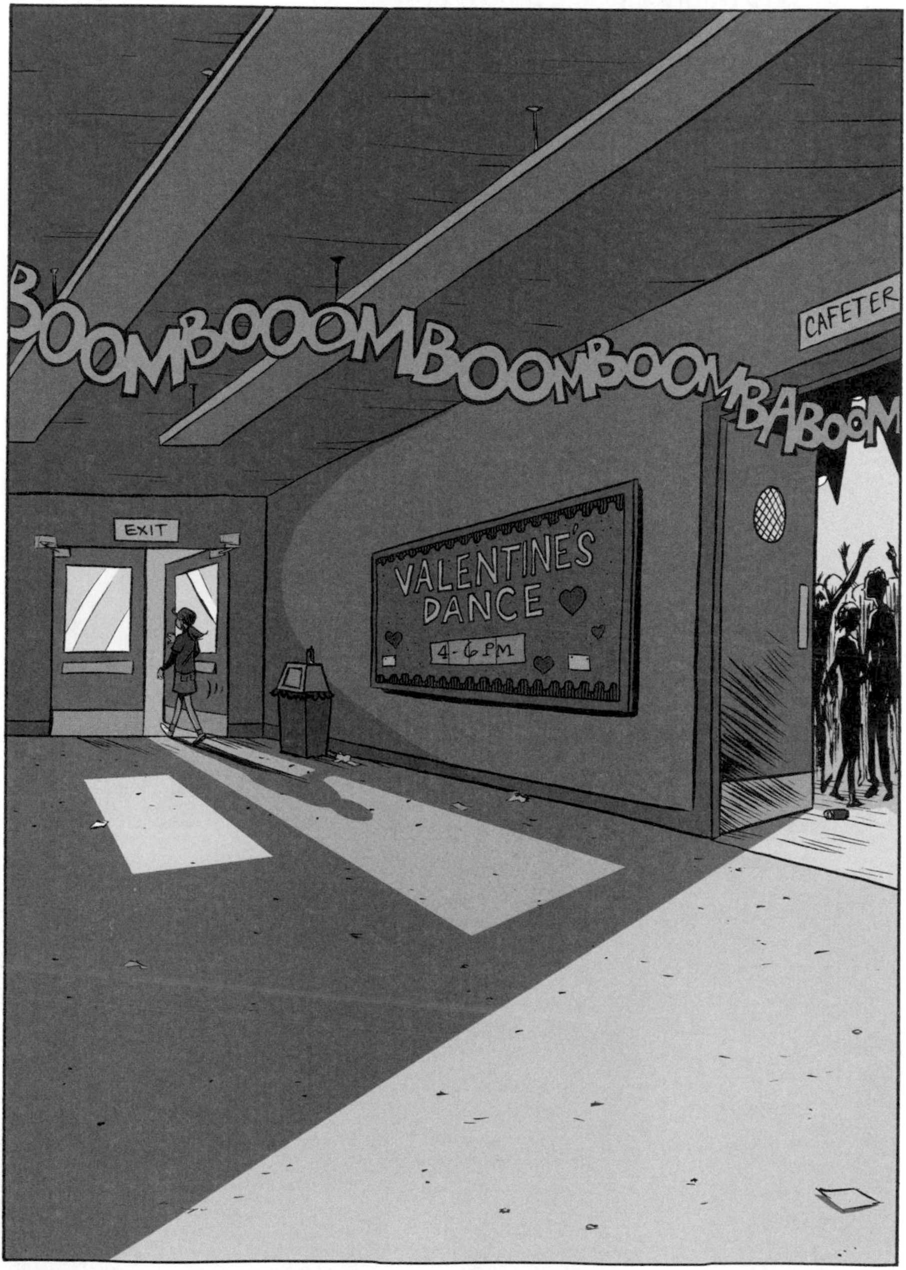
BOOMBOOOMBOOMBOOMBABOOM
CAFETER
EXIT
VALENTINE'S DANCE
4-6PM

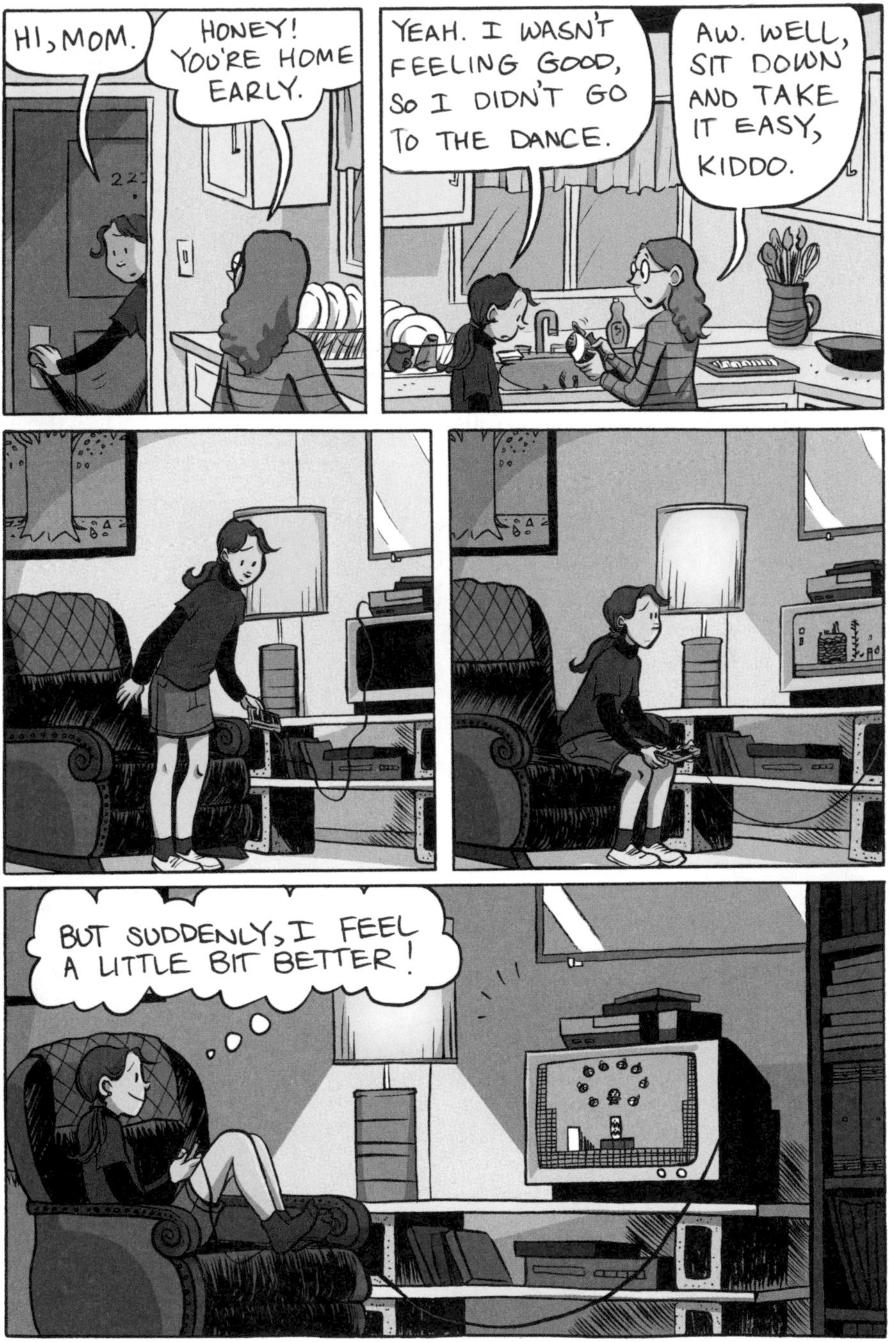
HI, MOM.
HONEY! YOU'RE HOME EARLY.
YEAH. I WASN'T FEELING GOOD, SO I DIDN'T GO TO THE DANCE.
AW. WELL, SIT DOWN AND TAKE IT EASY, KIDDO.
BUT SUDDENLY, I FEEL A LITTLE BIT BETTER!

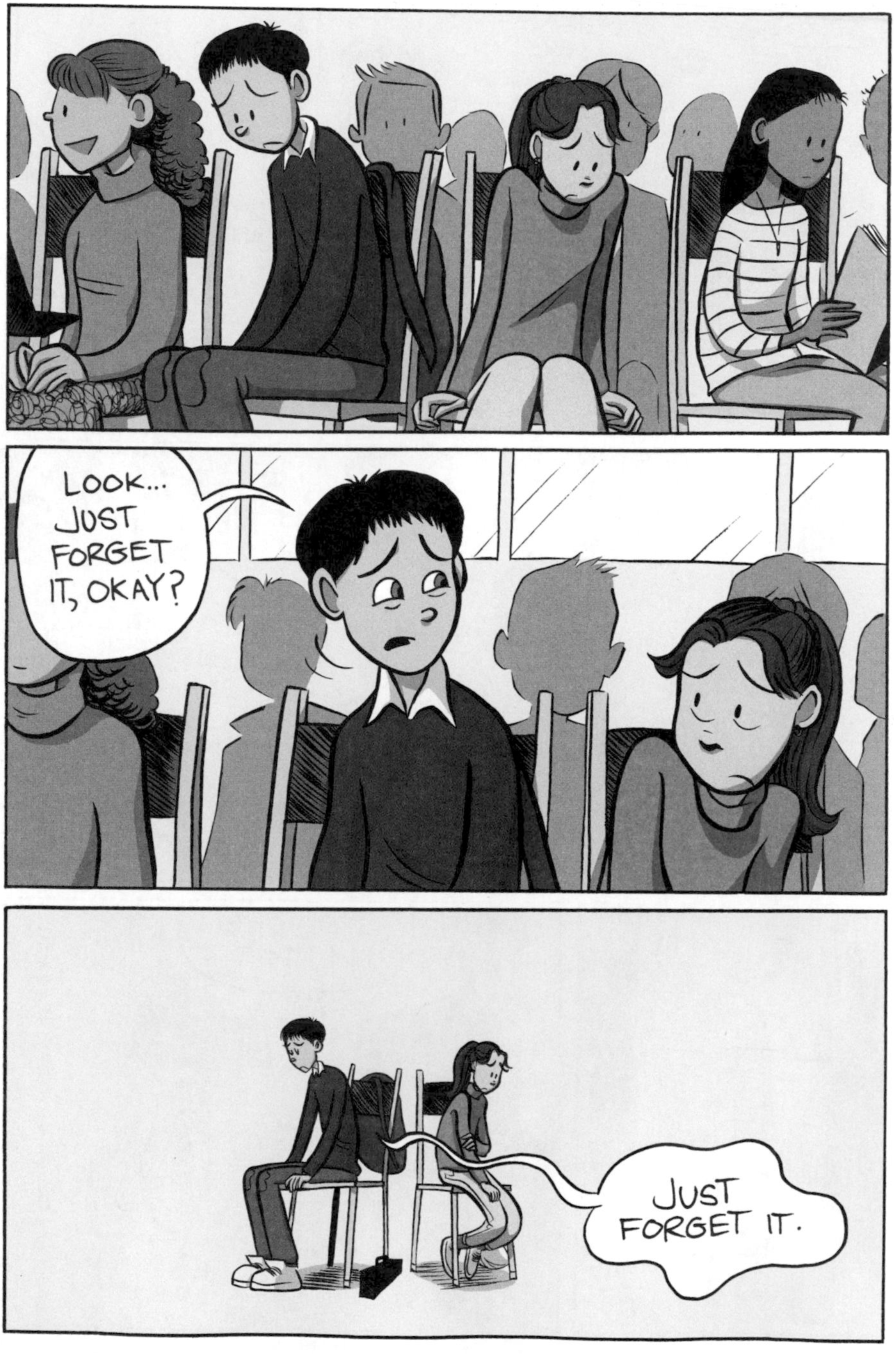
LOOK... JUST FORGET IT, OKAY?
JUST FORGET IT.

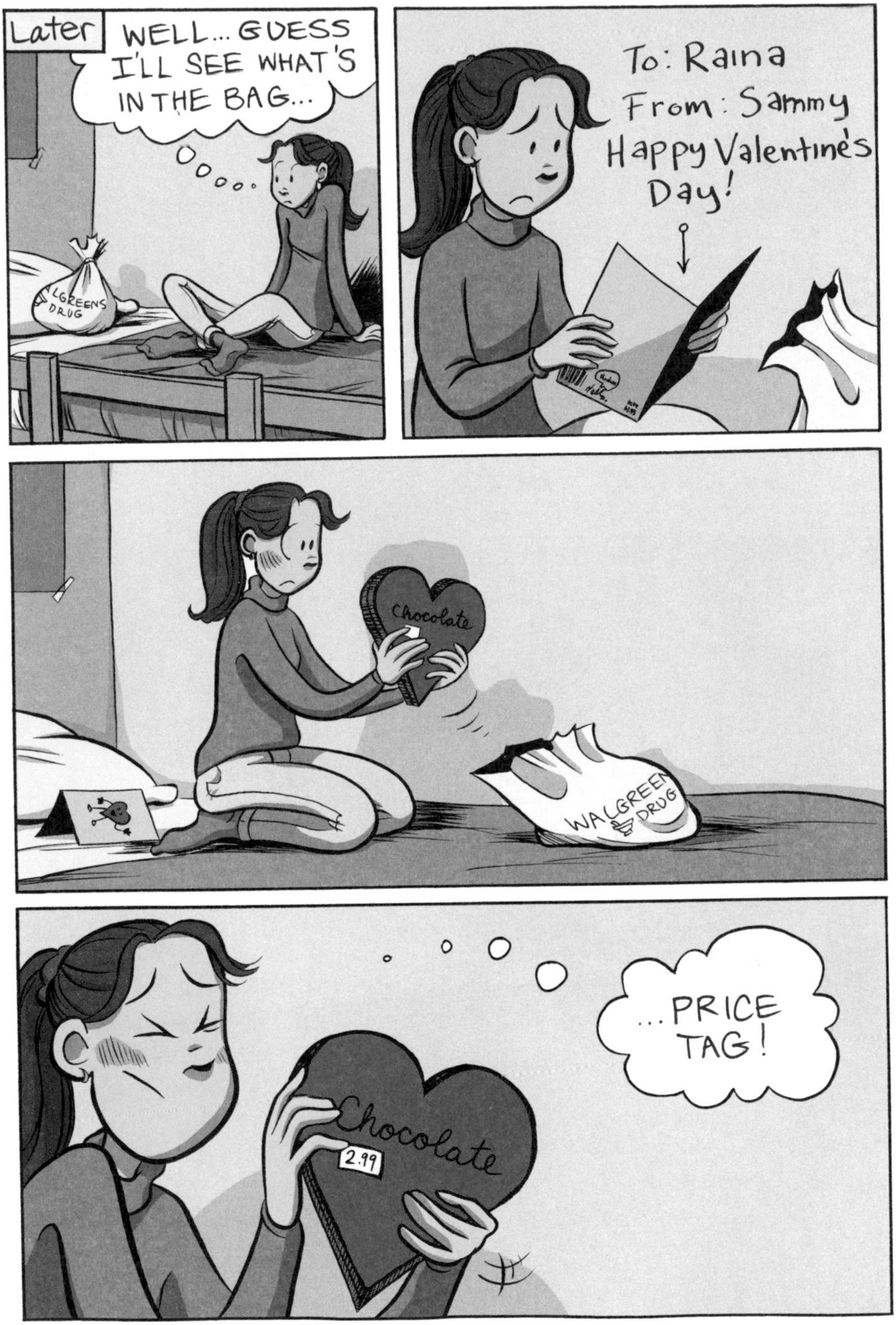
Later
WELL... GUESS I'LL SEE WHAT'S IN THE BAG...
WALGREENS DRUG
To: Raina
From: Sammy
Happy Valentine's Day!
Chocolate
WALGREENS DRUG
...PRICE TAG!
Chocolate
2.99

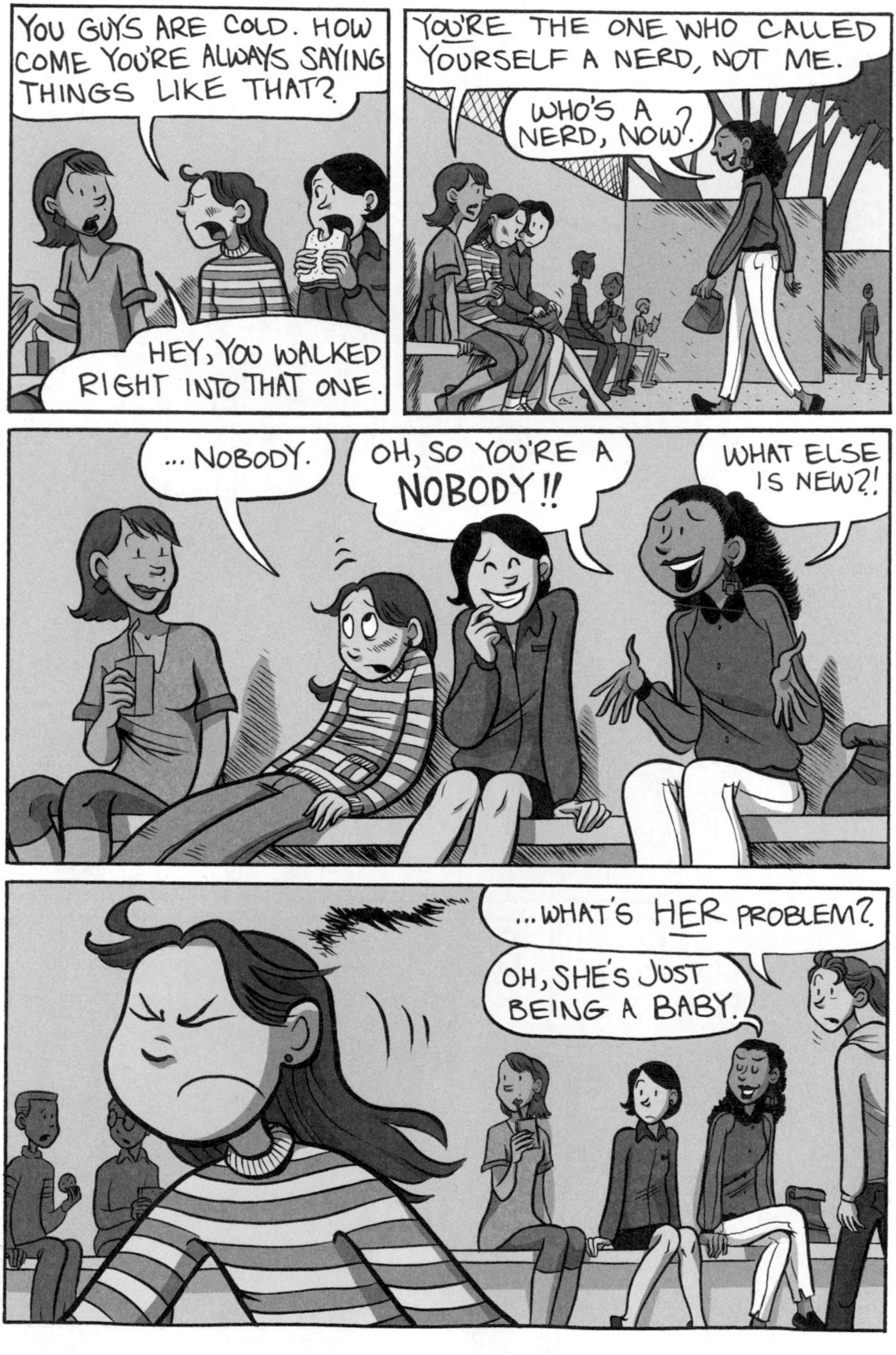
YOU GUYS ARE COLD. HOW COME YOU'RE ALWAYS SAYING THINGS LIKE THAT?
HEY, YOU WALKED RIGHT INTO THAT ONE.
YOU'RE THE ONE WHO CALLED YOURSELF A NERD, NOT ME.
WHO'S A NERD, NOW?
... NOBODY.
OH, SO YOU'RE A NOBODY!!
WHAT ELSE IS NEW?!
...WHAT'S HER PROBLEM?
OH, SHE'S JUST BEING A BABY.

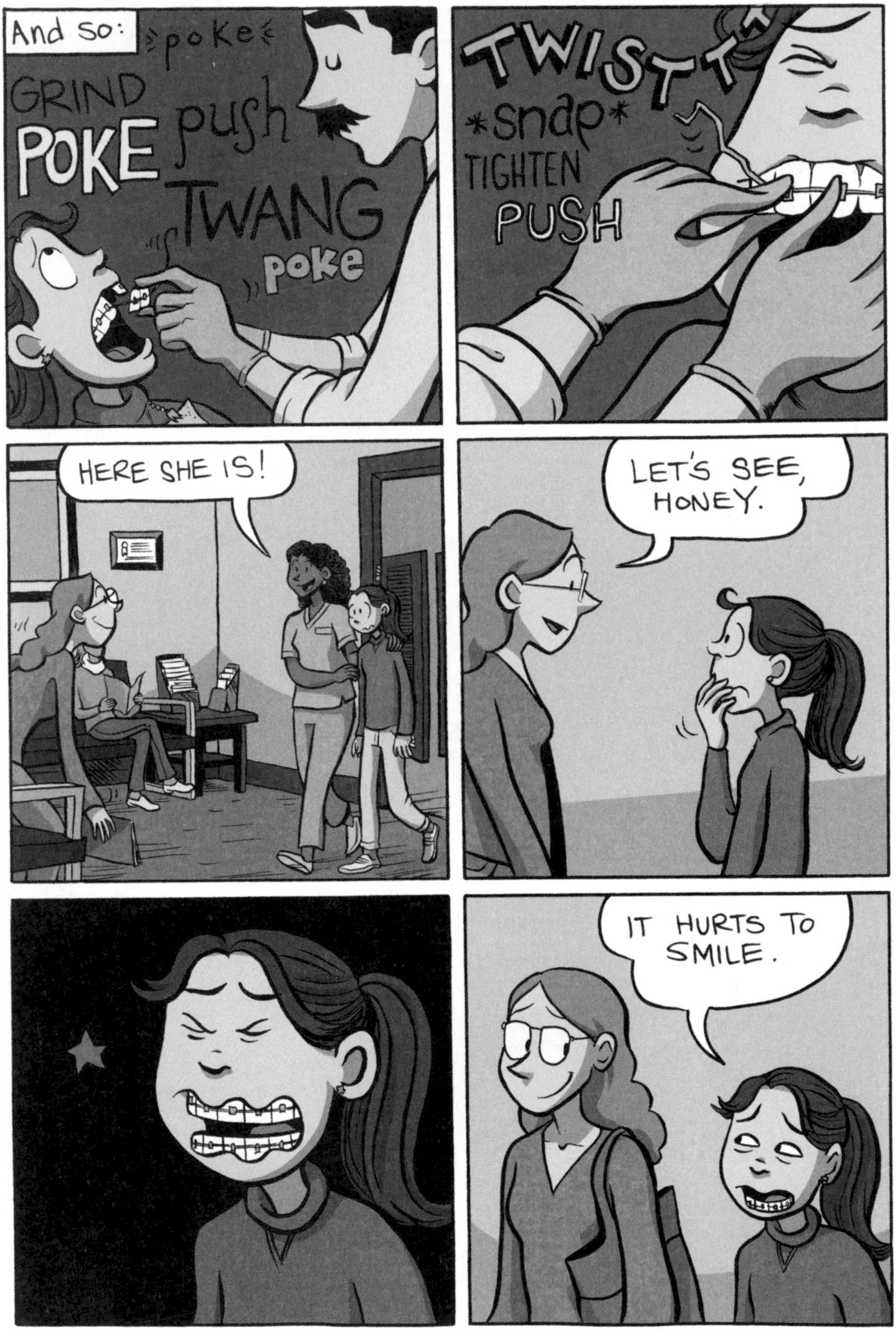
And so:
poke
GRIND
POKE
push
TWANG
poke
TWIST
snap
TIGHTEN
PUSH
HERE SHE IS!
LET'S SEE, HONEY.
IT HURTS TO SMILE.

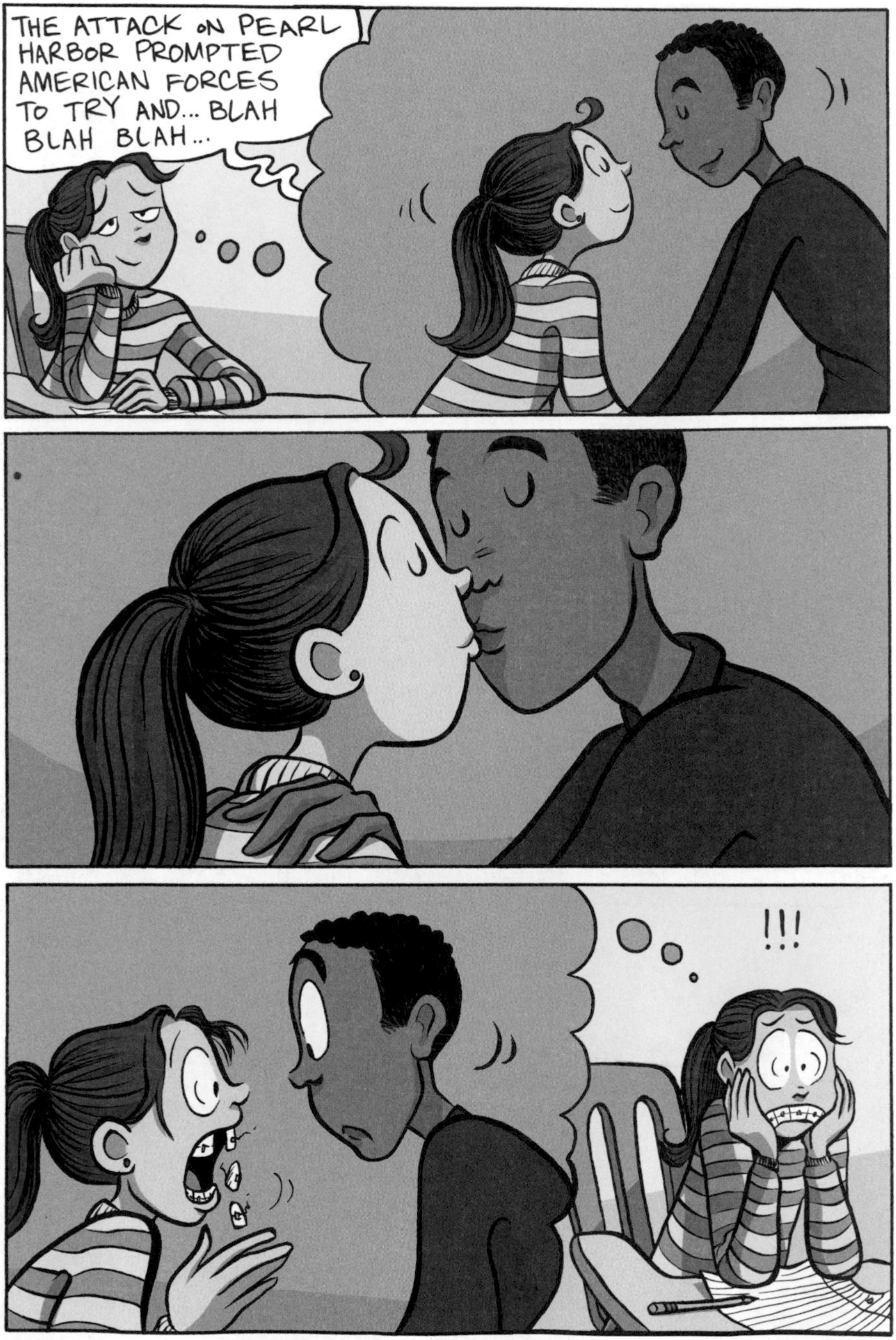
THE ATTACK ON PEARL HARBOR PROMPTED AMERICAN FORCES TO TRY AND... BLAH BLAH BLAH...
!!!

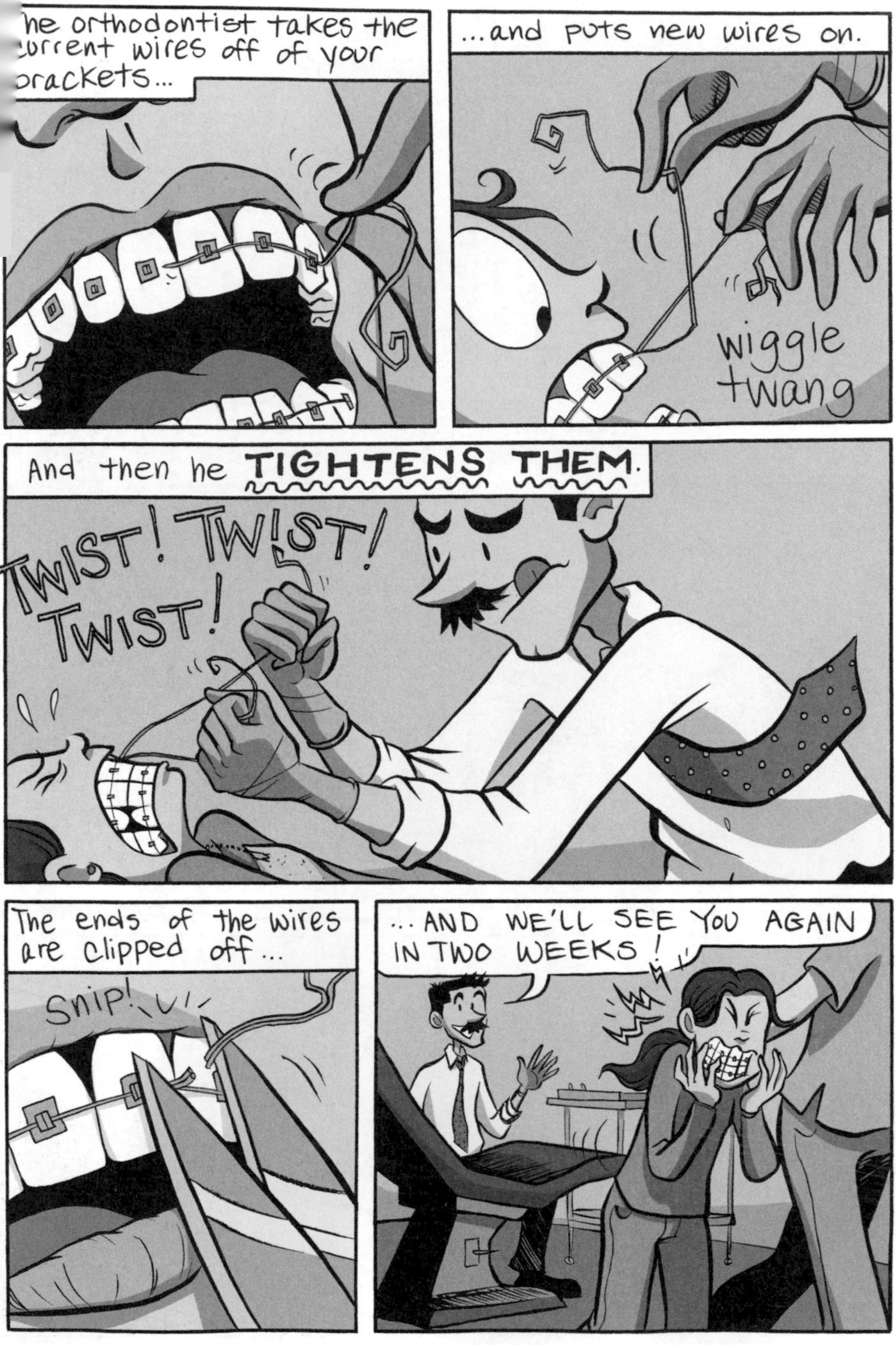

he orthodontist takes the
urrent wires off of your
rackets...
...and puts new wires on.
wiggle
twang
And then he TIGHTENS THEM.
TWIST! TWIST!
TWIST!
The ends of the wires
are clipped off...
Snip!
...AND WE'LL SEE YOU AGAIN
IN TWO WEEKS!

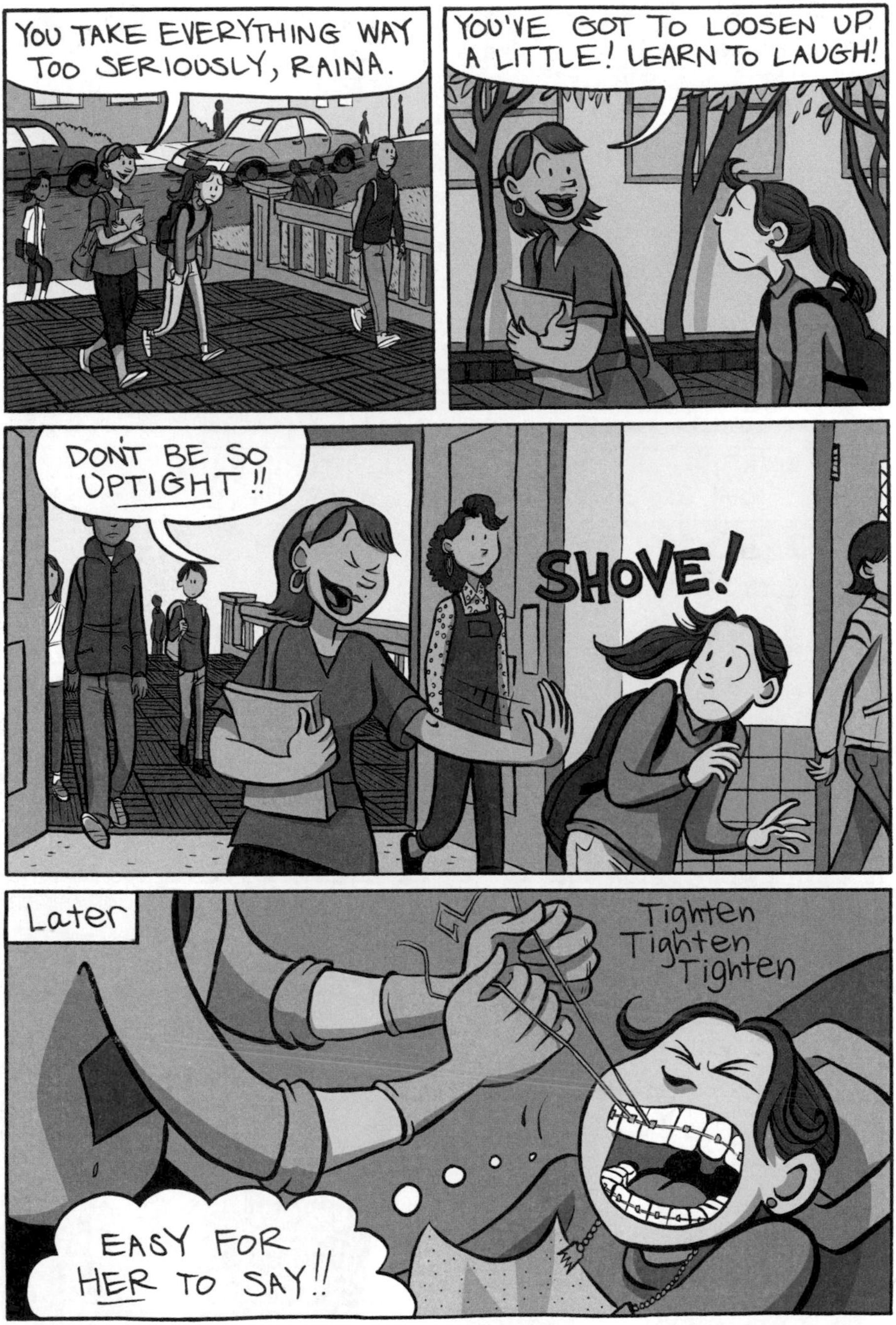
YOU TAKE EVERYTHING WAY TOO SERIOUSLY, RAINA.
YOU'VE GOT TO LOOSEN UP A LITTLE! LEARN TO LAUGH!
DON'T BE SO UPTIGHT!!
SHOVE!
Later
Tighten Tighten Tighten
EASY FOR HER TO SAY!!

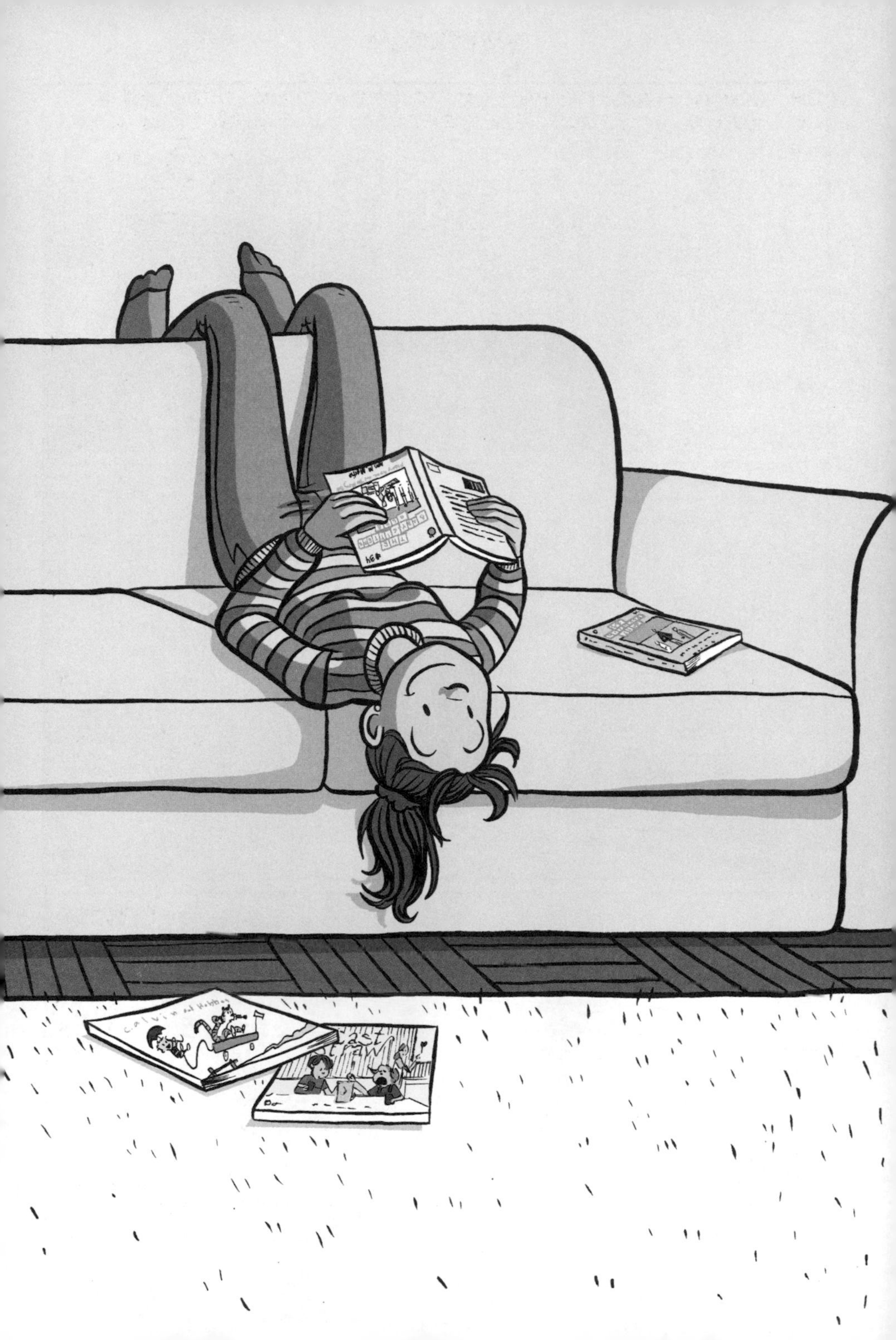

CHAPTER SIX

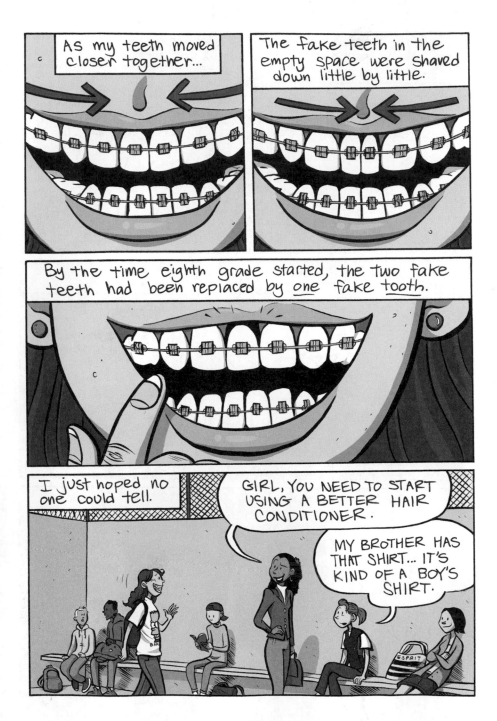

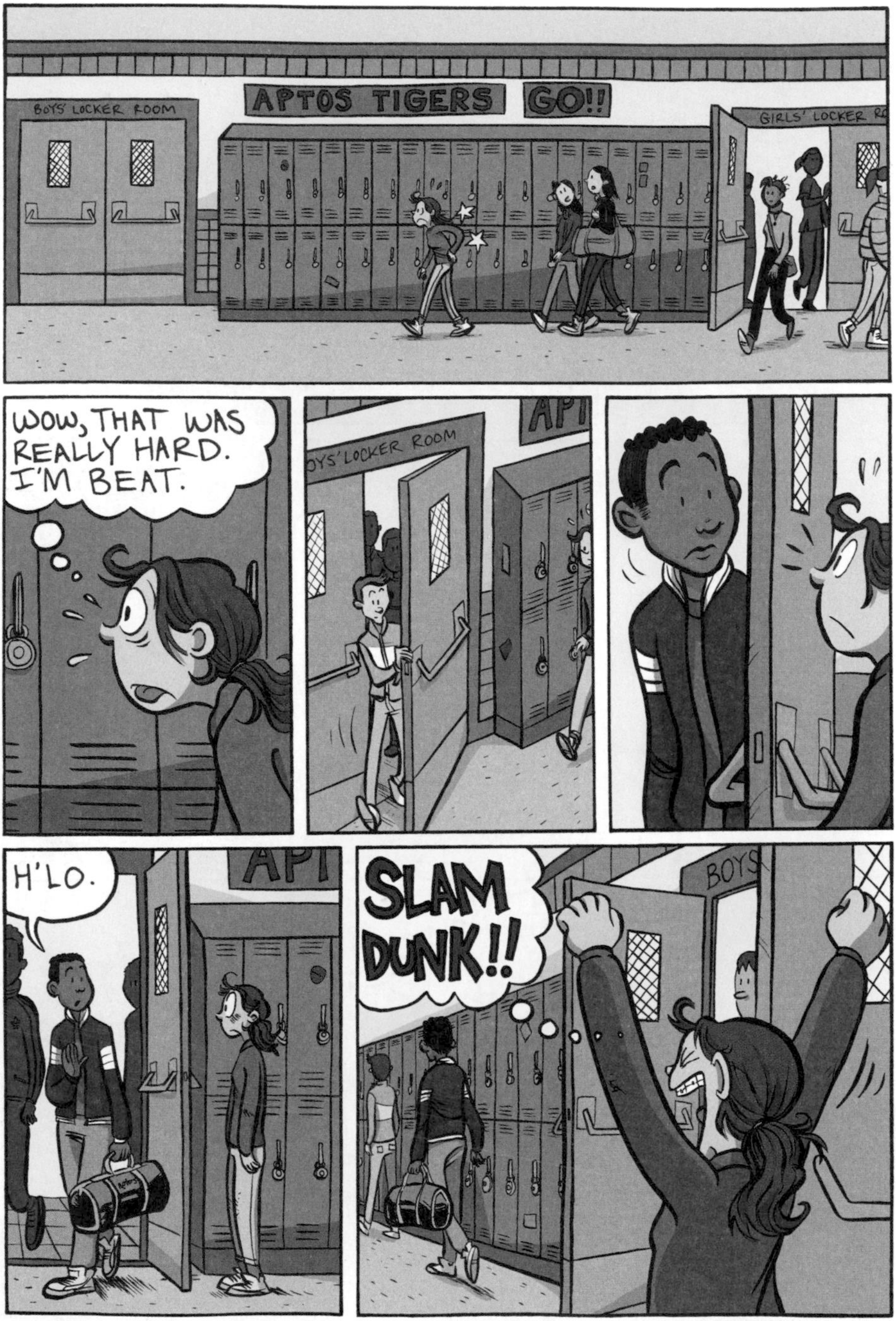
BOYS' LOCKER ROOM
APTOS TIGERS
GO!!
GIRLS' LOCKER R
WOW, THAT WAS REALLY HARD. I'M BEAT.
BOYS' LOCKER ROOM
H'LO.
SLAM DUNK!!
BOYS

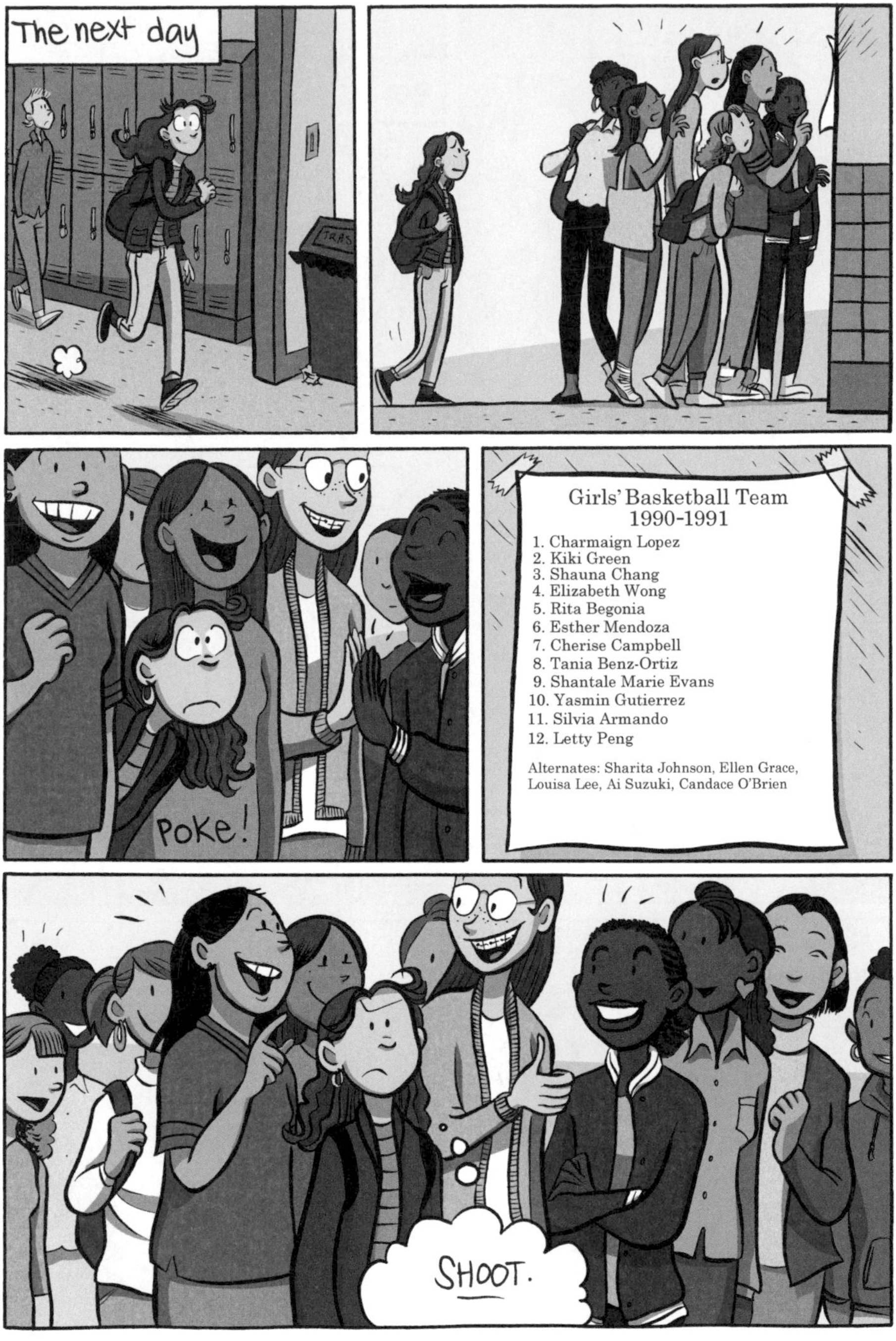

The next day
POKE!
Girls' Basketball Team
1990-1991
1. Charmaign Lopez
2. Kiki Green
3. Shauna Chang
4. Elizabeth Wong
5. Rita Begonia
6. Esther Mendoza
7. Cherise Campbell
8. Tania Benz-Ortiz
9. Shantale Marie Evans
10. Yasmin Gutierrez
11. Silvia Armando
12. Letty Peng
Alternates: Sharita Johnson, Ellen Grace, Louisa Lee, Ai Suzuki, Candace O'Brien
SHOOT.

... IN THE FUTURE, MISS TELGEMEIER, PLEASE DON'T PASS NOTES DURING MY CLASS. THAT GOES FOR YOU, TOO, MELISSA.
I CAN'T BELIEVE THAT JUST HAPPENED! I WAS SOOOO EMBARRASSED!!
HEY... AT LEAST SEAN ISN'T IN MR. F.'S CLASS WITH US.
crunch!
BUT NOW EVERYONE KNOWS I LIKE HIM! WHAT IF THEY'RE ALL TELLING HIM RIGHT NOW?
UHHH... WHAT IF NOBODY CARES?
WELL THAT WOULD REALLY SUCK.

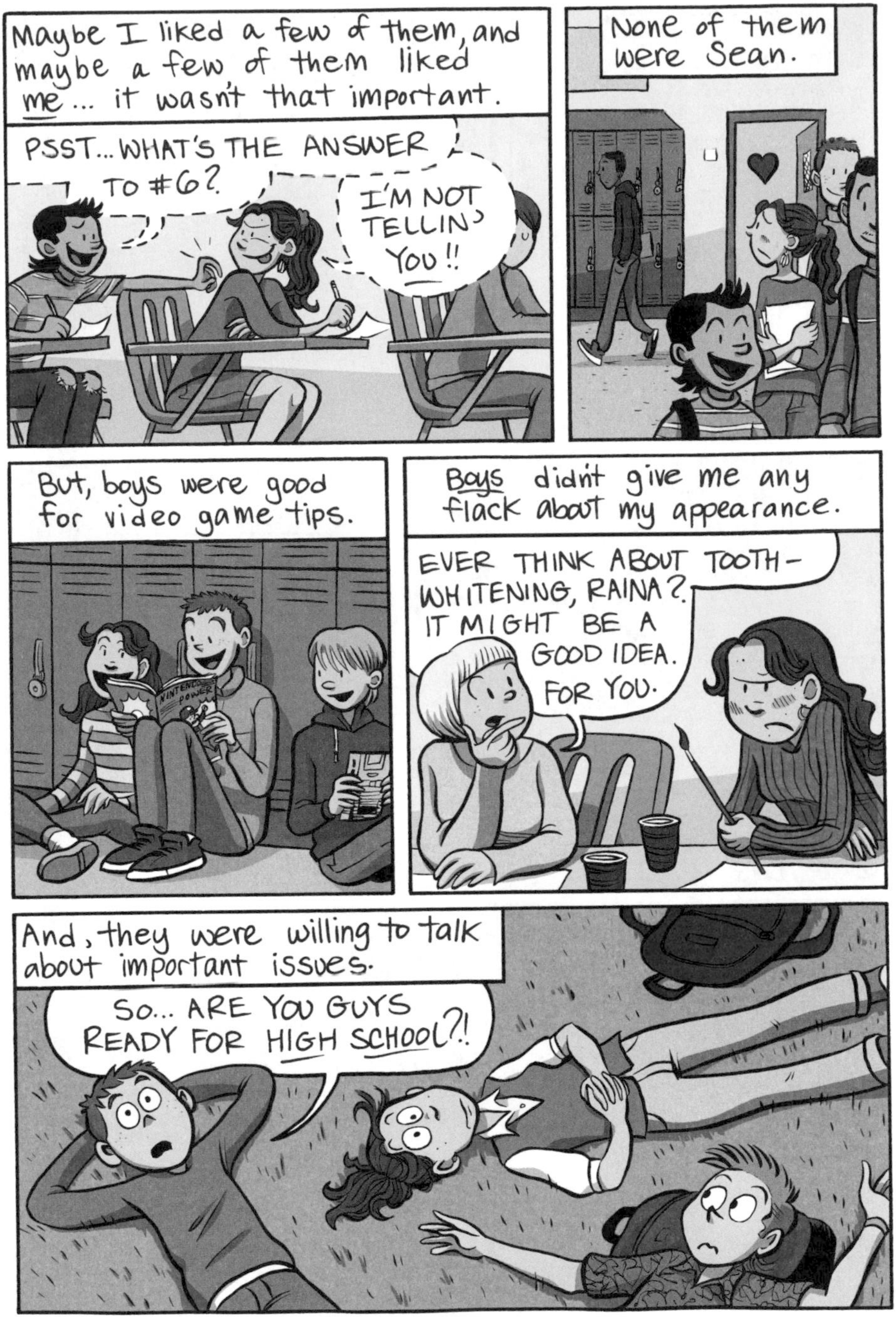
Maybe I liked a few of them, and maybe a few of them liked me... it wasn't that important.
PSST... WHAT'S THE ANSWER TO #6?
I'M NOT TELLIN' YOU!!
None of them were Sean.
But, boys were good for video game tips.
NINTENDO POWER
Boys didn't give me any flack about my appearance.
EVER THINK ABOUT TOOTH-WHITENING, RAINA? IT MIGHT BE A GOOD IDEA. FOR YOU.
And, they were willing to talk about important issues.
SO... ARE YOU GUYS READY FOR HIGH SCHOOL?!

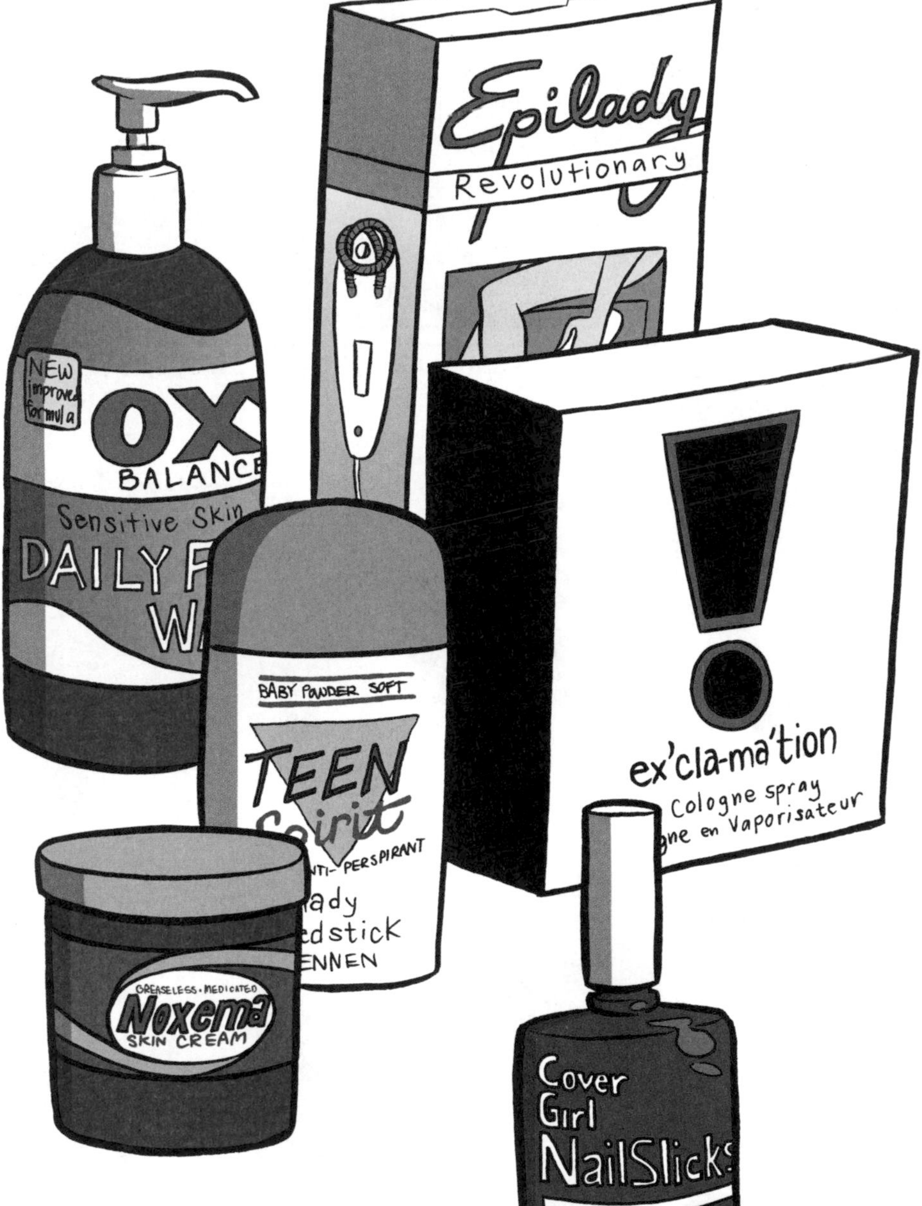
Epilady
Revolutionary
NEW improved formula
OXY
BALANCE
Sensitive Skin
DAILY F
WA
ex'cla-ma'tion
Cologne spray
gne en Vaporisateur
BABY POWDER SOFT
TEEN
Spirit
NTI-PERSPIRANT
lady
edstick
ENNEN
GREASELESS • MEDICATED
Noxema
SKIN CREAM
Cover
Girl
NailSlicks

165

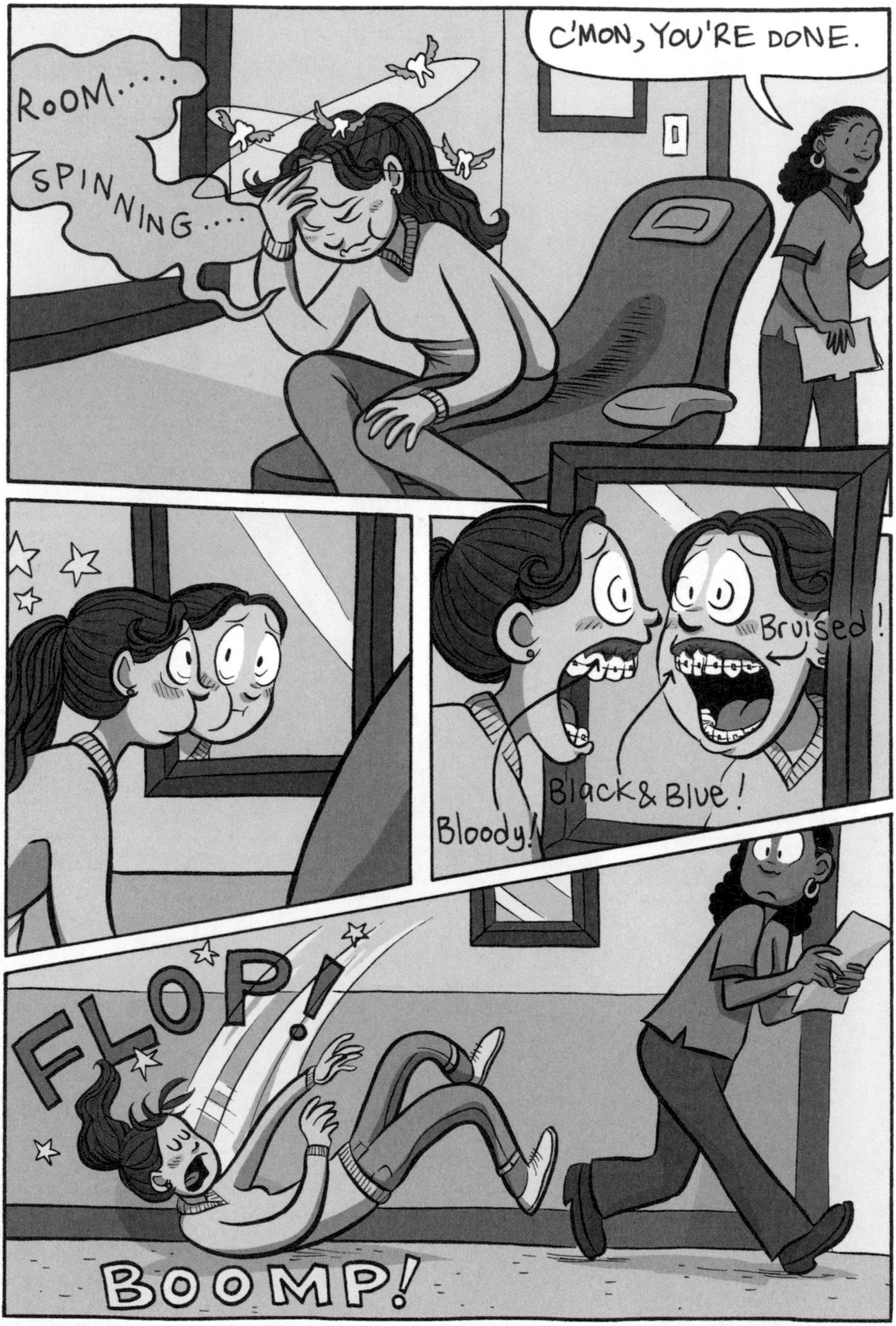

ROOM.....
SPINNING.....
C'MON, YOU'RE DONE.
Bruised!
Black & Blue!
Bloody!
FLOP!
BOOMP!

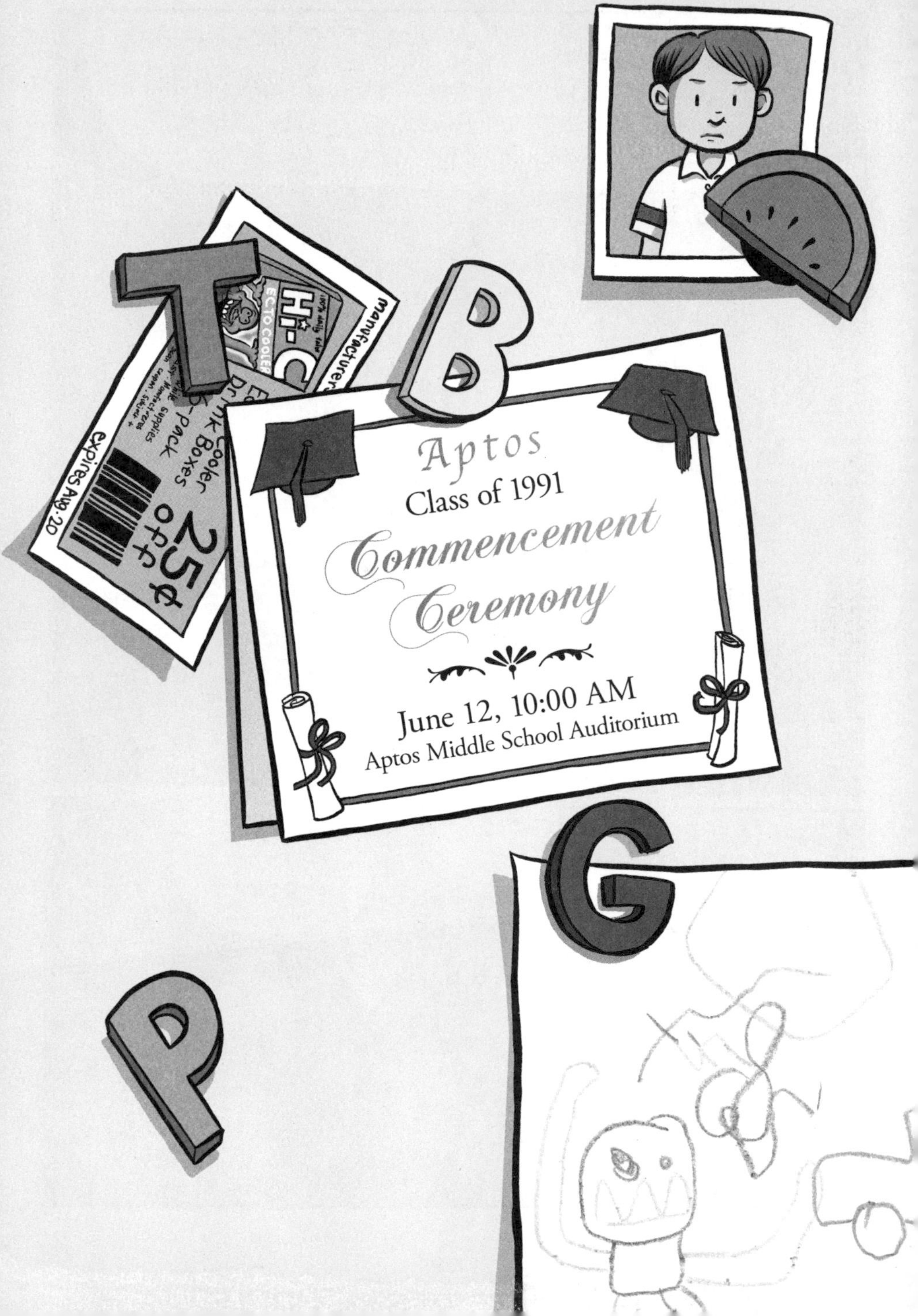
Aptos
Class of 1991
Commencement
Ceremony
June 12, 10:00 AM
Aptos Middle School Auditorium
manufacturer
Hi-C
ECTO COOLER
Drink Boxes
Cooler
5-pack
25¢
off
expires Aug. 20

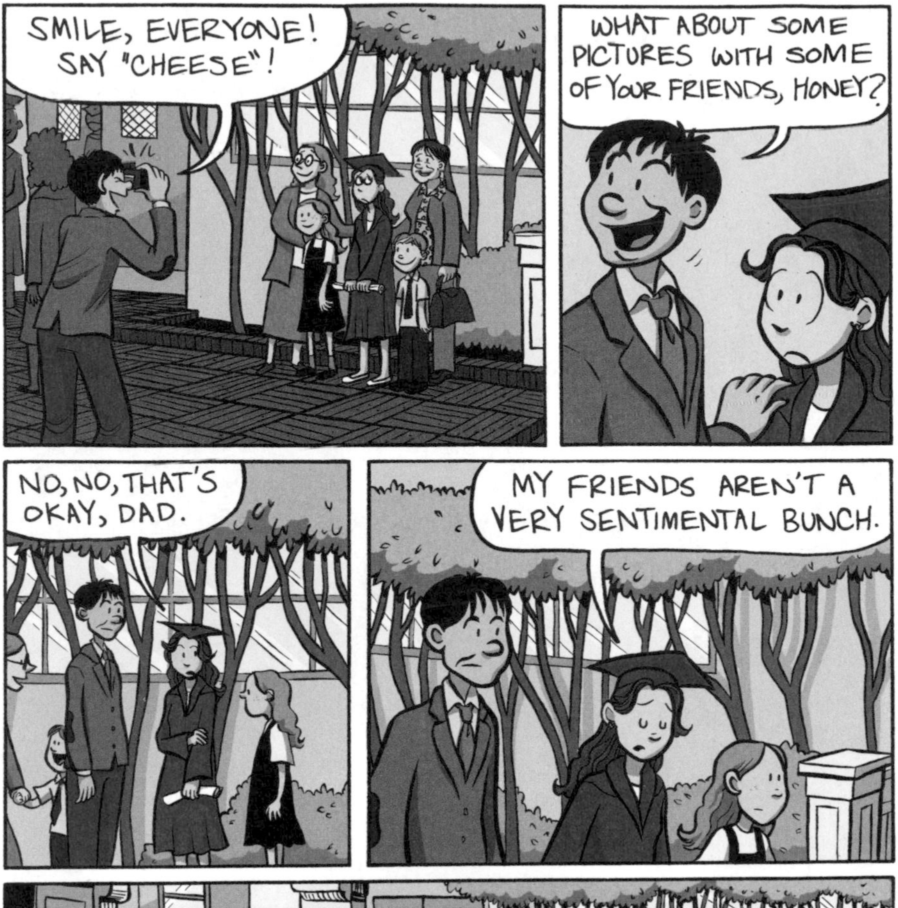
SMILE, EVERYONE! SAY "CHEESE"!
WHAT ABOUT SOME PICTURES WITH SOME OF YOUR FRIENDS, HONEY?
NO, NO, THAT'S OKAY, DAD.
MY FRIENDS AREN'T A VERY SENTIMENTAL BUNCH.

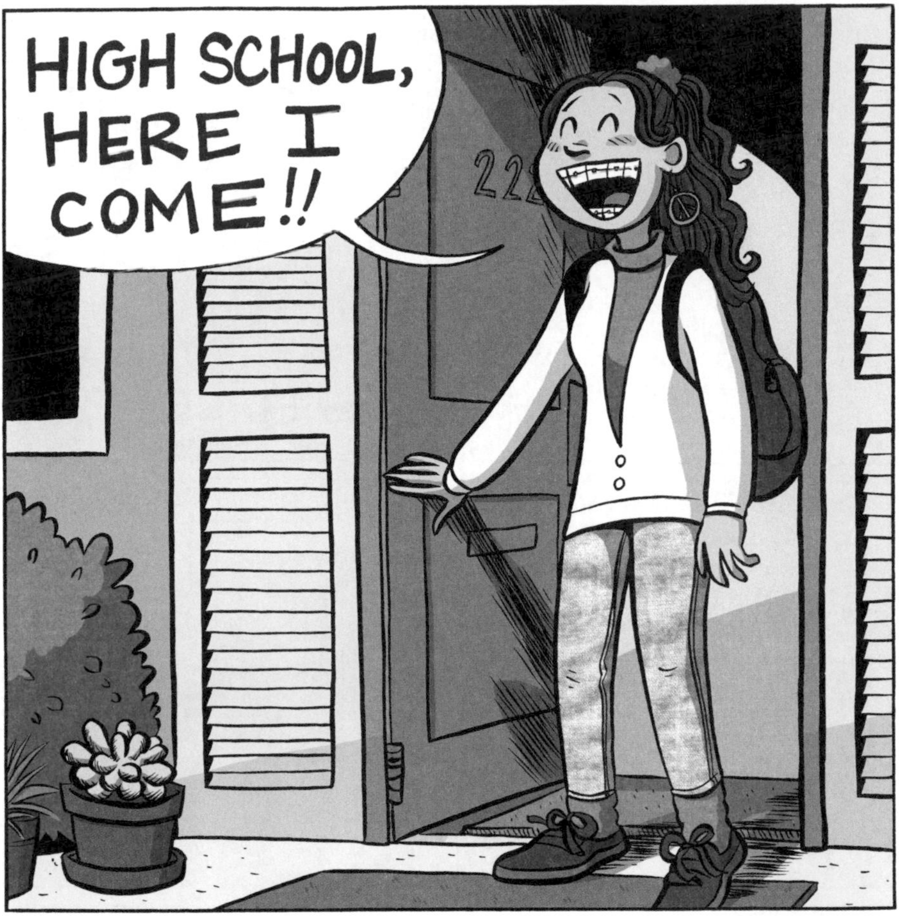
HIGH SCHOOL, HERE I COME!!

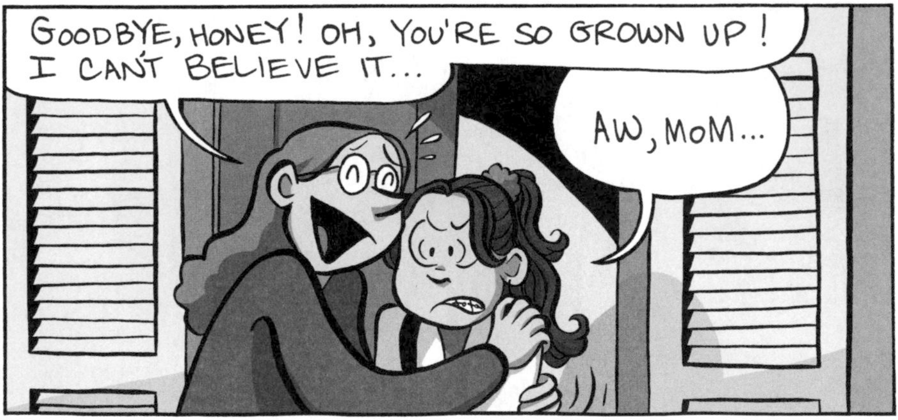
GOODBYE, HONEY! OH, YOU'RE SO GROWN UP! I CAN'T BELIEVE IT...
AW, MOM...

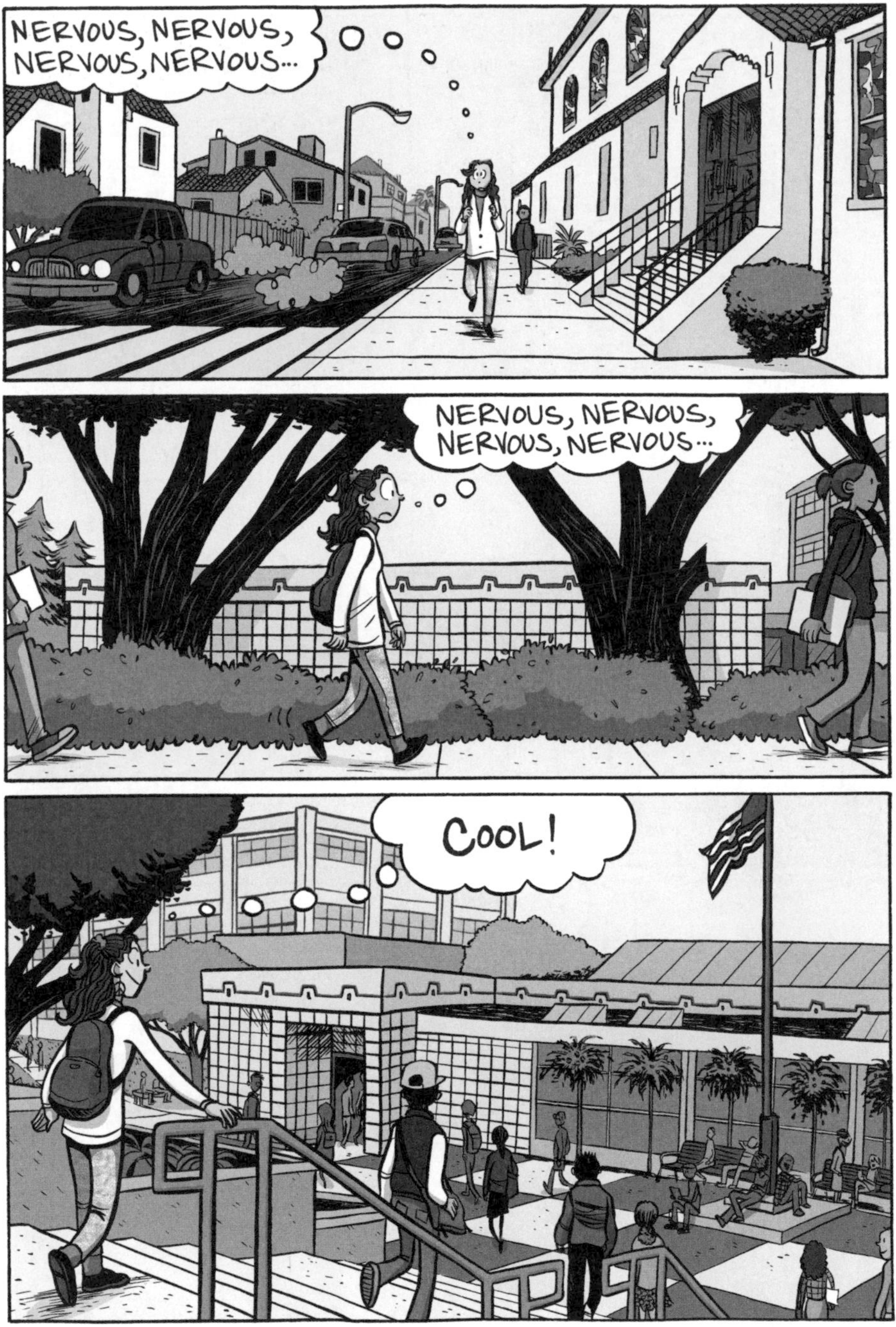
NERVOUS, NERVOUS, NERVOUS, NERVOUS...
NERVOUS, NERVOUS, NERVOUS, NERVOUS...
COOL!

The next stage of my orthodontic treatment was a fairly entertaining one, designed to correct my **CROSS-BITE.**

(That's when your top and bottom jaws don't line up.)

To fix this, little hooks are attached to specific brackets on the top and the bottom teeth...

①

②

...and a tiny rubber band is stretched between them.

I CAN' OPEN MA MOUF ALL TH' WEY!

Twannngg!

YOU'LL GET USED TO IT!

So, tiny rubber bands joined the contents of my backpack.

0.3

Jones + Jones
+ Waxed Floss
ie dentaire

PICK a PICK

N-Z Floss Threader

WAX

Fresh Mint BRITE ANTICAVITY TOOTHPASTE

Scope Mouthwash 44mL (1.49 FL oz)

Along with travel toothbrush and paste, dental wax, floss, floss-threaders, a little box of toothpicks, and a tiny bottle of mouthwash.

It was quite the spectacle when I went to get a pencil or whatever.

...OOP!

HA HA! LOOKS LIKE SOMEONE'S TRYING TO COVER UP THEIR DOG BREATH!!

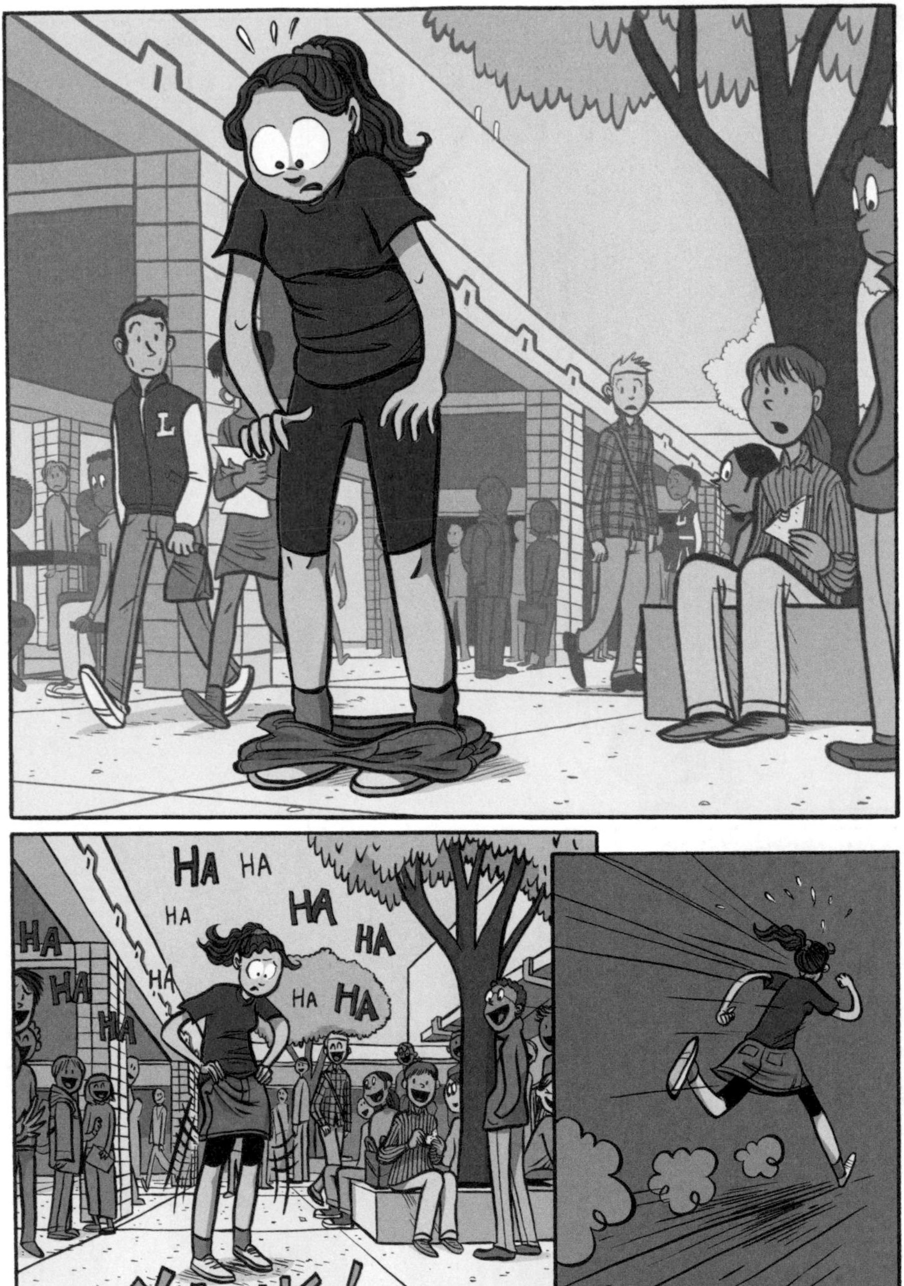
HA HA
HA
HA
HA
HA
HA
HA
HA
HA
HA HA
YANK!

189

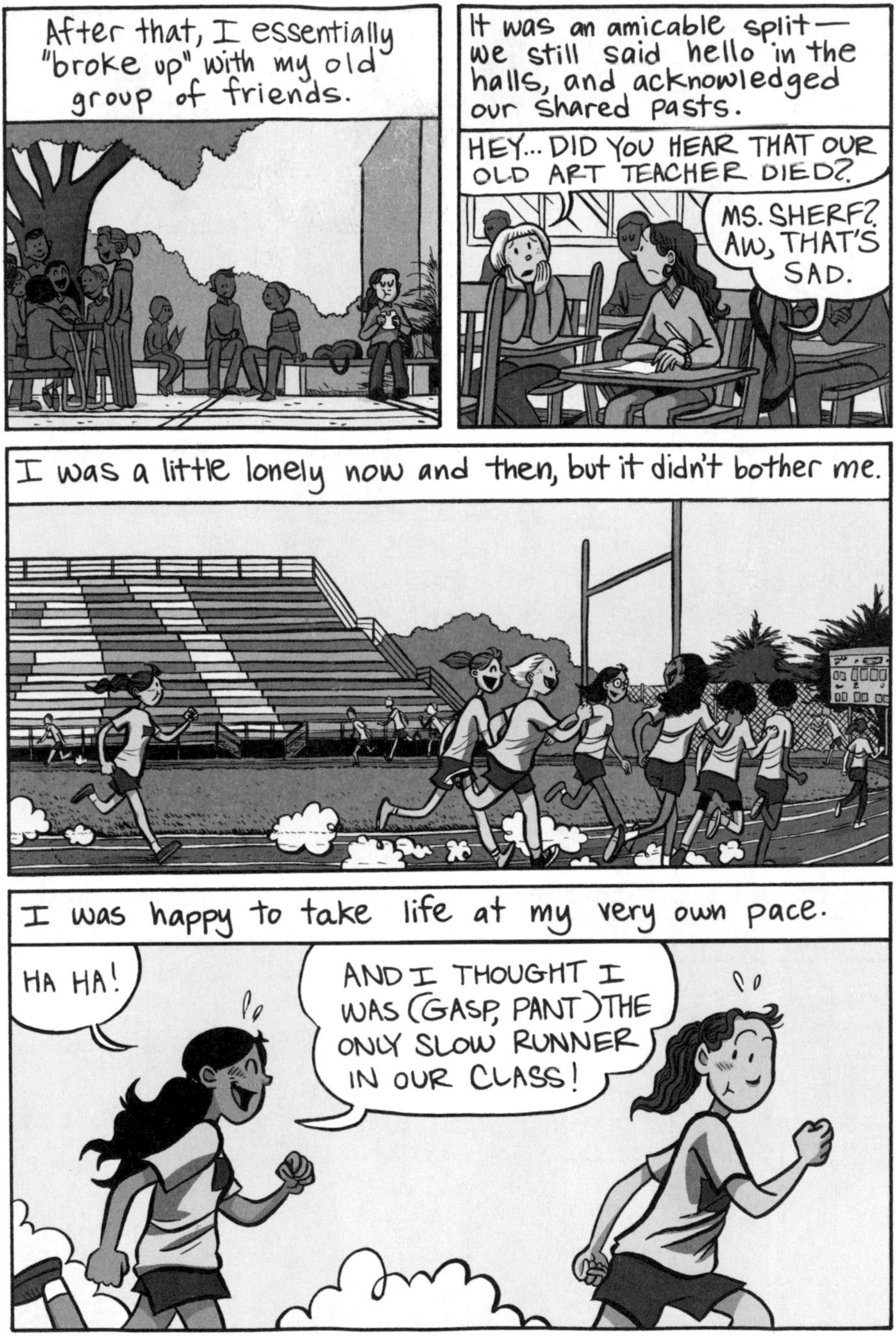
After that, I essentially "broke up" with my old group of friends.
It was an amicable split— we still said hello in the halls, and acknowledged our shared pasts.
HEY... DID YOU HEAR THAT OUR OLD ART TEACHER DIED?
MS. SHERF? AW, THAT'S SAD.
I was a little lonely now and then, but it didn't bother me.
I was happy to take life at my very own pace.
HA HA!
AND I THOUGHT I WAS (GASP, PANT) THE ONLY SLOW RUNNER IN OUR CLASS!

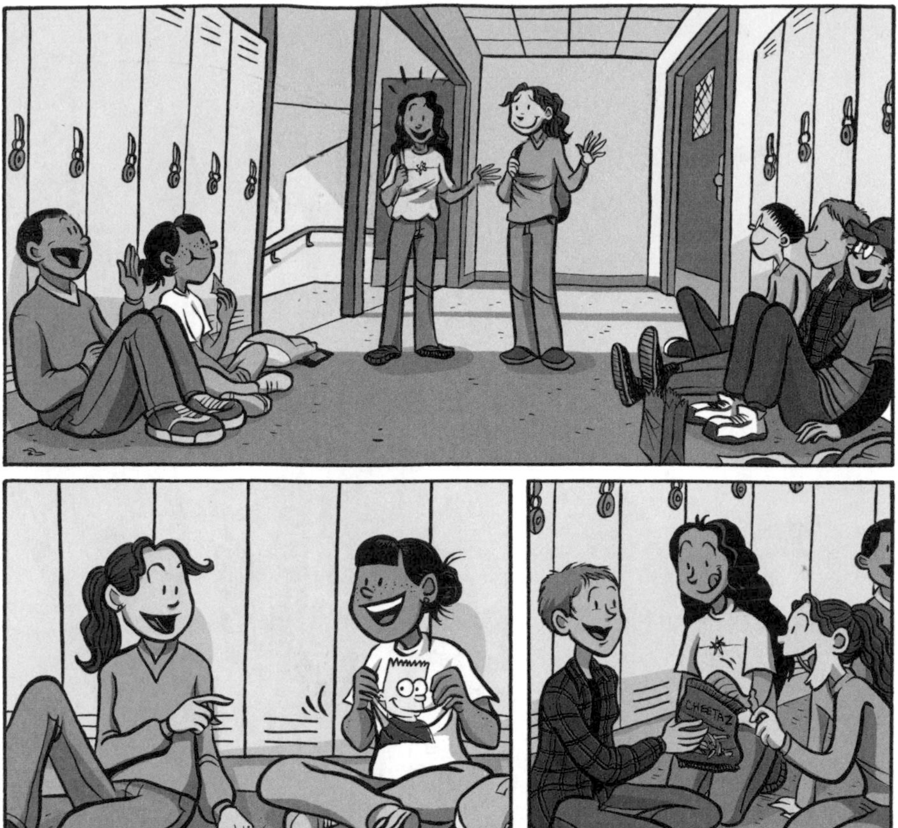
CHEETAZ
Dramatic Mono-logues

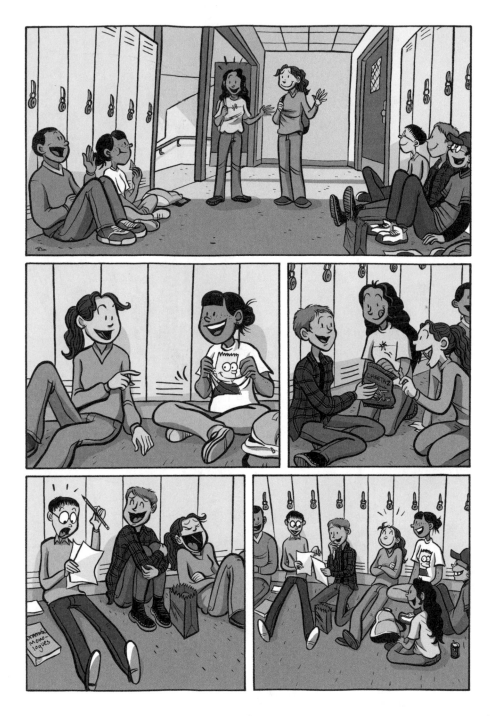

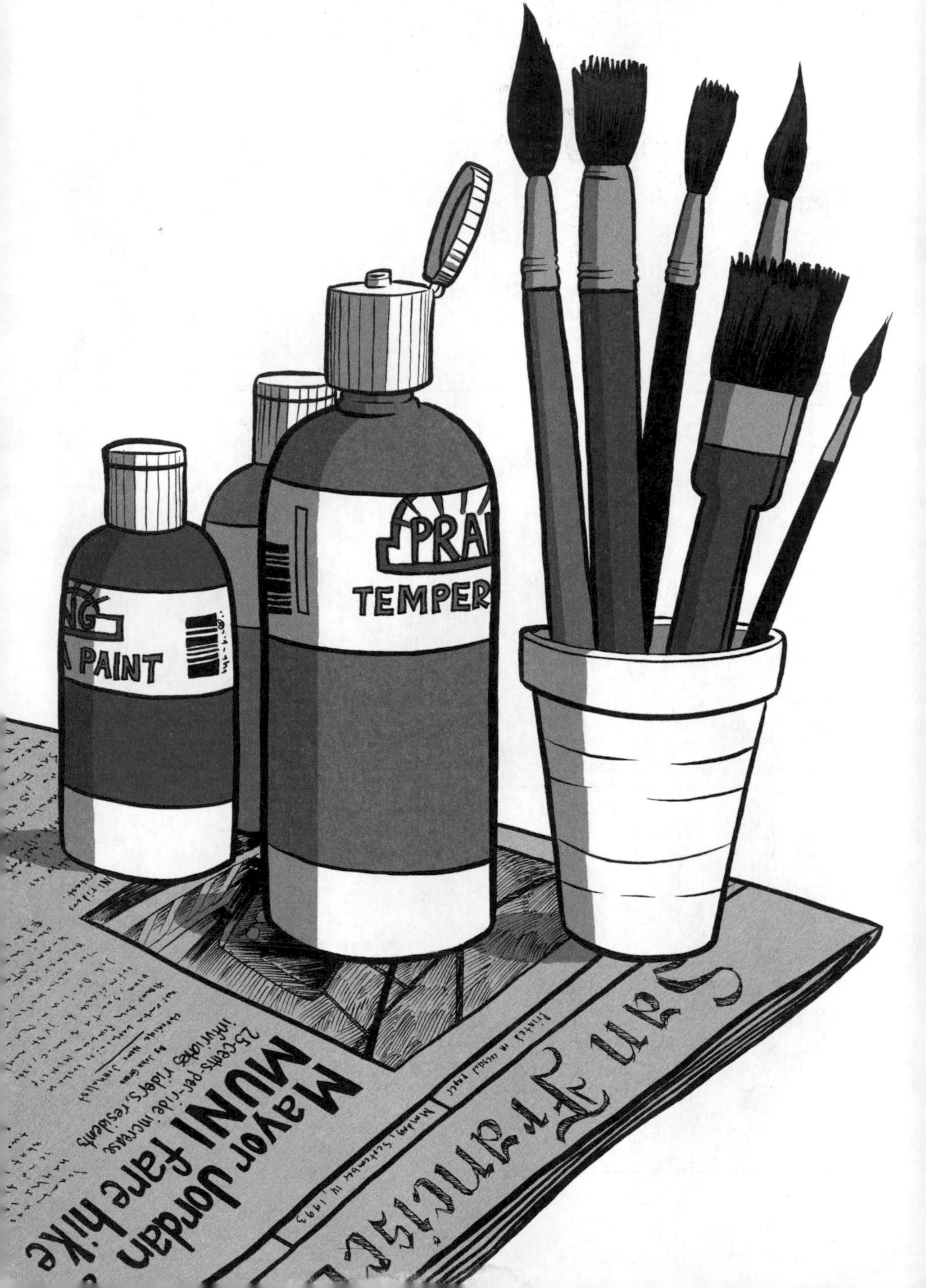

PAINT
TEMPER
Mayor Jordan
MUNI fare hike
25-Cents-per-ride increase
infuriates riders, residents

CHAPTER EIGHT

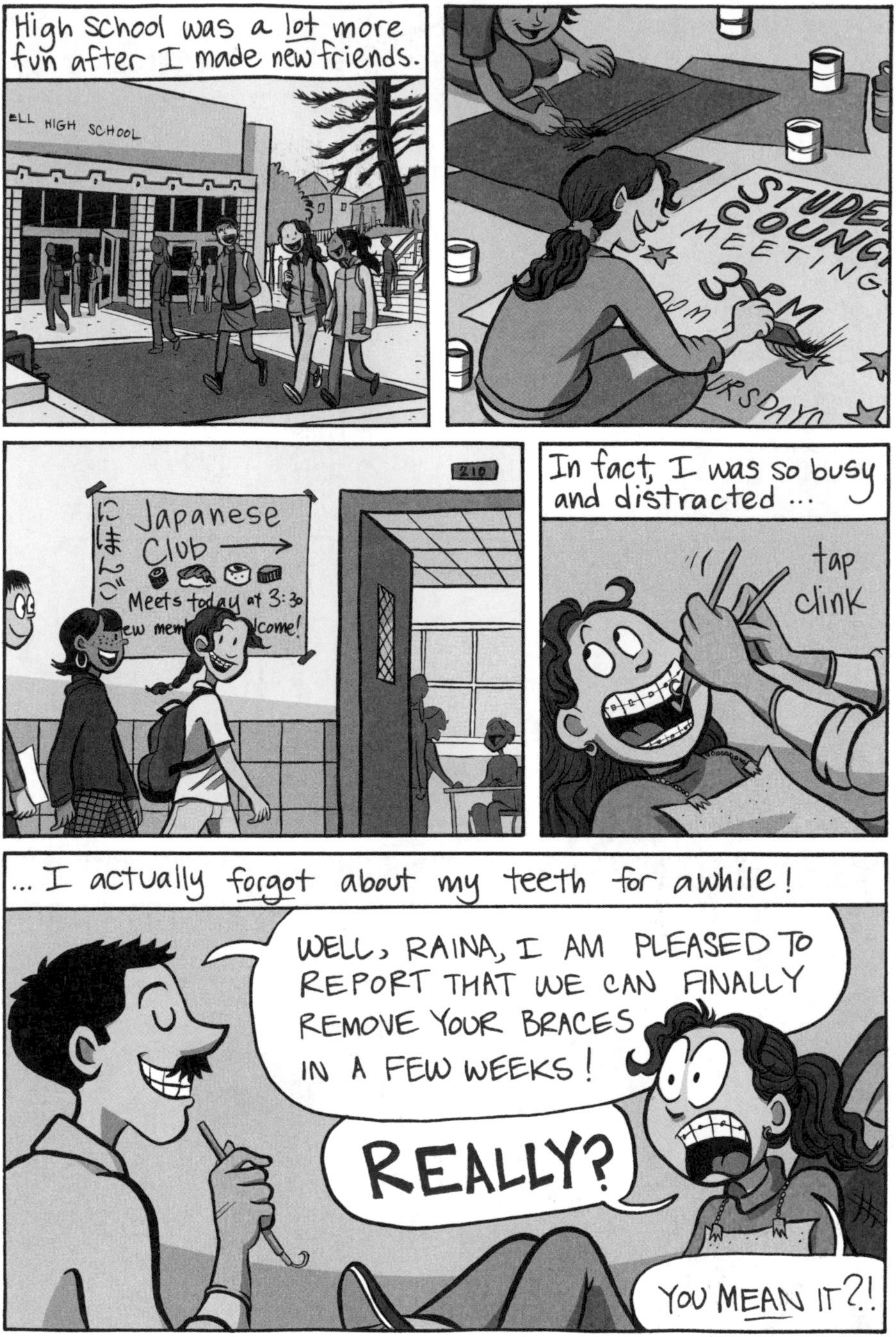
High School was a lot more fun after I made new friends.
ELL HIGH SCHOOL
STUDE
COUNC
MEETING
3 PM
URSDAY
210
にほんご
Japanese Club
Meets today at 3:30
In fact, I was so busy and distracted ...
tap
clink
... I actually forgot about my teeth for awhile!
WELL, RAINA, I AM PLEASED TO REPORT THAT WE CAN FINALLY REMOVE YOUR BRACES IN A FEW WEEKS!
REALLY?
YOU MEAN IT?!

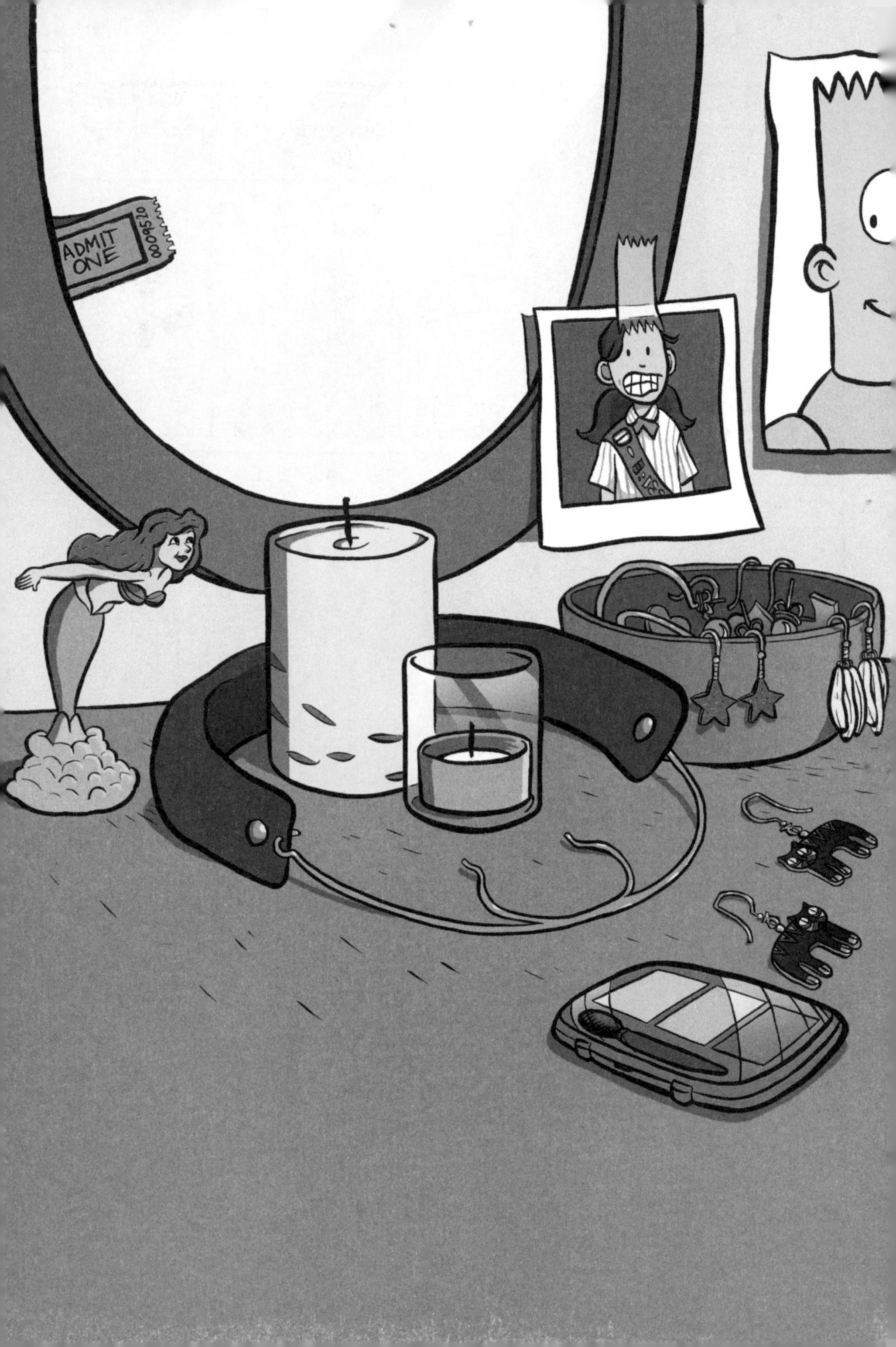
ADMIT ONE
00095120

But the more I focused on my interests, the more it brought out things I liked about myself.

And that affected the way <u>other</u> people saw me!

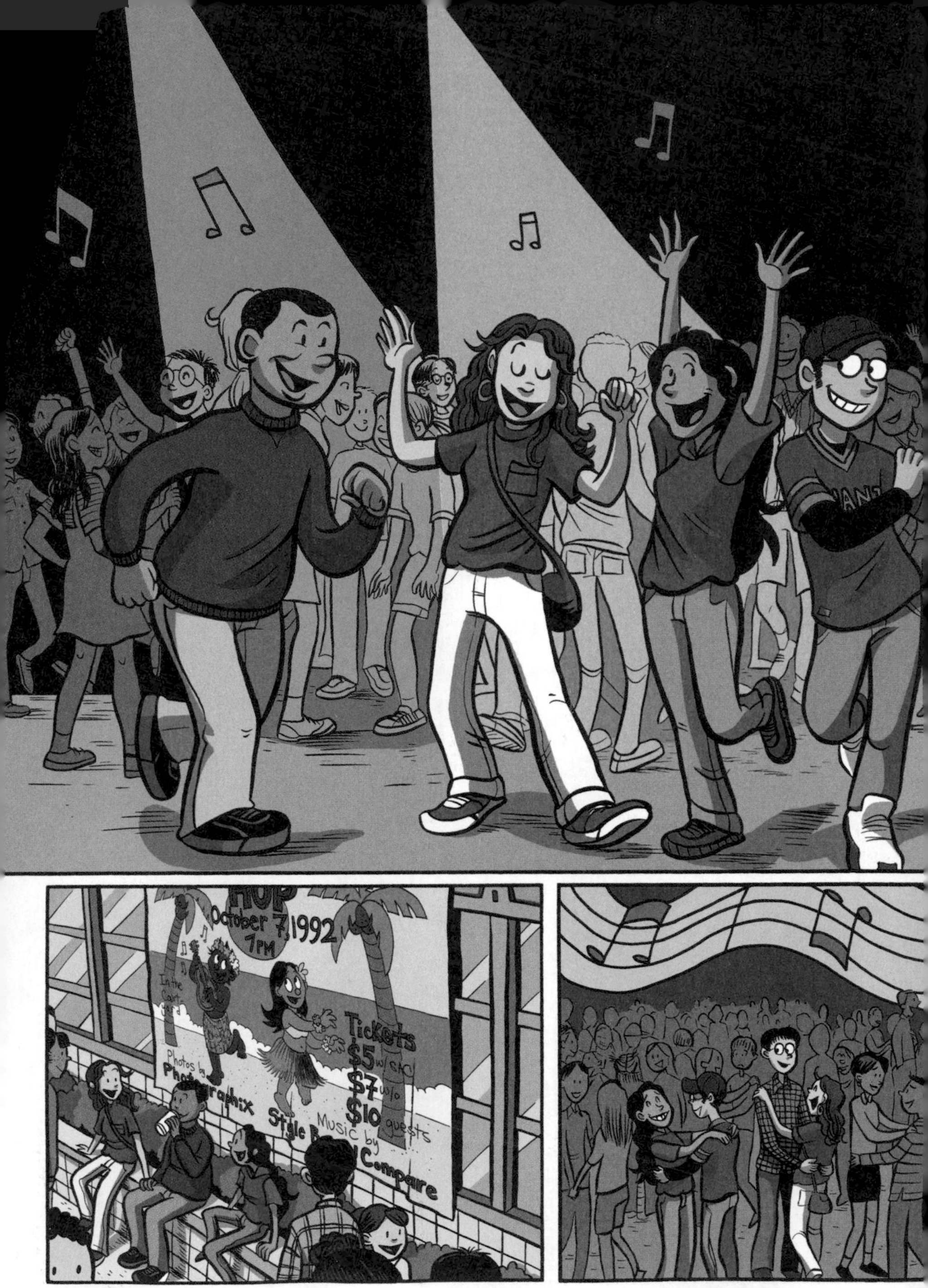
HOP
October 7, 1992
7PM
In the Courtyard
Tickets
$5 w/ SAC
$7 w/o
$10 guests
Photos by
Compare

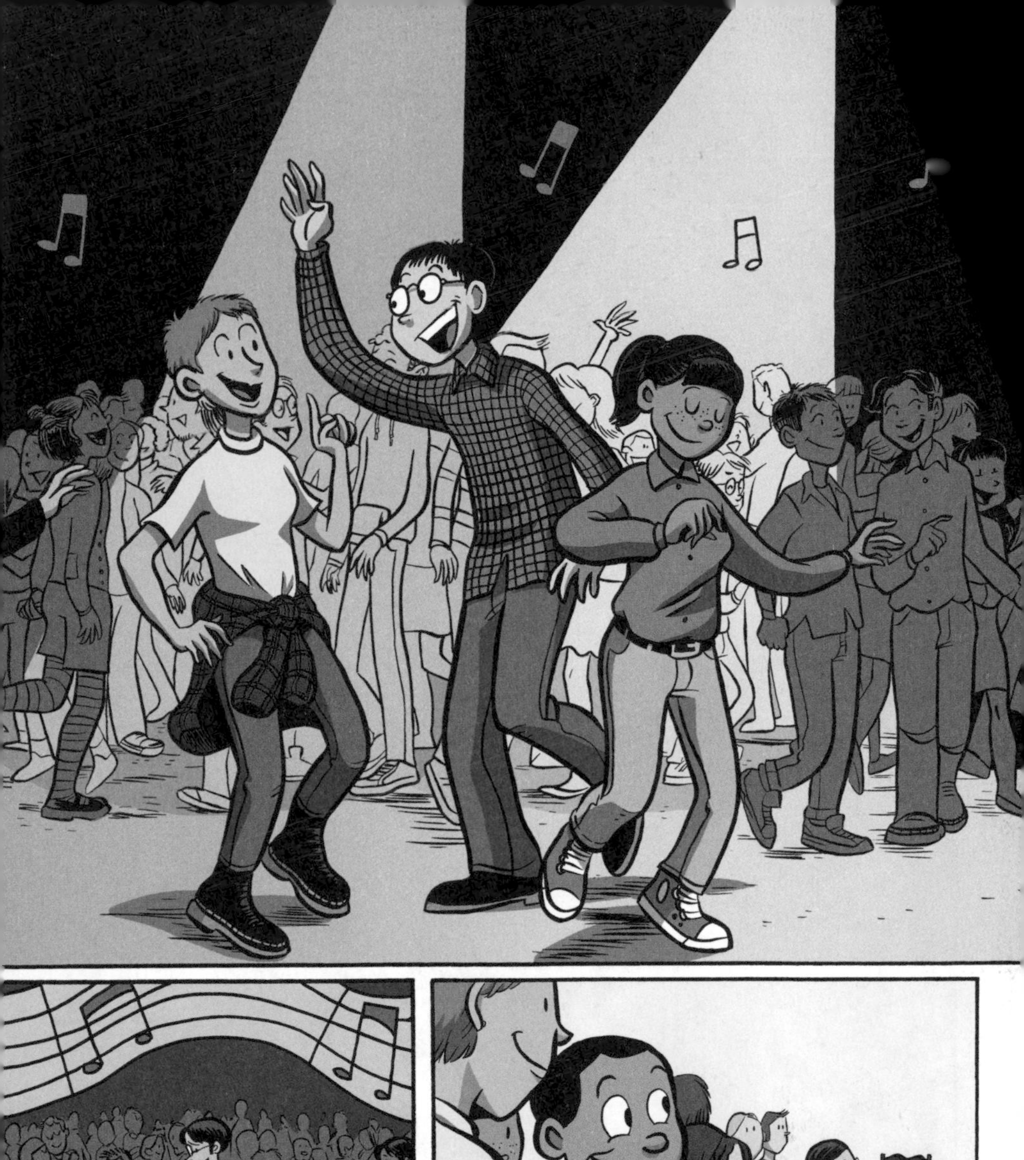

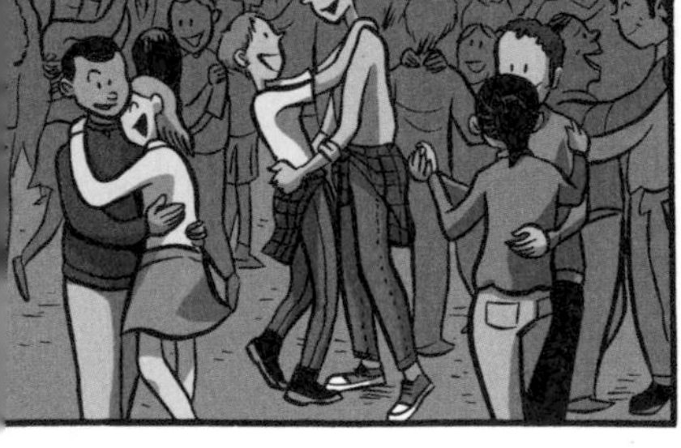

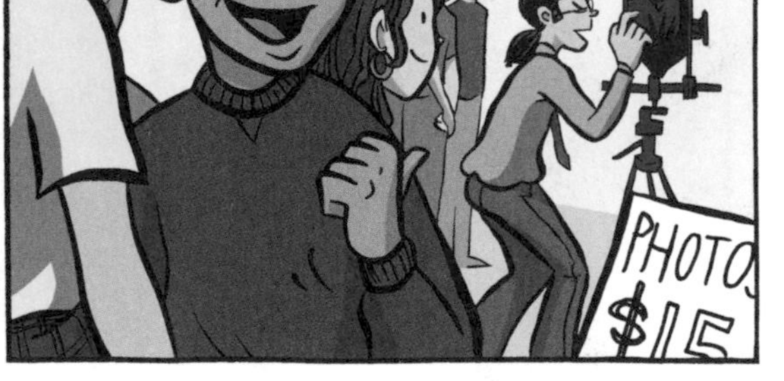
PHOTOS
$15

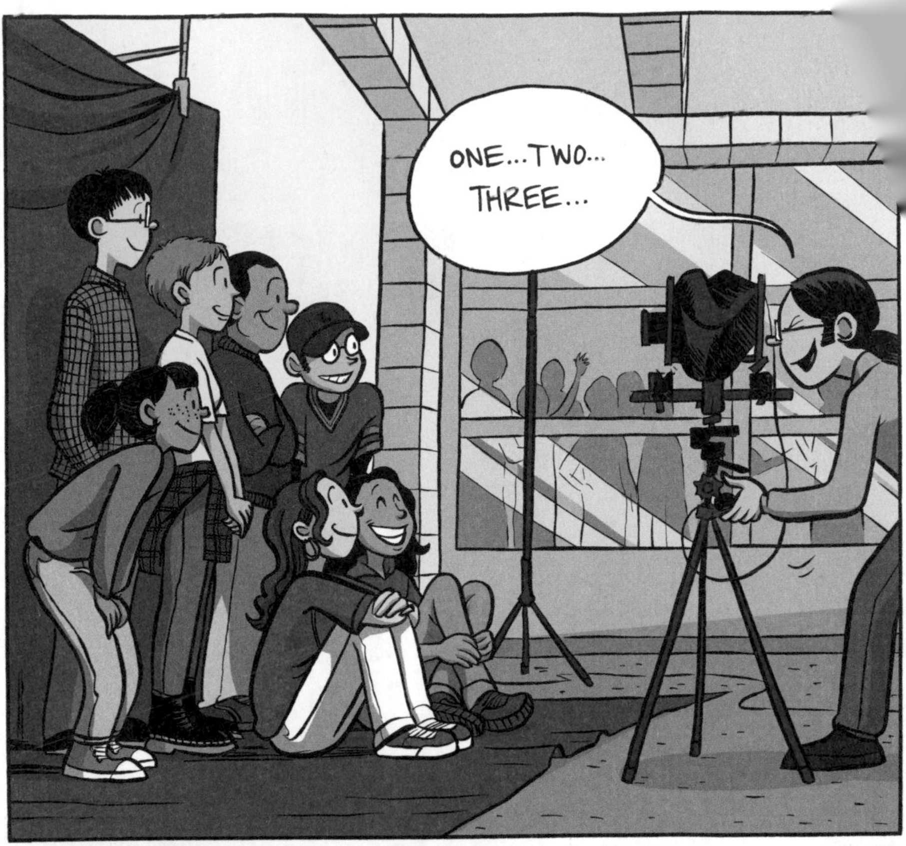
ONE...TWO...
THREE...

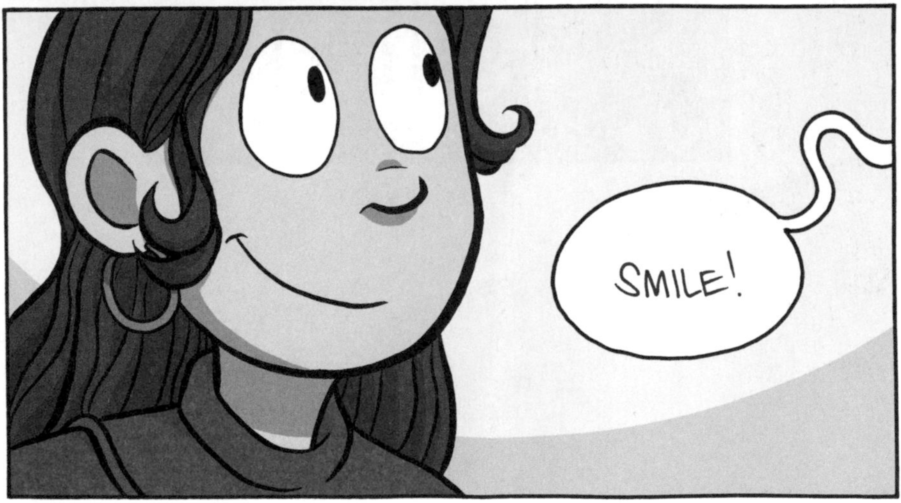
SMILE!

The End!

Thanks to ...

First and foremost, Dave Roman, who makes me smile every day.

Mom, Dad, Amara, Will, and Grandma, for being good sports and a great family.

Lea Ada Franco (Hernandez), Joey Manley, and everyone at Girlamatic.com, for giving a home to this project in its infancy. My friend and family dentist, Dr. Anne Spiegel, who evaluated the manuscript and gave me great encouragement along the way. David Saylor and Cassandra Pelham, for being a joy to work with. Phil Falco, John Green, and Stephanie Yue, for helping make my work beautiful. Judy Hansen, for being the best agent I could hope to have.

Alisa Harris, Braden Lamb, Carly Monardo, Craig Arndt, Dalton Webb, Hope Larson, Jordyn Bochon, Kean Soo, Matt Loux, Naseem Hrab, Rosemary Travale, Ryan Estrada, and Yuko Ota, for lending a helping hand during the final stages of production.

All of my friends who wrote me yearbook notes.

Everyone who has shared their own personal dental dramas with me.

The city of San Francisco, for giving me great backgrounds to draw!

Archwired.com, Janna Morishima, Heidi MacDonald, and Barbara Moon, for all their support and enthusiasm over the years.

Theresa Mendoza Pacheco, Marion Vitus, Steve Flack, Alison Wilgus, Zack Giallongo, Gina Gagliano, Bannister, Steve Hamaker, Seth Kushner, Neil Babra, and my extended family, wonderful friends, and readers, who have been invaluable.

Author's Note

I've been telling people about what happened to my teeth ever since I knocked them out in sixth grade. The story had plenty of strange twists and turns, and I found myself saying, "Wait, it gets worse!" a lot. Eventually, I realized I really needed to get it all down on paper.

I had been writing short-story comics for several years, and my tooth tale seemed like a good candidate for a longer narrative comic.

In 2004 I was invited to contribute to a comics-based Web site, Girlamatic.com, and decided to run *Smile* as a weekly Webcomic. This was at the same time I began working on The Baby-sitters Club graphic novels for Scholastic, so the two projects grew and evolved in tandem. By the time I completed the fourth BSC graphic novel, I had drawn, serialized, and posted over 120 pages of *Smile* on the Web!

As I wrote and drew the story, I was able to look back and actually laugh at some of my more painful experiences. What I went through with my teeth wasn't fun, but I lived to tell the tale and came out of it a stronger person. And once *Smile* started to receive reader feedback, I was amazed by how many people had dental stories similar to my own! The process of creating *Smile* has been therapeutic for me, and has also put me in touch with hundreds of kindred spirits. For this I am very grateful.

Even though my smile looks normal now, it's very possible I'll face more dental drama in the future. Amazingly, I'm not afraid of dentists, or dental work. I have a lot of faith and trust in dentistry, and how it can improve people's lives. And on the bright side of things, beyond the work I've had done on my front teeth, I haven't had a cavity since I was six!

Thanks so much for reading.

— Raina

Raina Telgemeier is the #1 *New York Times* bestselling, multiple Eisner Award-winning creator of *Smile* and *Sisters*, which are both graphic memoirs based on her childhood. She is also the creator of *Drama*, which was named a Stonewall Honor Book and was selected for YALSA's Top Ten Great Graphic Novels for Teens. Raina lives in the San Francisco Bay Area. To learn more, visit her online at www.goRaina.com.